My Take

My Take

GARY BARLOW

with Richard Havers

BLOOMSBURY

First published 2006

Bloomsbury Publishing Plc, 36 Soho Square, London W1D 3QY

A CIP catalogue record is available from the British Library

ISBN 0 7475 8764 7
ISBN-13 9780747587644

10 9 8 7 6 5 4 3

The author and publishers gratefully acknowledge the fair use of lines from the following songs: 'Don't Give Up', words and music by Peter Gabriel; 'Sailing', words and music by G. Sutherland; 'All I Have To Do Is Dream', words and music by Boudleaux Bryant; 'Only You Can Make The World Seem Right', composed by Buck Ram & Ande.

Endpapers: Images taken from the private collection of Gary Barlow

The paper this book is printed on is certified by the © 1996 Forest Stewardship Council A.C. (FSC). It is ancient-forest friendly. The printer holds FSC chain of custody SGS-COC-2061

Typeset by Hewer Text UK Ltd, Edinburgh
Printed in Great Britain by Clays Ltd, St Ives plc

www.bloomsbury.com

Contents

	Sitting Duck	*1*
1	Everyone Has to Start Somewhere	*5*
2	The Entertainer	*25*
3	And Then There Were Five	*48*
4	Manchester Mogul	*64*
5	Run for Cover	*84*
6	Bees on Heat	*103*
7	Mini Elton	*119*
8	The Grand Tour	*134*
9	The End Beginning	*158*
10	The Twist of Separation	*165*
11	Walking the Line as One	*179*
12	I'm Not Invincible	*204*
13	Writing It Out	*221*
14	Backstage for Good?	*229*
15	Take That Back	*243*
16	Take That Take Two	*257*
	Full Circle	*271*

For Nan Bo

Sitting Duck

7 March 2000

I'm driving down London's Edgware Road when my phone rings; it's my manager calling to say that BMG, my record label, have dropped me. It's a short conversation, what else is there to say?

I've often imagined how it would all end, but I never thought it would be like this and certainly not by phone. Fuck! I've really fucked it big time. So many things are going over and over in my head, all the things that have led to this. All the belief I started with, my total self-confidence – where has it gone? The fact is I've shared it around, handed it out to all the people close to me and let them lead my career off into the distance.

Even the music has become shit. The one thing I really care about is now overcomplicated, these last years everything I've written has been with a faded pencil so I can edit and re-edit my words. Where has the four times Ivor Novello winner gone? Maybe I can't write any more – no, that's not true, there's no maybe about it: I can't write any more.

I can imagine the chat they'll be having in Robbie-land tonight. The cheers, wolf whistles and belly laughs. There's no question now, mate, you're the winner, hands down, and it's not over yet. The time to get going is when your opponent's down – Christ, I'm a sitting duck!

I'm on my way to an interview at Heart FM, but there isn't much point. The only thing I want to do is go home. I turn the car around and head north; as soon as I hit the motorway I get on the phone. There are two people at BMG who always take my calls, whether they're in a meeting, out of the office or next to their wife while she's giving birth. 'No, sorry, they're busy right now,' is how their secretaries give me the brush-off. Then I try the next rung down, I call the people in the press and marketing departments. Again it's the cold shoulder: 'We'll have someone call you right back.' Wow, I've heard about this from other artists, but how could it be happening to me? I've sold twenty-four million records in countries all over the world for that company.

As I drive the 180 miles home to Cheshire, thoughts rush around my head, but I keep coming back to the same simple truth: it's over. It's really and truly over.

As I'm just about to exit the M6, I turn on the radio for no reason at all, and for no reason I turn it up loud. Instantly I go into a trance. The next three and a half minutes seem to go by in seconds – a voice is singing to me in my hour of need. The man is singing my story, the song's about me – my life, right here and now. Fans have often told me about how my songs have connected with them, how 'Back For Good' had changed their lives and made a difference to them. And now here's mine: 'Don't give up' sing Peter Gabriel and Kate Bush 'cause you have friends . . . don't give up, 'cause we're proud of who you are.'

In a haze of tears I've bombed it home. I want to go and pluck the Peter Gabriel album off my shelf and play it, but I can't. It'll be a long time before I listen to it again. In fact, the next time I listen to it I want to be back on my feet and back in the charts. But even that's not likely to happen in this lifetime, because I've decided I'm not going to look around and sign to an independent label or try to get a deal in Holland or Belgium. I'm finishing it right now. For me, it's over at the top level, where you get to roll the dice and gamble everything on your career. I don't want to play at any other level. It's time to find a new way to live my life.

I've just had a fax from my office with two offers of work. At the top of one of them someone has written, 'You see, it's not all bad.' The first is offering me the chance to be in Cinderella *in Liverpool this Christmas. The second is about a part in* Joseph and the Amazing Technicolor Dreamcoat. *Jesus! I played Joseph when I was ten years old and now I'm only good enough to play one of the brothers.*

So what is it to be? Neither.

January 2006

That was all six years ago, and a lot's come to pass since then. To be honest, much of it hasn't been that great, but then again, what's transpired has included some of the best things ever to happen to me, which must prove something. On 12 January 2000, a few months before my label dropped me, I married Dawn, and in August our son Daniel was born; two years later, in May 2002, we had a daughter we named Emily.

When I began writing this book I wasn't even sure if I would finish it. All I knew was that there were things I wanted to recall that would fade beyond recognition unless I wrote them down. I soon began to realise that time taints memories, too. What seemed like a disastrous day six or seven years ago was actually the point when my life began to turn around.

I was twenty-nine years old when BMG dropped me and I had lived the kind of life most people only dream of. I had experienced such amazing highs and, up until that point, very few lows, that I wasn't in the best position to cope with the disappointments that were to come.

I remember lying in bed at seventeen praying to be discovered, thinking how cool it would be for people to recognise me, or to be asked for my autograph. But the truth is it wasn't all it's cracked up to be. I even got to the stage where I was embarrassed to be recognised and I still can't understand why somebody would get so excited about having a scribbled name on a piece of paper. Yet without the fans I wouldn't have any of the things I have now, and believe me I'm very, very grateful. I'm thankful for the memories, for the luxuries fame has bought me, right down to the laptop on which I'm typing, but don't ask me to understand it, because I don't.

Being famous has highlighted two conflicting emotions in me. When I walk into a room and everyone stops to look at me, I'm flattered they all know who I am, but at the same time I can't help thinking, oh my God, please somebody break a glass, anything, just stop looking at me. Please let everyone's attention be distracted by someone more famous walking in.

Perhaps to spite the person I used to be I allowed my weight to balloon. At sixteen stones seven pounds I really lived up to what the papers said about me. But I found my way back, and learnt a lot about myself and life in the process. Now, six years since my career hit the buffers, life is wonderful.

1

Everybody Has to Start Somewhere

In Take That Take One we were always the five lads from the North. Robbie was from Stoke, Howard from Droylsden, Mark from Oldham, Jason from Wythenshaw and I was Gary from Frodsham. When I appeared at 12.20 in the afternoon on 20 January 1971, Frodsham was a Cheshire village; the year after I joined the band it became a town. I'm the second son of Colin and Marjorie Barlow; my brother, Ian, is three years older than me.

13 Ashton Drive, the house where I was born, was on a close-knit council estate on the edge of the village. Our house, like all other houses, had a garden at the front and another out back, where my dad used to keep pigeons (my mum hated them). With the exception of my mum's mum, who we called Nan Bo, everyone else in my life lived close by. My dad's parents lived 500 metres away in Clifton Crescent; my mate Graham, who I still know today, lived round the corner and we were in and out of each other's houses constantly. I still like having people hanging around the house, and I love it when the band is here working in the recording studio.

School, Weaver Vale Primary in Ship Street, was a seven-minute walk away. I can still remember my first day there, aged four. My mum walked me to the school gates, and as I left her and walked across the playground I looked round; through a haze of snot and tears I could see her face getting further and further away. Despite the shaky start, I settled in soon enough – a year in Mrs Whitfield's, then a year with Mrs Bowring, in whose class I made friends with some great characters. My first close friend was Chris Quinn. He lived opposite Weaver Vale and loved bikes, just like me. Quinny was mad, he'd jump higher on his BMX than the rest of us, go faster and do wheelies for the longest distance. He showed no fear and didn't seem to care if he hurt himself.

I loved music – I was one of those kids that's forever dancing in front of the TV looking at my reflection, and the first toy I really remember loving was a Fisher Price keyboard. I was five when I was given my first record – 'Living Next Door To Alice' by Smokie – and I played it over and over again. We lived next door to the Griffiths family – none of them called Alice – and they had some great music – their kids were slightly older than us and they were always playing the latest chart records. But the one LP that every house on my street seemed to have was Abba's *Arrival*. My parents also loved music and up until I left junior school I mostly listened to their record collection, which included Boney M, the Beatles, Motown, The Bee Gees and Stars on 45. The first record I bought with my own pocket money was 'D.I.S.C.O.' by Ottawan – that was Christmas 1980, just before my tenth birthday – and I followed it up with some Adam Ant – 'Ant Rap' – and Depeche Mode, Spandau Ballet and Duran Duran – no surprise then that I later became a real Frodsham New Romantic.

My first brush with playing music was in Mrs Bourne's class. She was the school witch; she took no nonsense from anyone and everyone was scared of her. The one good thing about her class was that a corner of the room was full of musical instruments – tom toms, cymbals, shakers, glockenspiels, xylophones and all sorts of things. When we were told we could play them there would be a mad dash to get to the best ones first – no one wanted to be left with the triangle. It was my first chance to play some real instruments.

I had gone from being a baby that never stopped crying to being a kid that never shut up. My mum and dad used to say, 'His tongue must be so glad when he goes to bed.' I loved attention. My Emily has the same bug – but with me for a dad and a dancer for a mum you can see where she gets it from. In my family it was a freak gene. My brother Ian couldn't be more different – never shine a light or point a camera at him.

After enduring Mrs Bourne for a year, I graduated to the second half of the school – the one for the big kids – where I joined Miss Brown's class. She was gorgeous, with long brown hair and olive skin, and she smelled really good too. For the next six months life was beautiful.

Then one day Miss Brown stood by the blackboard – she was wearing a patterned blue and tan dress, that's how big an impression she made on me – and said, 'OK, if everyone could listen.' Instantly all seventeen boys sat in total silence. 'When we all come into school on Monday my name will no longer be Miss Brown, it will be Mrs Gleave – I'm getting married on Saturday.'

The shock was too much. I sulked all afternoon until I could hold it in no longer – I had to talk to her. I headed straight towards her desk, pushing aside the chairs and banging into the tables that obstructed my path.

'Yes, Gary,' she said. 'What's the problem?'

She knew exactly what the problem was. This was a situation she must have seen coming.

'Miss Brown,' I said, as my bottom lip started to quiver. This was not the plan, big guy. Don't cry. She picked me up and sat me on her knee. I found myself overpowered by her perfume. 'Don't get married,' I said. 'I want to marry you.'

What a pro she was. She didn't laugh, instead she just smiled and said, 'Oh don't be silly', cuddled me and got ready for the next protester in line. So there it was, my first crush. It's probably good to get it over with early . . .

When I was five years old my mum returned to work. She bought herself a moped and off she went to be a lab technician at Chester City Hospital. It was then that I began to notice how hard Mum and Dad worked. My dad was a project manager for a fertiliser company and he worked shifts. He came home from a 10 p.m. till 6 a.m. shift, slept till 2 p.m. and then went off to work on a farm till seven in the evening. Looking back, I hardly knew him until I was older: he was always working. I suppose I learned the importance of hard work from them, not that they ever made a big thing of it. I never got the 'If you try hard and believe in yourself, you can do it' talks that I give my own kids; they just led by example.

My brother and I got out of school before Mum finished work, so we went to the Maddocks' house for an hour. They were a big, friendly family who lived halfway down Ashton Drive, on the opposite side of the street from us. Their house was different from ours: there were kids everywhere – there must have been six or eight of them – and Elizabeth and Rodney were my age. The Maddocks kids used to build motorbikes in their living room and there was always a pan of chips on the go. I'd retreat into the back garden to play – I never did like getting my hands dirty – and there was no hiding the fact that I didn't want to be there – I was so fed up with my mum for going back to work.

But there were compensations. When I visited other kids' homes I noticed we had a few extra luxuries that they didn't have. We had a colour telly and, even rarer, went on holidays abroad; Mum and Dad took us to Ibiza when I was five, which was really unusual then. And when we moved to a lovely bungalow on London Road when I was ten, closer to the centre of Frodsham and away from 'the Bronx' as we called the estate, I finally realised what they'd been working so hard for.

When I went to school I realised how rare it was that my family were so stable. My dad's quite quiet, and my mum's the boss of the house, but they are a perfectly matched couple. At the time it seemed boring – everyone else had a new stepdad who was going to buy them this or that, while I always has the same old mum and dad! But it's reflected on my brother and me. Ian's married with three kids, and he and Lisa are as inseparable a couple as Dawn and me. And when it came to being in the band, I realised that the stability of my home background was a fantastic thing to have to fall back on.

By age nine I was already honing my skills as a magician. I'd sit in front of Paul Daniels' magic show every week and Siegfried and Roy every Christmas, completely fascinated. I guess the reason I liked magic so much was that there was an audience and it was on TV. My parents would never have encouraged me to hog the limelight, but I got good enough at the magic for my dad to take me along to his pigeon club evenings as the entertainment. It didn't matter what I was doing – it could have been Irish line dancing for all I cared – it was the audience I loved.

In my last year at Weaver Vale we had a new headmaster. Mr Walker was a breath of fresh air: he took us on school trips and fancied himself as something of a musical producer. He decided we were going to stage *Joseph and the Amazing Technicolor Dreamcoat*, and as I was always singing and acting, as well as being a bit of a joker, everyone expected me to get the lead – no one more so than me. I knew I needed to work at it, though, so I spent the whole summer listening to a record of *Joseph*, learning it back to front and inside out. I'm always well prepared for things. Even on our most recent tour, ten minutes before the show I'm all ready, earphones plugged in, suit on, dusted off and ready to go. Next in line is Mark – he's got his shirt on but no jacket, and he hasn't finished his hair. Then there's Howard, he's just got his trousers on, he's doing his exercises and he's hardly ready at all. And then there's Jason, still in his underpants. Some things never change.

By the time the autumn arrived, I knew the entire cast's lines, and yet I still had to go through the audition. I tried to play down the effort I'd put in.

'I'll be stopping late tonight, I'm auditioning for *Joseph*,' I told my mum casually.

'OK,' said Mum.

The next night it was the same. On the third night when I got home Mum asked, 'How did you get on, Gary?'

'Got it. I'm Joseph.'

I'd secured the lead in Weaver Vale's first production. I think there would have been trouble if it had gone to anyone else. Andrew Lloyd Webber and Tim Rice's musical is what got me started on stage, and I have to say I loved every second of it. The showman in me had emerged.

At half past seven on a Thursday night in the early eighties, there wasn't anywhere else to be but sat in front of *Top of the Pops*. One night in October 1981 three keyboard players and a singer opened the show. The sound they made with their synthesisers was incredible; I'd never heard anything like it. It was 'Just Can't Get Enough' by Depeche Mode. Mum and Dad had been asking me what I fancied for Christmas, and I'd been umming and ahhing over some new wheels for my BMX, but now I knew exactly what I wanted – I wanted a keyboard and I wanted to know how to make a sound like that.

I was so certain I dreamt about it that night, and in the morning I announced it to my mum and dad, who agreed to do some research, which is how we ended up in Chester at Rushworths Music the following Saturday. We entered the shop, went down the narrow stairs and there they were: fifty synthesisers, just like the ones on *Top of the Pops*. The salesman wore a thin little tie with a keyboard on it, had long white hair to his collar and was fifty-five at least – he'll never understand, I thought, as I reluctantly told him about Depeche Mode.

'I think I've got what you're after. Come over here, lad.'

We followed him to the counter. He took a keyboard with half-size keys from the stand, placed it on the counter, plugged it in and turned it on, a smile hovering around the corners of his mouth. Suddenly the drum machine kicked in – what a sound, what a beat! It was just like Depeche Mode. The guy's left hand played a bass part – I was staggered: it was the riff from 'Just Can't Get Enough' – and then to finish it off he played the melody with his right hand. I felt like honey was being poured into my ears. My heart was beating faster than the drum machine, I wanted the synth so badly I'd have given my legs and arms for it. In fact, I wanted to be that guy – except for his hair, his tie and his age! The oldest swinger in Chester had sold his first synth of the day. What a blinder.

But Christmas was *weeks* away. I begged my parents to let me have it before then, but there was no deal. On the morning of 25 December I woke up on the couch, because Nan Bo, through from Liverpool had my bed, and there it was, my very own Yamaha PS-2.

It was out of the box and plugged in in no time. I turned on the keyboard and started to fiddle with it. Within five minutes my left hand began talking to my right and an hour later I could pick out three or four carols. A few hours more and I had the drum machine and a bass line going, while my right hand played the melody of Scott Joplin's 'The Entertainer'. I was surprised at how fast I'd picked it up, but not half as amazed as the rest of the family. I could change sounds in the middle of a song, pressing the button to get a fill in before the chorus – it was pretty impressive stuff.

After three weeks of constant hammering I'd mastered everything the PS-2, with its two-octave range, had to offer. While I worked hard at playing my new keyboard, it didn't feel like work and it wasn't something I found difficult. I realise now that it must have been partly down to natural ability, although where that came from no one's quite sure. It's not something that runs in the family, although Nan Bo did say that her next door neighbour's husband played the piano . . .

I was hatching a plan. I wanted to go back to Rushworths to see what the next step up from my little synth was. For a while I kept it to myself, but more often than not Mum and Dad would go to Chester on a Saturday, and one week I asked if I could go too. From the kitchen I heard my mum say to my dad,

'Let's take him. He doesn't want anything at the moment.'

Wrong, wrong, wrong. Once in Chester, I said to Dad,

'Let's go and have a look in the window of Rushworths, see what they've got in.' It was the back-door strategy as I knew that Dad was a softer target than Mum. As we walked into Rushworths there was the oldest swinger in Chester, welcoming me with a big grin.

'Back already?' he said. He led us down to a different corner of the shop.

These synths were nothing like my little Yamaha; they were more like pieces of furniture. Each one had two keyboards, with full-sized keys that spanned three octaves. He turned one on, sat down and started to play. This was in a different league to his pre-Christmas demo – this was big boys' stuff. Not only was he playing the bottom keyboard with his left hand and the top keyboard with his right, he was playing the bass notes with his *feet*. The swinger had turned into one fat cat. He drifted from beautiful sounds and textures to samba, salsa, disco and rock – I was in heaven. Fortunately Dad was blown away too. There who only snag: the price tag. The synth was £500. It wasn't something I could beg for. We thanked the man and headed out. When we met up with Mum and I excitedly began telling her what had happened, she just tutted.

'Honestly, Gary, it's far too much money.'

I knew this to be true, so I didn't make a fuss.

Later that evening they both sat me down at the kitchen table.

'I've been working some of my days off and I'm due quite a lot of holiday, so I've decided to sell it back to the company,' said Dad. 'With the money they'll pay me we can afford to buy you the synthesiser.'

For once I was truly speechless. What a thing to do. Looking back I can see it was a turning point. I decided I was going to have to get so good at playing this new synth that I could make enough money to pay them back one day.

Two weeks later a colossal box arrived. This was no synth, this was an organ! Fast forward three months, counting every day, and most nights, as time spent playing the Yamaha A-45, and once again I'd hit a crossroads – I'd reached another level. Mum thought it was time for lessons, although I have to admit I was none too keen: doing my own thing seemed much more fun than being told what to do. On my own I'd make up melodies and change bass notes in chords, and while I often had no idea of what I was playing, I used my ears to tell me what to do.

During my last year at junior school I was in the chorus for the Frodsham pantomime, which that year was *Jack and the Beanstalk*. A week before the first night we started stage rehearsals; I was standing in the wings with the rest of the chorus – mostly girls – waiting for the show to start when suddenly the music began. It sounded really good. What was it? A record? A band? I put my head around the curtain. One guy was generating all that sound from a huge organ. As soon as rehearsals finished I looked at the call sheet to find out his name: Christopher Greenleaves.

'Chris Greenleaves?' said my mum when she picked me up from rehearsals. 'He's Barbara's husband. They only live around the corner from us.'

Sure enough he lived about 300 metres from our house. The following night at rehearsals I tried to talk to him, and then again several times during the pantomime's run, but it was clear he didn't know that I could play the organ too. So one day after the panto ended I decided the best plan of attack was to call at his house.

His son, who was a year younger than me, answered the door.

'Is your dad in?' I asked.

'He's on the organ,' said Paul.

'Can I come in and listen?' I almost begged.

'If you want,' said Paul, trailing back into the house. I followed him into the kitchen and sat down at the table so that I was right behind Chris. I'm not certain that he even knew I was there at first. I was transfixed; I could have sat there all day. After about an hour of pure bliss, Chris turned to me and said, 'Wanna have a go?'

I was in there like a shot. He could see my enthusiasm, and maybe after I'd played a little, a glint of talent. Whatever it was, it was the start of Chris teaching me to play the organ properly. We didn't have set days or evenings for lessons, but I was over there at least one night every week. He'd make up tapes of pieces for me to learn, which I'd take home and play over and over again until late into the night. Before long I realised I needed to learn how to play the bass pedals with my feet, so Chris taught me how to play 'A Whiter Shade Of Pale', which was a great way to learn as the bass descends all the way down in an uncomplicated run. I had to sit right at the edge of the stool to reach the pedals, and the lower down the scale I got the more I had to stretch my legs. For the next four months I played the organ while watching my feet, but soon I could move them around without looking down.

After I cracked the pedals I felt I was on my way to becoming a musician, and by that stage that's exactly what I wanted to be. With my hands and feet flying around all over the place, I played songs such as 'Tico Tico', 'Fame', the theme from *Hill Street Blues*, 'Love On The Rocks', 'Just The Way You Are' and a new one by Lionel Richie called 'Hello'. Old songs, new releases, chart songs, I had a bash at just about everything, and I'm glad I did as those early years playing every kind of music were invaluable when I became a songwriter later. By playing my way through the standards of contemporary music, I was seeing how the songs were crafted and beginning to understand their structure – I became aware of their DNA.

Unlike some kids I had no worries about starting 'big school'. By now my mum was working at Frodsham High School, a mixed comprehensive, as a lab technician and brother Ian was already there. He met me in the playground on my first day. My clearest memory of that day was that there was a boy in my class who had a beard! I had no hair anywhere on my body, and even now I have trouble growing a full beard.

It was easy for me to be good enough at school, because by this stage Ian was being bad enough for the both of us. He started smoking at eleven and riding motorbikes without a crash helmet at twelve – he was a really naughty kid, who was always in trouble. When he was fourteen, the year I started secondary school, he met his female counterpart, and they were like Bonnie and Clyde; inseparable, feared by the teachers and always and in out of the headmaster's office, we even had the police round once. It was hard on my mum, working in the school labs just down the corridor, and it put years on her. In fact the only trouble I ever recall at home was my parents arguing about my brother. Then he left school, set up his own building business and has never caused a concern since. School just didn't agree with him.

I, meanwhile, never made a ripple. Sometimes I think I sleep-walked through school – my real life was in my head and in my music. Mum, Dad, schoolfriends, everybody came second to my passion. I'd get up in the morning and play for an hour before school; then I'd come home for lunch and play again for an hour and after school I'd play until bedtime. Nobody heard a squeak out of me apart from the t-t-t-t of my hands on the keys.

One evening in early 1984 I found my mum looking through our local paper. 'Here it is,' she said, 'someone at work told me about a talent competition.' It was being organised jointly by the *Chester Observer* and Greenall Whitley the brewer, and they were looking for that year's Club Act of the Year. I was all up for it – it would give me the chance to play the organ in front of an audience. And yes, to be honest, a part of me wanted to show off how well I could play by then.

Two weeks later, on Thursday 15 March, my mum and I headed off to Connah's Quay, a forty-five-minute drive from Frodsham. My mum's friend lived very close to where the competition was being held and she let us park at her house, then from there we walked to Dee Road and found the Labour Party Social Club.

On the door was a large older man who asked, 'Can I help you?' His voice had a distinctly Welsh lilt. We told him why we were there and he entered my name in the book along with the other contestants. I was the fourth on the list and was due to perform just after the break. We took a seat so we could watch the acts before me. First up was Big Little Island, a husband-and-wife duo, and they were definitely going to be tough to beat as they were very professional. He played the keyboards and she sang – a really polished act. They were followed by the Hazel Jay Duo, a pair of vocalists, and after that came a seven-piece group called Table for Seven.

It seems surprising now, and it was out of character, but my mum had taken in how all the acts fared and noted how their level of performance compared to me, and she decided I needed to talk in between the songs I'd chosen to play. My mum's not one of those pushy mothers, she just wanted me to do the best I could. During the interval she fed me a few witty intros and cheeky comments to fill the gaps between the music. It helped me feel a little more confident. Not that I was nervous; it felt quite natural. I couldn't wait to get on stage to sample the atmosphere; I knew I was going to enjoy it.

The compere of the show came and found me. 'OK, son, you're on next.'

'Good luck,' said Mum and off I went to the side of the stage where I met the resident drummer.

'Do you want me to accompany you?' he asked.

Without hesitating I said, 'Yes,' although I had no idea how we would fit together – I hadn't even seen the organ at this point. I didn't even know how to turn it on or what sounds to use. If I were attempting this today, knowing what I know now, I'd have a heart attack about taking such a chance.

Fortunately there were three or four minutes before the show restarted, so I sat behind the organ and quickly figured it all out. I decided on what sounds I was going to use for the different songs and even had time to tell the drummer what the set list was. He seemed cool, so we were ready.

'Ladies and Gentlemen, please welcome a young lad who plays the organ – thirteen-year-old Gary Barlow.'

I could hear clapping, but there was no way I was going to risk looking over the top of the organ. I just concentrated on playing as best as I could. I can recall very little of the next fifteen minutes. The drummer, who was superb, really enhanced my playing, my jokes and intros seemed to go down great and there was lots of clapping from the audience – the rest was a blur.

I came off stage feeling fantastic. I know now that I was experiencing the buzz you get from performing. I loved the surroundings, the stage, the audience, lights and the music. Never mind that it was an old social club with peeling paint and a bar selling warm beer, I was on a high. My mum, sitting in the audience, was almost as excited as I was.

We were waiting for the winner to be announced when the guy who was on the front door came over. He said his name was Norman.

'I enjoyed your act, son, got any plans for the future?'

'Well, this was my first time playing in public, but it's definitely not my last,' I replied.

'Why don't you let me have your phone number, 'cos I might have something for you.' My mum wrote it down for him and off he went.

The winner was the husband-and-wife duo and they certainly deserved it. I hadn't expected to win, but I was more than pleased with the way it had gone. My mind kept turning over what Norman had said – would I really get the chance to play again soon? We left the club and headed for my mum's friend's house, where we had a cup of tea and told her all about our night. By the time we left it was very late, and besides being tired I had a funny taste in my mouth. That night I was sick, not just once, but over and over again. I'll never know if it was the tea or all the excitement.

A week or so later the call came.

'Hello, it's Norman from Connah's Quay Club. I liked your playing, Gary, and I was wondering if you'd like a job as our resident organist in the bar? I could pay you £18 a night and if possible we'd like you to start next Saturday – you'll be on from 8 p.m. until 10.30 p.m. – and then we'll have you on every week after that.' I was thirteen. £18 seemed like a fortune.

The first thing my mum said was, 'You'll need more songs if you're going to play all evening.' Of course she was right and from then until Saturday all I did was to learn new tunes – loads of them. I practised current songs, old songs, just about anything I thought people might like. Norman said I was to do three spots, so between us – Mum, Dad and I – we worked out some links, as well as some jokes, to fill in the gaps between songs. By Saturday I was ready for what I assumed would be my big night, playing to a packed club.

On the journey to Connah's Quay Labour Club I was more excited than I had been for the competition. Dad came with us this time and when we got there Norman was waiting to greet us. I really liked Norman, and not just because I knew he was the guy I had to please. He reminded me a bit of my dad: quiet with a quick sense of humour.

Connah's Quay Labour Club was the social club for the local steel works, but as all the steel works were closing down at that time it was quite depressed and business wasn't booming. Not that I noticed at first, I was too blown away by the wooden sign hanging above the small stage where the organ sat: it said 'Gary Barlow'. Smiling from ear to ear, I was itching to get going, even though we were thirty minutes early.

'No point in waiting around is there, Norman?' I said, and sat down and started to play.

It was the same organ I'd played on the night of the talent competition, so I had no difficulty getting stuck in. I was in a haze of happiness, too absorbed in my new tunes to look over the top of the organ. When I finally did I realised there were only two people clapping. Mum and Dad were sat proudly at the back of an empty bar. Every now and again Norman would look in from his doorman's seat, and by the time the evening finished there was a grand total of four people in the bar. I suppose it's a realisation that everyone has in a new job – once you've got the job you've got to come up with the goods. What Norman needed was thirty-five tables filled – and he'd taken a gamble on a teenager.

'Don't worry about it, son,' Norman said. 'You played great. I'll see you next week.' All the way home we talked about what had happened and how I needed to learn even more songs. I wasn't deterred – I wanted the place to fill up right there and then.

I couldn't wait for the week to be over and for Saturday to come round again.

For the next three months I played at Connah's Quay Labour Club every Saturday night. It pains me to admit this, but after all that time the audience only increased by about eight people, two of whom were my mum and dad, who gave me a lift each week. Norman had showed so much faith in me that I felt like I was letting him down. So I desperately tried out some new ideas. I tried singing and ambitiously chose Paul McCartney's 'Pipes of Peace' as my first song – big mistake. Undaunted, I tried including some magic – bigger mistake. I watched some comedians on the TV and wrote down a few of their jokes. Saturday night came and I tried stand-up – biggest mistake of all. Disheartened, I didn't know what to do to get people into the bar. All I could rely on was what had got me the job in the first place, playing the organ. My set list grew and grew until it was vast, so I started taking requests since as often as not I knew them off by heart.

One Saturday evening I noticed four people sitting at a table to the left of the stage; I'd never seen them in the bar before. By then I'd perfected the art of playing while watching the room, and for some reason they caught my eye as they chatted and sipped their drinks. They seemed to enjoy my playing, and as I finished my first song of the second spot, one of the guys approached the stage.

'Hello,' he said. 'Do you know "All I Have To Do Is Dream" by the Everly Brothers?'

'Yes.' Of course I knew it, in any key.

'Can I sing it?' he said.

I didn't know what to say, so I just started to play as he took the mic off the stand and stood beside me.

'Dream, dream, dream . . .'

The guy had a nice voice and I realised I hadn't taken my eyes off him since he'd started singing. I looked out into the room. By the time he'd finished singing there were about thirty people standing at the back watching. There was complete silence, except for my music and this guy's singing, and we were rewarded with great applause.

'More!' a few people were shouting.

He put the mic back on the stand and the other guy from his table approached the stage.

'Do you know "Feelings"?' he said.

Another favourite of mine, so off we went. This guy was also a good singer. There were now more people coming into the bar from the club next door. In the four minutes it took for him to sing the song every table had people sitting around it. We finished and again there was loud applause.

I got on the mic and said, 'Anyone else like to sing?'

Everyone was too shy, so the first guy got up and sang 'Let It Be Me', another Everly Brothers song.

It was like that scene in *Jaws* where everything comes slowly into focus. This is how I do it, I thought. These people want to come and sing. I'd found my solution: open mic every Saturday night. I went over to where the two guys who had got up to sing were sitting and thanked them for helping to make it such a good evening. The guy who had sung first was called Trevor and he turned out to be a great guy; I found out later that he was a Justice of the Peace. The following week, Trevor was back with his friends, and so were many other people who'd heard about the previous Saturday. As the weeks went by more and more people got up to sing and I came to know what they liked singing and sometimes I harmonised with them. By this time my voice had dropped, and from listening to Trevor I learned some vocal tricks such as adding a vibrato to my voice. It got to the point where I wasn't happy until Trevor showed up on a Saturday night.

With the improving crowds the club decided to put in some stage lighting and dim the main lights when I was on. Atmosphere at last! Connah's Quay became the local place to be on a Saturday night and some weeks minibuses full of people came from surrounding towns. Instead of audiences in single figures we were filling the bar to capacity with sixty people. Norman was a happy chap, and my money went up to a whopping £20 a night.

I started to get other gigs in the area, mostly through word of mouth. I was soon playing Friday nights and Sunday nights as well. A few small write-ups appeared in local newspapers, and with my pay rise from Norman I bought an Italian-made Elka keyboard. I also started working on my voice. I didn't just want to develop my voice for the clubs – on *Top of the Pops* everyone sang, even Howard Jones, who was who I wanted to be at the time. To begin with I sounded terrible, but after listening and practising, and putting my poor mum through hell, one day it happened. The first song I ever got to grips with was 'You'll Never Walk Alone' in honour of my football team, Liverpool, and my Nan Bo.

Not only did I get a new keyboard, I also got my first proper girlfriend, Heather. She was in the year below and when we met the principal object of her affection was a horse called Philip – I soon changed that. We'd go to the Mersey View under-eighteens disco every Monday night and kiss and cuddle all evening. At school we'd rush out at breaktime to find one another. We spent all our time together so it wasn't long before she became party to my music obsession. Heather had a reasonably nice voice, so we got an act together, with me playing the keyboards and both of us singing. 'Karisma' was born.

Besides playing the Union Church Coffee Morning, we also entered the annual talent competition organised by Greenalls and the local paper. The first heats for Starmaker '85 were in April and our heat was on 24 May. The songs we played included the Carpenters' 'Top Of The World', 'Flashdance', 'I Know Him So Well' and 'Waiting For A Star To Fall'. We didn't qualify for the final, but we did win £100 as the 'Act Showing Greatest Potential'.

I was sure that all that was standing in our way was my equipment. There was another duo in the competition and they had a Yamaha DX7 and a Roland SH101 – their kit made them seem so much better than us. With my half of the prize money, along with my savings from working at Connah's Quay, I went and bought an SH101 – serious noises at last.

When I played the SH101 live I could programme it mid-song with my left hand as I went from verse to chorus. It marked the beginning of my fascination with the art of recording. I wanted to learn how every sound got on to every song I liked, what made the individual noises and how records came to sound the way they did. Often Heather would come to my house at seven in the evening and just sit there until a quarter to ten when it was time for her to go – I'd be so busy experimenting I wouldn't have spoken to her at all.

The guy that organised Starmaker '85 was called Mike Bain and he was a local agent and manager. He got us more gigs in Liverpool, at social clubs and legions as well as at Frenchies in Victoria Road, Widnes – 'neat and tidy dress essential' as it said on the poster. We did shows everywhere, all over Liverpool, the Wirral and Runcorn, and even locally in Frodsham. We were making £40–50 a night, not bad for a couple of teenagers. With the proceeds of our gigs I bought an amplifier, two massive speakers and mics for us both. The peak of my aspirations was the Yamaha DX7 organ, which was £1,300, the equivalent of £3,500 today. My mum took a deep breath and put it on her Access card. It took me fourteen months to pay her back; I still can't believe she did that for me. Heather's mum and dad were great, too, and helped me buy a PS-360 keyboard. We began to sound a lot more professional.

My mum and dad and Heather's mum and dad were probably our most loyal fans at this stage. They'd come to all our shows and proudly watch us. My dad used to complain that Heather's dad was classic Frodsham – he'd time all the rounds so he only had to get one in while my dad got two. They came along to one gig in Accrington, where we were booked to play three spots. We did all our usual material, which went down really well wherever we played and afterwards, as we were packing up the gear, two members of the committee came over and said, 'I'm sorry, kids, but the fact is you weren't very good, not what we were expecting at all, so we're not going to pay you.' I couldn't believe it, I knew they were trying it on. Both my dad and Heather's dad spoke to them, but they would have none of it. They refused to pay us a penny. I was utterly embarrassed by the whole thing – but I'm ashamed to say that it made me doubt Heather, not myself.

A while later I got a call from Mike Bain, who asked me if I'd be prepared to do a gig in Austria. His daughters had a dance group and he wanted me to support them, but he only wanted me, not Heather. This went down very badly with Heather's parents. They reminded me that they had paid for one of my keyboards, which was now a vital part of my equipment. It was a kind of ultimatum: no Heather, no PS-360.

In the end the gig fell through, but it caused a rift in my parents' friendship with Heather's parents and it was a watershed in my relationship with Heather. From then on we stopped working together and began seeing each other in secret because her parents disapproved. And they huffed and puffed about the PS-360 so much that I told them to stick it; I'd buy one of my own.

2

The Entertainer

There's no question that working a club, faced with an audience who don't really care whether you're there or not, is just about the best training there is. You learn how to win them over, make them laugh and entertain them to the point where eventually they begin to enjoy you in spite of themselves. Believe me, performing to a stadium is nothing compared to playing to a hostile audience in some of the clubs in the north of England.

With the gigs I got through Mike Bain, and a few I'd cultivated myself, it felt like time to leave Norman and Connah's Quay Club. I also had a piece of real good fortune. Chris Greenleaves was the regular organist at Halton's British Legion Club, the local premier league. One afternoon I was round his house when he said, 'Gary, I'm quitting the Legion, why don't you try out for the job? They're holding auditions this coming Saturday.'

The club was over five times the size of Connah's Quay and I'd have to work every Friday, Saturday and Sunday night, as well as Sunday afternoons. In addition there was a compere, a star turn featuring either a top-flight singer or a comedian every night, and I'd get the chance to play with a drummer. It would be a big promotion from the lower-division clubs I was used to playing.

The audition was around midday. Mum dropped me off outside the Legion. This was the first time I'd been inside; it was *huge*. There was a massive stage with a circular gantry above it, on which were suspended loads of lights; it was the biggest and best-decorated stage I'd ever seen. It had two tiers – the top was for the organ and drums and the second was where the guest artists would perform. There were no chairs and tables dotted around, just semi-circular booths with seats covered in dark red velvet. It looked very flash, but it also felt awesomely professional.

There to take the auditions were the four gentlemen of the committee. I recognised one of the guys – his name was Jimmy Gill and he was a shortish frightening-looking character. When you looked at him you thought just one thing: tough. Another guy introduced himself as Bernie Collings. He was older than Jimmy, with thick glasses and a slightly bald head. The other two didn't seem too involved with the audition and didn't even bother to introduce themselves, but I could tell they all loved the power of being on the selection panel. Social club committees are all about self-importance – not that I knew that then.

There were four of us there for the audition; the first man was already playing and thankfully he was pretty crappy. By this time I was a very good keyboard player – much better than I am now because all I'd done for the previous three years was play. The second guy proved to be little better than the first and then it was my turn. I said something that made them laugh as I made my way to the stage – so far so good – but as I sat behind the organ and looked at what was facing me I thought, oh boy, this is big. It had three keyboards, not the usual two, and hundreds of buttons. Within thirty seconds I had the thing talking – it wasn't clever; it was what I did every day – and over the fifteen minutes I got the organ's drum effect going, the guitar, the piano – it was a great piece of kit. By the end of my three songs I was happy with my audition and walked back to my seat.

As I sat there thinking over how it had gone, I realised that the drum machine had been playing for some time, but nothing else was happening; there was no tune coming from the organ. It was clear the fourth guy didn't know how to turn it off. Everyone was looking round and he was looking down from the stage for help. I stood up, ran on to the stage and stopped the noise instantly. 'Thanks,' said the guy. 'Thanks,' said all four committee members in unison. I was a hero. Once the guy started to play I realised he was good – technically much better player than I was – but he hadn't mastered the organ, so texturally it didn't sound as good as it should have done.

We all left our phone numbers and waited for a call; and a few days later Jimmy rang to say the job was mine. I was really excited and so was my mum – especially as Halton was a lot nearer than Connah's Quay and she would have to drive me there!

There was just one problem: I was still only fourteen.

When I'd gone for the audition I hadn't mentioned the fact that I was under age, and I still couldn't bring myself to say anything. The first time I went to play at the club one of the committee bought me a pint and I had real difficulties losing it – I didn't drink at all until I joined Take That. This ritual went on for a few weeks until things finally came to a head and Bernie asked me for my National Insurance number.

As usual Mum came to the rescue.

'Bernie, this is Gary's mum. I need to come and see you, we have a bit of a problem.'

Mum and I went to the club.

'He's not fifteen until next month,' said Mum.

Bernie went cross-eyed.

'Is he not, love? You'll have to leave me thinking about that.'

The solution was simple: they paid me less, so I avoided the threshold for tax and National Insurance.

Playing in the club was an altered reality. This was a working men's club and the audience was full of real salt-of-the-earth types who liked to have a drink, a game of bingo, a dance and that was it. It was 1985 – the Pet Shop Boys' 'It's a Sin' was in the charts and Wham! was huge, but they weren't interested in hearing current stuff: they wanted to hear 'Sweet Caroline', and 'Amarillo'. There was no respect for the stage – you were just there to cater for their needs.

It was shortly before Christmas when I got the gig, and almost right away Jimmy Gill told me I'd be required to work a lot over the holiday period.

'Gary, on Boxing Day afternoon you'll be playing for an open mic session,' said Jimmy.

'No problem, I've done plenty of those at my last club,' said I, all cocky.

For the first time since starting at the Legion, Dad came along too. He was there to witness a fiasco. It was the first Legion gig where I played without a drummer and with no other artist to accompany. It was just me, the keyboard and an audience of middle-aged and older men, almost all of whom seemed the worse for wear. I had barely got going when out of the corner of my eye I saw a guy climbing lopsidedly on to the stage. Next thing he was belting out, 'Pleaz-a, release me, letta me goa . . .'

I didn't really know the song, and as I fumbled around, trying to find some of the notes he was singing, he would change key, so my notes and his song only collided randomly at intervals. He was hardly off the stage before another guy was up.

'Only yoooou can make this wooorld seem right . . .'

Again I desperately tried to find the notes but couldn't, while he waved at me trying to get me to join in – I was trying dammit!

'This kid can't back anyone,' was his abrupt dismissal.

The nightmare went on. If only they'd ask me if I knew the song first I might stand a chance. Hang on, here comes another one . . .

'I am saaailling . . . I am saaaaaaaaaai . . .' Ah good, this one I know. This time the challenge was to find the key he was singing in. Got it, I thought, I'm safe. And on they went for two hours – two hours of non-stop hell. Some of the songs I knew; some I'd never heard before or since. Sometimes they sang lyrics to songs I knew, but to tunes I didn't. Others were in mad keys neither I nor anyone else had ever played them in. And you wouldn't believe the abuse I got from those I couldn't join in with. I wasn't ready for this. I looked down and Dad was cringing. So this is Christmas . . .

And as if the embarrassment of the afternoon session wasn't enough, I had to be back at the club at 7.30 p.m. to play through the evening. At the end of the night Jimmy Gill came over. I knew everyone was disappointed in me.

'That was a real test for you, wasn't it?' he said.

He wasn't wrong; my expression said it all.

'Don't worry, Gary, there's a whole year till the next one. Plenty of time to practise.'

For someone so young, it was a huge responsibility doing these gigs – I had to be consistent and reliable; no wonder I felt like I was fourteen going on fifty. Even now I'm always the responsible one, and I hate it! With Take That, when the guy comes in from the label, it's always me saying, 'How you doing, do you want a cup of tea?' Coming from my kind of family, you always feel you have to do your best and do everything properly so it wasn't long before I could see improvements that could be made at Halton. The drummer at the Legion was called Brian and he'd played there when Chris had the gig. He was kind to me and a good drummer – better than most – although he had a tendency to speed up and would get annoyed if any of the acts criticised his playing. One thing about him really bugged me, though: he was always scruffy when he came to work at the club. I was still buzzing from getting the gig and chuffed to be working such a great stage and venue, so I couldn't understand it. I decided to set an example and started wearing a shirt and dicky bow as my stage gear – that was the look in the clubs. Brian took the hint and soon we had matching wardrobes. It looked so pro, the backing band in the same attire. Some nights we did black shirts and red dicky bows, others blue shirts and white dicky bows. Soon I began hearing comments around the club like, 'Gary's really changed this place.'

It made me proud. Now all we needed was a decent compere.

One night, not long after Christmas, I was playing away when it dawned on me that there were no women in the club that night. When I'd finished my first short set I was surprised to see Jimmy Gill and one of the other committee members bolting and locking the doors. Jimmy told me to get back to the keyboard, handed me some sheet music and asked me to start playing. Seconds after my opening chords a girl came out of the wings on to the lower part of the stage and started dancing. I immediately knew what she was. Next, as I'm playing away, a feather floated down from somewhere and landed on my arm. I didn't dare look up, in fact my eyes never left my sheet music. All the while I was thinking, so this is what they meant when they talked about a 'Gentlemen's Evening'!

Smartened up or not, the Committee soon decided that Brian the drummer had to go. One evening I arrived at the club to find there was a different set of drums on the top tier next to my organ. It was a nice kit, with more drums than Brian had had. Standing over them talking to Jimmy was a podgy black-haired guy twiddling two drumsticks. 'This is John Tedford; he's your new drummer,' said Jimmy.

I liked him immediately; he was bubbly, easy to get on with and he was smartly dressed.

We fired into a song and he was pretty good – steady rhythm, no speeding up – and it sounded fine. John had been playing at another big club in the area with a girl called Lisa, who I'd heard people talking about. Everyone said how great she was and I worried that John would think she was better than me. I wanted to prove how good I was to him, so I tried everything – Latin, samba, rock, disco and ballads – I really put him through it. By the end of the night I looked over and poor old John was as red as a tomato.

'You can play, kid,' he said, wiping his brow.

I guess John was playing the same game: he wanted to be sure it was a step up for him too. We were both happy. We needed a head start on the following weekend, so I suggested we put in a couple of nights' rehearsal in the week.

'No problem, kid.'

We rehearsed at the club on Wednesday night and all went well. The following night we were just getting ready to start when a good-looking guy in his late thirties came walking towards the stage.

'Hi, I'm Chris Harrison.'

He handed me some music, took the microphone and started to sing – he was great. When he finished he told us he was the new compere at the club. The next night was our first as the resident trio and it was really slick. Chris was fantastic, and from the start the three of us just gelled. His chat between numbers was brilliant, in fact, he was a fantastic all-round entertainer. Even as a fourteen-year-old veteran I knew that from then on Halton Legion would be talked about as a top-class venue.

In a way John Tedford and Chris Harrison were my best friends then. Sure between gigs there was school and I had friends there, but I had no time to see them outside school – I kept it all separate. Heather and I were still seeing each other in secret. I think originally we kept on meeting to spite her parents, but now that I was working so much at Halton we began drifting apart. The music always came first. My mum was concerned that I should be applying myself more at school; she worried about how I'd make a living from music and used to say, 'Gary, don't you think it would be good if you got a job in a bank?'

But one day the Head of Physics, Ted Walker, came round to the house, heard me playing and said, 'Marge, don't put him in a bank.'

Years later Ted came back into my life. We needed a choir to sing on 'Never Forget' when we played ten nights at Manchester's MEN Arena. I rang my Mum and asked her if she knew of one and she suggested Ted, who is now a headmaster and a member of the Warrington Male Voice Choir – they did a great job.

Ted wasn't the only teacher at school who noticed my passion. Mrs Nelson, my school music teacher, told me about a competition called A Song for Christmas, which was organised by the TV programme *Pebble Mill*. She encouraged me to write something – my first serious stab at composing – and I recorded it at home on what was by now pretty sophisticated equipment. When I played it for my mum she said it was a bit slow; Mrs Nelson on the other hand said I should go for it. The two weeks after sending in a tape of 'Let's Pray For Christmas' proved to be just about the longest fortnight of my life. Finally a reply came from *Pebble Mill* when I was in the gym doing some rope climbing. Mrs Nelson walked through the door and I didn't need her to tell me that my entry had been accepted into the finals, her face said it all.

A week later I went to *Pebble Mill*'s studio in Birmingham, where I met the producer Bob Howes, whose brainchild the competition was. He was incredibly kind to me from the start. He must have been in his mid-thirties then – he'd just had his first child – and was a real BBC type: a cuddly guy with a big beard, a grand BBC voice and classical training. He knew just what to do with my recording. My tape was over four and a half minutes long and Bob edited it down to make it shorter and better.

Another week went by and Mrs Nelson and I went down to London, her navigating the tube, me following behind, the wide-eyed small-town boy in the big city. We made our way to Bob's studios, West Heath Studios in Hampstead, where, after a bit of chat, he said, 'We've got half an hour to record the song.'

'What? Is that all?'

In a flash I was taken into the studio proper, where thirty musicians were sitting waiting. I was placed in front of a microphone, and the next thing I knew a pair of headphones were being shoved on my head. This kind of thing is second nature to me now, but back then I was scared to death. To be honest, I had no idea why I even needed to wear the headphones.

Two, three, four . . . and the orchestra began playing *my* song, it was unbelievable. It was one of those special moments that can never be repeated – thirty musicians were playing a song I had written and it gave me such a kick. I did my vocal accompanied by three girl backing singers. When we finished, some of the musicians tapped their music stands with their bows, which I discovered was their way of showing their appreciation. It was incredible.

A couple of weeks after that I went to the TV studios, where I was filmed singing to the track on a set covered in fake snow. I won the semi-final, but not the final. Of course I was disappointed, but I was still pleased to have done so well.

The most important part of it all, however, was meeting Bob Howes. After the competition he said, 'You should carry on writing songs; you've got a real talent for it. Keep in touch and let me know how you get on.' It was the encouragement I needed. I went home to write more songs, which I then recorded as demos to send to Bob. He sent me a handwritten letter back, saying,

'Why don't you listen to this . . . try listening to that . . . and let's not do this by post, come down and see me.' He had a perspective I was never going to encounter in the clubs.

That first time I made the trip with my mum, and we all sat and listened to the songs. Bob critiqued my songs, often criticising them, but at the same time encouraging me, making me feel I had a future. I've never forgotten him saying, 'Gary, if you're successful and you eventually get a record deal, you won't have time then to write songs. Think of it this way, you have a lifetime to write that first album, and probably only a few weeks to write your second, so keep writing whenever you can.' He was bloody right.

And I did keep on writing. Mum would come home from work, get herself a cup of tea and settle down to listen to what I'd written that day, because most days I wrote something. Three months later I went down to see Bob again, on my own this time, with a new tape. It became a routine – Bob would pick me up from Euston and we'd stick the tape in the car stereo and start right away. One of the first songs I sent Bob was one I had just written and recorded called 'A Million Love Songs'. It seems amazing now to think that I wrote it in my bedroom in Frodsham, aged fifteen. I think it was inspired by working in the club and playing all those smoochy Lionel Richie ballads and Neil Diamond songs. Somewhere in my fifteen-year-old mind all those love songs had mingled into something original. At the time I didn't know it was a big one – I didn't learn that skill till much later – so it was just tucked in among loads of other stuff I'd come up with that week, but my mum used to take tapes of my songs over to Nan Bo's to play her, and one day she came home and said, 'Your nan loves that Million Love Songs, she does, she thinks it's brilliant and I do too.'

With reactions like that, it began to climb its way up my demo list moving from number seven to number two.

It was a shame my mum and Nan Bo weren't A&R people. I was starting to send people demos, albeit with Bob's advice 'Never, ever, sign anything without telling me first' ringing in my ears. Bob had a few good contacts in the business and on one of my trips to London he put me in touch with a guy at Rocket Publishing, one of Elton John's companies. I had visited some other publishers, where the guy who listened to my tape would give me a polite brush-off after a couple of songs. At Rocket the guy listened to all six songs, including 'A Million Love Songs'. He sat behind his desk with his back to me and stared out of the window as he listened. When the tape finished he got up, went over to the cassette machine, took out my tape, walked back across his office, opened the window and threw my tape out of it. He then turned, and without smiling or showing any emotion, said, 'Don't come back here with any of your music ever again.'

I was gutted. Years later I told Elton about it and he remembered the guy. Apparently he left Rocket without telling anyone, and it was only after two months that they noticed he'd gone. That made me feel slightly better.

With John Tedford on the drums, working at Halton was a wonderful experience. The acts that John and I backed almost always brought their own music with them. They would come into our dressing room before the show and say,

'Here's the dots, any problems?'

The dots is what they called their sheet music. Luckily I was able to sight-read any of the music the acts brought with them thanks to my lessons with Chris Greenleaves. On a typical night, John and I would play from 8–8.30 p.m., and after a five-minute break the main act would go on. One guy we backed gave us the dots, I took a quick look and it all seemed straightforward. Everything was going fine when suddenly what he was singing and what we were playing were at total odds with one another.

We managed to get to the end of the song and through the rest of the set with no further problems, but I was baffled as to how we'd gone so wrong. When I asked him afterwards what had happened he opened up the sheet music,

'You missed the BTT,' he said, pointing to the bottom of the page.

'BTT? What's that?' I thought I knew all the fancy musical notations.

'Back tut top.'

We backed old-school stand-ups at Halton, including Jim Davidson and Russ Abbot – they were big names to us then – but there was one man we dreaded: Ken Dodd. It ought to have been a breeze as Ken only did six songs and he would come into the dressing room before the show and give us our cues: 'When I say, "You can go a long way on a shuttlecock", that's your first cue and I'll sing "Happiness", so you'll need to start the music there.'

It all seemed simple enough, except for one problem. The head Diddyman went on and on and on, twenty to forty minutes between songs was not unusual, and we had no idea at all when the cue was coming, which meant John and I had to concentrate bloody hard. Sometimes he would be on stage for four hours – the audience could come and go, but neither John nor I could even take a leak. After five nights waiting on Ken to sing about the bloody Diddymen I was totally wiped out. The other end of the spectrum was Bob Monkhouse, who was absolutely brilliant and a total professional. He would do five nights and on each night his jokes would be different.

It wasn't just comedians and singers that worked the clubs, one man who I appeared with a few times was a clairvoyant called Bentley Evans. One night after the show he came up to me and said, 'Gary, I'm desperate to talk to you. There are some things I really want to tell you. Give me your hand.' He looked at my palm and exclaimed, 'I knew it! You've got some life ahead of you. Between fifteen and thirty you'll have an amazing time, but I need to warn you that for the next few years after that, things will be difficult. Something is going to happen to you. It might be that you break your leg or have some kind of a fall. But don't worry, after you pass thirty-five and head towards forty, things will get better and better.' At the time I hardly gave it a second thought and I forgot about it completely until very recently. But it popped into my head the other day and I thought he might have been on to something.

It was my last year at school, but school felt like an inconvenience. I certainly wasn't focusing on my five O-levels (I'd already passed my music O-level the year before). I was backing gigs three or sometimes five times a week and John and I were busy entering the 1987 Greenall Whitley/*Weekly News* Club Act of the Year together. We called ourselves Stax and beat a Liverpool group called Fizzy Drinks who had already appeared on TV's *New Faces* by just one point, and walked away with the £500 top prize – my first.

At the same time I entered the National Schools Make Music Competition, which is sponsored by EMI. Three weeks after winning the talent contest I heard that out of thousands of hopefuls, I was down to the last ten. The local paper came round to interview me and take my photograph – I still have that cutting. I told them it was my lifetime's ambition to appear on *Top of the Pops*, and added rather optimistically, 'Eventually I would like to go on and record great records, that is my dream.'

A couple of weeks later I heard that my song 'Now We're Gone' had won and that I was invited to London to receive the prize. It was a big moment for my whole family – first I went to EMI's headquarters with Dad, Mum and Nan Bo, and after that we went to Abbey Road Studios, where I recorded my winning song. I was really excited by all this, but I wasn't phased by it. I'd been doing so much performing I'd started to think of myself as a pro.

EMI brought in a couple of guys to do some programming and, probably because I was so used to working on my own equipment at home, I took over in my usual way. It took longer than they had anticipated to finish, and I never did get to see the record pressed at EMI's factory; I'd been too busy being a perfectionist. Back home our local newspaper interviewed me and I told them that the song wasn't very good, but my headmaster said, 'Gary has a great natural talent.'

One afternoon, after we heard that I had won the prize, I went to his office and said, 'Mr Brown, you know all this gear I've won for the school? Well, I was thinking, it's worth a thousand pounds, which is quite a lot, I mean it'll buy a fair bit, but I need some new gear for my studio, too, so how about writing me a cheque for half?'

He was good guy, Mr Brown, and he didn't flinch. He didn't say, 'Gary, this is your chance to contribute to the school and the community,' he just wrote me a cheque and handed it over with a smile.

Every time I earned money, it never went into the bank, it just went on more gear – more synths, an Atari music computer, a drum machine, you name it. It was never a case of do I need it? More, do I want it? And I wanted it all. It had reached the stage where there was no room in my bedroom for a bed, so for three years I slept on the couch in the lounge, which, as you can imagine, my mum loved.

It might not have been cool but I found all things techy completely compelling – it was like an addiction and still is. By now I was doing a Wednesday night gig in a pub near Wigan, where I'd just play instrumentals like *War of the Worlds*, Shakatak, Jan Hammer and the theme from *Miami Vice*. I'd take all my synths and have a fantastic time. There was a whole group of techy keyboard players who used to come each week, and in the break we'd talk about the delights the YS185 – what an enjoyable night that was! But it wasn't just about synths. At home I was developing my demos. Rick Astley was from my area and I remember seeing him on the local news, *Look North West*, and feeling really pissed off that he'd been discovered by Stock, Aitken and Waterman and I hadn't. They seemed to be behind everything: Mel and Kim, Bananarama, Sinitta and, a few months later, Kylie and Jason Donovan. It was as if they'd discovered the hit formula – suddenly pop was a sum with a plus and an equals. I wanted my demos to sound just like theirs. but Bob Howes wasn't so sure; he used to say, 'Listen to Peter Gabriel and Sting, listen to Phil Collins . . .' But I was heading towards manufactured pop, even if I had to manufacture it myself.

I passed my O-levels that summer – just – and left school. Suddenly life was wide open before me. I was busier than ever, performing almost every night. With my spiky hair and impressive array of keyboards I would open with 'Phantom of the Opera', follow it with 'Love Changes Everything' and then do some Lionel Richie and Neil Diamond. I had my set down to a fine art; I knew what they liked and they knew what they liked, but most important of all they liked what they knew.

A few agents began to take notice of me and offered me gigs, which was a real bonus. As soon as I was seventeen I began learning to drive, and soon after I passed my test, which allowed me to travel further afield. With my own car, my own speakers and my keyboards in the back, along with my homemade backing tapes, I was a self-contained one-man band. I did a Monday, Tuesday and Wednesday in Blackpool for £50 a night, a local gig on Thursday for the same money and then Friday, Saturday and two shows on Sunday at Halton, for which I would pick up between £90 and £120 per night. I was making more money than my dad! I was also making a lot more than my brother, who had just finished a YTS scheme. Our lives were very different, particularly because he needed to be careful with his money. I'd been earning since I was thirteen and had always had the luxury of being able to buy whatever I wanted – I was renowned for it. On my eighteenth birthday my mum organised a surprise birthday party for me, with all my friends there. They had got a branch of a tree and taped eighteen pound coins to it, then they'd written on it, 'To the man that thinks money grows on trees', because that was me. Then I spent it all on equipment, now my great pleasure is spoiling my family – taking the kids on a Disney cruise or treating my whole family to a grand Christmas gives me a real buzz.

More than the money, working was about learning. When Take That played live in the early days, we'd have found it much harder if I hadn't spent so long doing the circuit. I was the only one in the band who was used to performing live. When we stepped up a level, my ability to sing night after night helped our live shows to happen. Added to which, my experience gave me a lot of self-belief to fall back on and an ability to ride out the tough times – I knew I had what it took to work even the most difficult audience.

In June 1989 I finally left Halton British Legion, having had a brilliant time working with many great people. I began playing lots of different clubs, sometimes quite a way from home. I played the Valor New Home Social Club on Merseyside, Clock Face Labour Club in St Helens – 'Gary Barlow – welcome return of the teenage sensation!' – Wargrave Labour Club in Newton-le-Willows, Laporte Recreation Club in Widnes, and as far south as Lakeside Country Club in Essex. I became a performer like those I'd backed at Halton. At some clubs I took my own dots with me and the house duo or group backed me, while at others I used my homemade backing tapes.

At home there was some tension, though. Mum and Dad

thought I should be working – at a proper job. They didn't get the fact that I was sleeping in until eleven in the morning and working late at night. For them work happened between nine and five, and my life, well, I guess it seemed short-term to them. So when I talked about being famous . . . It made no sense to my dad, but I think my mum turned a blind eye because she secretly believed I might be the one in a million it would happen for.

Looking back, it was quite a solitary time in my life. Heather and I were still seeing each other on and off, but the relationship was limping along. What was in it for Heather I'll never know. I wasn't very nice to her. I never took her out for dinner, I never complimented her or told her I loved her, although I think underneath it all I must have done. It was one of those classic first relationships where the boy uses the girl but the girl keeps coming back for more. I'd also met a girl called Nicky. Nicky was made of different stuff from Heather. Her mum and dad had split up, she was tougher, liked to argue and had made a bit of a name for herself at school for being lippy with the teachers. She had a much brassier look than Heather – blonde, blue-eyed and always in short skirts – and to meet her you'd think she was hard and cold, though underneath she was anything but. Needless to say my mum didn't approve of her one bit and banned her from coming to the house, so now I had two relationships to carry on in secret.

To offset the loneliness of gigging as a solo act, I had a crack at joining my first group. They were called Passion and we got a write-up in the local paper as an 'up-and-coming Chester rock band'. I only did a few gigs before deciding my own work was more lucrative and, for me, more satisfying. As often as not I found it difficult to make rehearsals and gigs because I already had a booking. I was gigging most nights and Nicky used to come and watch – she was fascinated by the music business and by show business in general. She used to talk about being an actress and that's exactly what she does now: sometimes I catch her in *The Bill* or on *Coronation Street*.

One night an agent got me a double, that's to say two shows on the same night. Apart from the fact that it was hard work, one of them was Bernard Manning's Embassy Club in Manchester and they paid crap money. The other was a big new club that had just been refurbished. I arrived full of confidence, knowing that my money was steadily going up, which only happens when you get better. The car park was full and as I walked into the club the guy on the door smiled and said, 'Full house, kid.'

'Just the way I like it.'

Inside I found lots of older couples dancing ballroom-style, accompanied by a lady sat on a nice-looking stage, playing the piano. The manager spotted me and immediately came over.

'What do you think? It's taken me ten months to get this place right.'

'It looks pretty good, but I don't see any speakers,' I said, feeling slightly worried.

'It's OK, I've got a microphone,' he replied, producing a mic with a long cord and, in place of the normal jack plug, a three-pin plug.

A little questioning from me revealed that he thought you just plugged the microphone into the mains and the sound magically came out from somewhere. I told him not to plug it in under any circumstances – it was a miracle he hadn't fried himself already.

'I can't perform without amplification and there's no way my Dad can get my equipment here in time,' I told him. 'We'll just have to call it off.'

He was mortified; his big night was about to be ruined. Eventually I agreed to go on with the pianist as my accompanist. They shut the bar to keep the noise down and I stood in the middle of the dance floor and sang for forty-five minutes without a mic while she played the piano on stage. I got four encores and it turned into one of my best nights as an entertainer.

Midweek gigs were the worst, especially if it wasn't a club I knew or played regularly. I particularly dreaded young audiences. On more than one occasion I was forced to beat a hasty retreat from a club after being accosted by some drunken guy. 'You fuckin' looked at my girlfriend,' was the usual line of attack. Sometimes I got myself into hot water all by myself. One night I had a booking at the Metal Box Social Club near Speke, which wasn't far from where my nan lived. I got my car close to the back door of the club so I could unload my gear and finished setting it all up just as the bingo started. I wasn't due on for about an hour, so I thought I'd nip round to Nan Bo's to see how she was. Where I thought I'd been told to park was a patch of grass and as I drove off I did a few hand-brake turns and wheel spins – actually it wasn't a few, it was a lot! When I got back I did my spot, which went fine, and then as I was loading my equipment back into my car, one of the committee came up and asked if I'd seen anyone driving around earlier.

'Some bloody hooligan has completely ruined our bowling green,' said the man. He was red with rage. I, in contrast, turned white. I didn't have the guts to own up.

One midweek gig that initially appeared to be promising was at Mabbs Cross, near Wigan. The first time I went there I was met by a well-dressed man in his late fifties who ran the place. When I finished my first night he said, 'Gary, we'll definitely have you back again, you're a nice young man.'

Next time I played there he invited me to have dinner, and as we chatted he said they had a health club and sauna if I was interested in using it. Then he said, 'Do you know Dorothy?'

'Dorothy who? Well, no, I don't know anyone called Dorothy.'

'OK, that's fine. I just wondered.'

Now I can see that he was gay and that was some kind of test question. I had no knowledge of his world; I don't think I'd even met a gay guy at that point, and thankfully he never followed up on his remark. I took my mum and dad there once and she was fascinated by him – my mum loves gay men.

I often played clubs in Sheffield and other parts of Yorkshire. You knew it was a good club when there were two acts on the bill, although some of the clubs in Yorkshire had a disconcerting way of showing their appreciation after you finished. The compere would get on the mic and say, 'Come on ladies and gentlemen, show your appreciation for Gary. I think you'll agree he's well worth sixty quid.'

At another Yorkshire club, I was halfway through 'Love On The Rocks' when a guy got up on the stage, walked right in front of me, switched on the compere's mic and said loudly, so as to drown me out, 'Pies 'ave cum.'

Every chair in the place was scraped across the floor as, en masse, they all stood up and got in line for their food.

On another night I was on with a duo from London, a couple of black guys who were really good.

'Ladies and gentlemen, we've got a couple of darkies who've come all the way from London. We didn't really want 'em, but now they're 'ere, show 'em some appreciation.'

As I say, working the clubs was an amazing experience.

My name had begun appearing in the local what's-on guide and word had started to spread. I was acquiring an image, even if it was one that appealed to the over-forties. I'd turn up for an evening in my white shirt with the black stars, my hair freshly bleached and gelled, doused in Jazz aftershave and feeling pretty good. People had started coming up to me after the show and talking about becoming my manager or agent, about their contacts and sometimes about how they could make me a star. One of them was called Barry Wooley, a sociable guy who worked for the Leo Agency, which booked me into some of the clubs in Wigan. He was always on about people he knew in the record business. One day Barry told me that 'some people in the biz' who he knew down in Nottingham had a track they wanted to release as a single and they were interested in me doing the vocal.

'I'll take you down there, but you have to sign a contract with me,' said Barry.

'I'm not sure about that, Barry.'

'Well you have to sign, otherwise I can't take you. I'll tell you what I'll do, if it doesn't work out with the record, you can walk away from the contract.'

I knew it wasn't a good idea, so much so that I didn't tell my mum and dad I'd signed it, let alone Bob Howes.

The studio in Nottingham was great and I started to feel like I was getting closer to something big happening with my career. The song they wanted me to sing was a remake of 'Love Is In The Air'. I did my vocal overdub, which turned out fine, or so I thought anyway. They all said they liked it, but added that they already had a good vocal and would I be prepared to be in the video and front the recording instead? I was to be 'Kurtis Rush' for the purposes of this project. I suspect that was the plan all along, but I agreed and the following week I was in London in a studio full of the latest equipment, with a video director and, best of all, two eighteen-year-old dancers, Priscilla and a blonde girl called Dawn. Dawn was very thin, with short curly hair, and painfully shy. Whenever I looked at her she went red. We finished the shoot, said our goodbyes and I went home to Frodsham. I didn't see my future wife again until Take That played the Children's Royal Variety Show, then she did the BRITs and toured with us.

In the end 'Love Is In The Air' didn't get released, but I enjoyed the experience. However, that wasn't the last I heard of Barry Wooley. Once I found fame with Take That, he came around clutching his so-called contract and demanding a piece of the action. Despite the fact that there was no proper agreement, it was easier to pay him off than fight it.

At home I was getting careless in my two-timing love-rat ways. Nicky and I were still going out – she was a great gal and we had some fantastic times together – but I couldn't bring myself to come clean with Heather. It was my brother Ian who finally told Heather that I was playing around. One night the family was out and Nicky and I were at my house together when Heather knocked on the door. Nicky and I were both shocked to see her and I think we all froze.

'What are you doing here?' said Heather, although she knew she'd catch us. She looked at Nicky and said, 'I think you'd better go.'

Nicky looked at me.

'You bastard!' said Heather. She turned and tore out of the house in floods of tears, and this time I knew it was the last time.

There were so few nights I wasn't working back then that it was surprising that Heather even caught me at home. I was driving all over the place – a three-hour drive to Whitehaven in Cumbria on a Wednesday was nothing unusual, although the drive home was knackering. But working the club circuit was a good living and a lot of fun, and, besides that, was giving me experiences that were priceless both personally and professionally. Those clubs are the heart of what happens in the north – they are the centre of the community, and the communities are very close knit because of them. Week in, week out, people turn up, sit in the same seats and wait to be taken out of themselves for a few hours. And they usually have a good time – even if they don't always show it.

Perhaps the most telling comment I ever received while playing the clubs came when I was working in the north-west.

I finished my set and no one applauded, they just sat there. As I was leaving the venue one of the committee said to me,

'Have a good night, lad?'

'Well, it was a bit odd because I worked my arse off and no one clapped,' I said.

'No one claps me when I come out of the pit either,' he said. It kind of put it all into perspective.

3

And Then There Were Five

Some time around 1990 I wrote a list of goals in my Filofax, the things I wanted most in the world:

To appear on *Top of the Pops*
To go to Disneyland
A Ferrari Testarossa like the one on *Miami Vice*, or failing that a Ford XR3i
A Saisho CB radio
To have my songs published with 'Words and music by Gary Barlow' on the cover
To turn on the Blackpool lights

Top of the Pops was the big one, but more and more I couldn't see how the clubs would ever connect with that world. The longer I spent in the clubs the more I took on the club act mentality – a little bitter, a little bitchy, very 'Ooo, what does she think she looks like in that dress?' It was time to get out.

Doing the rounds of the clubs I met a lot of other acts, and one that I saw regularly was a great husband-and-wife duo who I became quite friendly with. The wife's name was Jeannie Gray and she was always saying to me, 'Gary, you need to find a manager.'

Early in 1990, not long after my nineteenth birthday, Jeannie began to put together a list of local guys who managed artists; I think she'd looked through *The Stage* to come up with their names and addresses. With her help I put together a package to send to each of them. In it there was a photograph of me (it was horrible), a biography and a tape of my songs. There were also some packages without the tape which we sent to casting agents as I'd always fancied being an extra on *Brookside* or some similar show, and thought a few walk-on parts on TV could earn me some extra money to supplement the £400–500 a week I was making in the clubs. I posted them off and waited for the offers to flood in.

It was a while before I heard back from anyone, and when I did it wasn't what I was expecting. A Manchester casting and model agent, Boss Agency, contacted me and asked me to go in for a meeting at 3 p.m. the following day. They were one of the agencies who just had my biography and photograph, no tape, but I agreed without hesitation. I roughly knew my way around the centre of Manchester from playing some of the clubs, so I had no trouble finding my way there. I parked my red Ford Orion, wandered down to Half Moon Chambers in Chapel Walks and found a big brown building with the words 'Boss Agency' above the door. I stood for a moment or two looking up at the sign, though at the time I couldn't have told you why.

I wasn't that excited because I'd just been offered a twelve-month contract on the SS *Canberra* and the chance to cruise around the world. One of the guys on the club circuit had said, 'Gary, you have to do it – it's a shag fest!' Besides, getting a manager wasn't like getting a record deal, I was wise to that by now. It was just something that might help move me on to the next rung of the ladder, on the way to who knows where.

As I climbed the stairs to the first floor I looked at the walls covered in black-and-white images of beautiful girls and a few guys – I guessed they must be their models. I, meanwhile, was sporting the Gary Barlow 1990 look, which was the 1986 look for anyone else: white shirt, thin tie, a nice pair of Phil Collins-style pleated trousers, white socks, slip-ons and my hair gelled and spiky at the front, long at the back – why have one hairstyle when you can have two?

Sitting behind the reception desk was a gorgeous girl. She didn't smile.

'Hi, I'm Gary, I'm here for a meeting with Nigel Martin-Smith,' I said.

'OK, take a seat,' she replied without looking up.

A thought flashed through my mind, I wonder if she's waiting to be discovered? Opposite where I sat down were two stunning blonde girls of about seventeen or eighteen; they were probably models. To my right sat a handsome guy in his early twenties. He had amazing arms and an equally amazing hairstyle. I didn't fit in, not in any way. I was as white as white could be, while they were all tanned and buffed. Shit! I wanted out of there. This is why I'm not on TV, I thought. I'm not cool, I'm not styled, I could never look like them. My inner man was saying, 'Walk out now, before you make an even bigger fool of yourself.' I had grown used to rating myself pretty highly and thinking I was one step ahead in the race – but that was in the clubs where I was the boy wonder hanging out with people thirty years older than me. It was a shock to come face to face with people my own age, all of whom were just as likely to be talented as I was.

As I stood up to leave a stunning Chinese girl, I later found out her name was Ying, put her head round the corner and said, 'Are you Gary? Nigel's ready for you now.'

'Oh, right,' was all I could say as I made to follow her, my head down, hoping the models wouldn't look as I walked past. She led me through a small packed office in which six or seven harassed-looking people were crammed around a big desk, barking into phones, and into an office. Across the room, sitting behind a big desk, was Nigel Martin-Smith. We shook hands and I sat down.

Jeannie had told me that Nigel was gay, so I was instantly watching him, watching me. He was smartly dressed in jeans, a good shirt and cufflinks; I remember noticing his pierced ear and fast-moving watery green eyes. You just knew he was sharp. He looked very powerful; it was the way he sat and spoke – very softly, as if he didn't need to speak loudly, drawing you right in to hear what he was saying. And he was very charming.

Nigel explained that he was putting a band together.

'Oh, right,' I said, 'bands aren't really my thing. I was in one once and I hated the gigs – all that loading stuff in and out of vans is not for me.'

But as we were talking I couldn't help noticing a gold disc hanging on the wall above Nigel's head. The artist had a man's name – Damian – which seemed a little strange because he looked like a woman in the picture. The title of the song was 'Time Warp'. I dimly heard Nigel say, 'Had a number seven hit with Damian and he was on *Top of the Pops*.'

It was those four magic words.

All of a sudden my head began to buzz. This was my chance. Nigel had done it all before. This could be it. He was my passport to the big time. Logically, none of these thoughts made any sense, I knew it took more than talk to make things happen. Talk is cheap, and in the music business it usually ends up costing the one who's listening. But this felt different. It was Nigel's way of talking about something that hadn't yet happened as though it *had* happened, *was* happening. He was so certain this band was going to be big there was something almost overwhelming about it.

'Gary, you could be a part of the band, are you interested?'

I said I was and Nigel took my number and gave me his card. As I got up to leave I said, 'Here's a tape of some of my songs, why don't you have a listen?' He took it, but I could see a vacancy in his eyes. I knew he'd been given a hundred tapes before.

'Just have a listen . . . please.'

As I reached the door of his office I saw him toss the tape to one side of his desk.

Walking back to my car, I felt quite exited. That gold disc was a sign that this guy was serious. In my naivety I thought only really successful people got a gold disc. Imagine owning one of those, one with my name on it. Wow! I drove home, and for the next eighteen hours life remained exactly the same. It was business as usual – another night, another gig.

Next morning I was on our front drive washing my car when the phone rang. As I answered it a soft voice said,

'Gary, it's Nigel. I've just listened to your tape. It's very good.' He sounded less cool than the day before, less 'couldn't care less'. Nigel continued, 'So, who have you done this with?'

'Er, no one, just me,' I replied.

There was silence.

'Yes, but who helped you write the songs?'

'Er, no one, just me.'

The next silence went on even longer than the first.

'OK, well who recorded this stuff and played all the instruments?'

I was beginning to sound like a broken record.

'Er, no one, just me.'

'I think you'd better come back in to see me. Is this afternoon OK for you?'

A few hours later I headed into Manchester in a very clean red Ford Orion. I parked and made my way to Boss. Up the stairs I went and into reception. This time I was taken straight through to Nigel's office, no waiting. This felt better. No sooner had we said hello and sat down than Nigel flicked play on a big remote control. On to the TV screen came five guys who were all singing and dancing.

'This is an American band called New Kids on the Block,' said

Nigel. I'd never heard of them. 'They're massive all over the world, and I want to put together Britain's answer to them.'

Great, I thought. No instruments. No lugging gear up fire exits. I like this. Nigel then revealed a little more of his master-plan.

'I want to build the five-piece band around you, Gary. Your songwriting will give the whole thing credibility.'

He went on to explain that he had found three members already. Had he had these three lined up before he'd met me yesterday or had he found them since listening to my tape? It wasn't entirely apparent and I didn't like to ask.

Nigel then showed me a card with a guy's photograph on it.

'His name's Howard,' said Nigel, 'He's one of the three.'

He was a good-looking bloke with curly brown hair and a great body – he had a real model's look.

He then played me a video of the TV show featuring Pete Waterman and Michaela Strachan – *The Hitman and Her.*

'The lad that's dancing is called Jason. He's already getting fan mail,' said Nigel. 'He's one of the best dancers I've ever seen.' Then he passed me a photo.

'This one's called Mark, he's been a child model at the agency and is only about seventeen. I actually haven't completely made my mind up about him yet – he might not be in the band.'

Well, this all sounds pretty good, I thought, maybe this guy really does have a plan. We talked about the tape and Nigel said there were three songs on it that he thought were great: 'Waitin' Around', 'Girl' and 'A Million Love Songs'.

Nigel said he was truly impressed that I'd done them all by myself; he asked me to tell him how I got started as a performer and where I'd been working. What struck me most was the fact that he seemed interested in every word I said. Suddenly I felt at home and I thought there was something different about him compared with the run-of-the-mill club agents and managers I had come across. I was intrigued by him. He wasn't just telling me what he could do for me, he was showing me. He wasn't just saying I was going to be a star, he was explaining how it was going to happen. I'd found the man to take me where I wanted to go.

As we finished Nigel said, 'I'm going to arrange an audition to find the fifth member, and possibly the fourth member too, if I decide against including Mark in the group.' Somehow I felt that, although there was an air of uncertainty about the whole process of putting the band together, I was in already.

Nigel hadn't said much about the audition, apart from where it was going to be – La Cage nightclub in Manchester. I had no idea how many lads were going to be there, maybe quite a few from the sounds of things, but there were no queues of hopefuls waiting round the block, just a couple of boys and their mums. The club was nothing special – it looked like all those places during the day: nasty. I walked down a flight of stairs and found a stage, a dance floor, lights everywhere and a long bar; though even at that point something said gay club to me. A smiling DJ in the booth was playing Madonna's 'Vogue'. By the time I'd weighed up the situation Nigel was gathering everyone around him and introducing us all.

There were just five of us. There was Jason, who I'd already met at Nigel's office a week or so after my first visit. He was dressed in his *Hitman and Her* uniform, in red trainers, red socks and a red vest. The DJ couldn't take his eyes off him. There was Mark, who was much smaller than Jason. He was friendly, too, warm and enthusiastic and quite good-looking. Then there was a tall kid called Robert. He was friendly, but in a different way – other than that he made little impression on me then. Last, and least, was a real non-event guy, so non-event I can't recall his name. I don't know why Nigel had asked him to come along, he just didn't look right; though if I'm honest he didn't look right because he looked too much like me. The other three looked cool; they had the latest clothes, the latest hairstyles and were definitely *not* the kind of guys who had sat in their bedrooms playing a synth for eight years. Nor had they been appearing in social clubs six nights a week.

I was going to have to work at this.

There was another thing I was going to have to work at – Nigel wanted us to dance. The DJ put on a track and off we all went. Jason shone. He was such a natural, the way he danced was really graceful and effortless. Mark just seemed to look right, even though he wasn't up to Jason's standard. Robert danced like the star of the under-eighteens club. There was a dance about at that time called the running man. If you were really good you could do it in every direction, turning 45 degrees every few bars, and Robert could do it every which way. Bet that was the result of many hours in front of the mirror. That left the two guys with two left feet. For me, used to sitting behind a synth or crooning with a mic, it felt like this part of the audition went on for ever. Song after song came on with no let-up. Pretty soon Jason went into his TV routines and everybody copied his moves – my dancing then was in time, but small moves, nothing flash. It was funny, because one side of me really wanted to be good at dancing while the other side thought, 'I don't need to do this; I'm a singer and a musician.' In fact, I think I got worse as time went on.

The music was just coming to an end when Howard arrived – I recognised him from the picture Nigel had shown me; he lived up to his photo. He looked friendly, although next to him I felt a bit self-conscious about my appearance. Nigel, who seemed totally relaxed that Howard was late, walked over to the DJ and gave him a tape, the same one he'd sent to all the boys. It was a backing track to 'Nothing Can Divide Us', Jason Donovan's first hit record; he had asked everyone to learn the song except me. I guess it had been obvious to Nigel that I could sing even if I couldn't dance.

The five other guys all had a bash, but it was clear that no one other than Robert had much previous experience of singing. He at least could hold a note. Just before the singing stopped, Nigel said to me quietly, 'I need to get rid of him,' and nodded in the direction of the boy-with-no-name. Why was he telling me this? He got up, walked over to him and just dismissed him. There was no emotion, no apology; it sent a chill up my spine. It was the first time I'd witnessed Nigel's cold business side, something I was to see hundreds more times over the coming years. Next thing I saw, the lad was putting on his coat and making for the exit sign . . . and then there were five.

Strangely, Nigel said nothing about the outcome of the audition. He was putting together a five-piece band and there were five of us left – and yet he couldn't, or wouldn't, give us an answer as to whether we were in or not. Perhaps he still hadn't made up his mind about Mark? He just said, 'Come on, get your coats, I'll take you for something to eat.' We headed out of the gloom and off to the British Home Stores cafeteria, where we filled our dark brown trays with crisps, sandwiches and chocolate bars; all except Jason that is, who was on some kind of health kick and ate a Ryvita. In fact, Jay's always been like that; he's the only person I know who has water on his muesli.

We sat around a six-seater table and made small talk. Everyone was slightly on edge.

'I wonder when we'll find out whether we're in or not?' Mark asked me.

'Who knows?' was all I could offer in response.

Howard just kept talking to Nigel about modelling jobs and didn't seem that bothered about how the audition had gone. Even though I still felt like the centre of Nigel's attention – his reaction to my tape had given me an extra layer of confidence that the other boys might not have had – it was noticeable that Jason and Howard received a different kind of interest from him; Nigel had a real eye for them both. I didn't understand why, but I felt slightly jealous. Trying to dissect this feeling now is strange, and trying to put myself back inside that time and place and emotion is

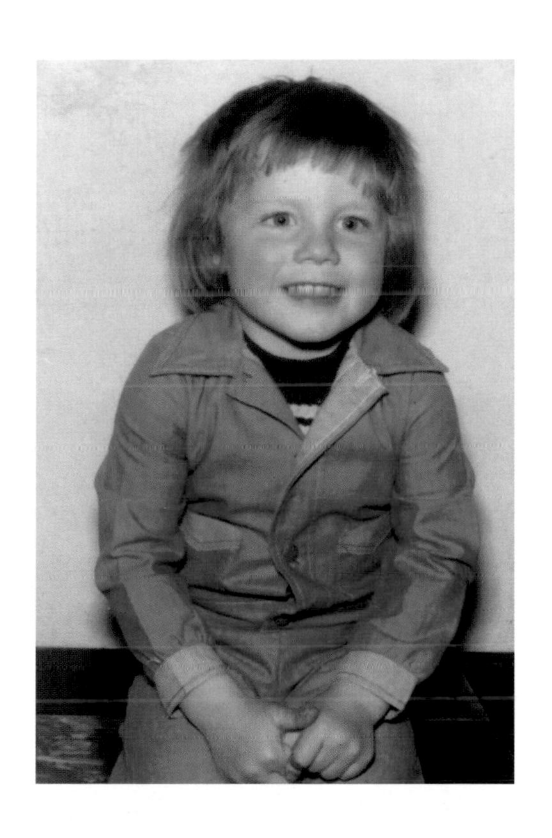

Top: Me, age three

Bottom: Wearing the technicolour dreamcoat

Dad and me living the good life

Mum and Nan Bo

Top: Me in my bedroom studio

Bottom: Heather and me as 'Karisma'

Looking the part at Lakeside Club, Essex

Entering 'Club Act of the Year' with John Tedford

Top: Me, in Nick Kershaw mode

Middle: Nigel Martin-Smith, the man who made it all happen

Bottom: On my trip to Florida with Nigel

The band transformed at Pierre Alexander's Manchester Salon

impossible. My only explanation is that Nigel was my knight in shining armour, the one I'd been waiting for. He was really impressed with my talents and believed in my future. He wasn't the first believer, but he was the first with the vision, determination and contacts to take me to where I wanted to go. He was also the first gay man I'd got to know, and that gave me a buzz. I sensed that the girls who worked in Nigel's office thought I was gay and I did nothing but play on that. I also knew that I wasn't gay, and was never going to be, but I enjoyed playing the part; it was a bit like borrowing an expensive car for the day. For the next twelve months it was a role I played for Nigel.

We finished our food and said our farewells. At this point I didn't know when, or even if, I'd see any of the others again. While I desperately wanted to have faith in the whole thing, I couldn't quite get a handle on Nigel's vision for the band. But it sounded as if it might be a good launching pad to a solo career, so wherever he was going, I was up for it.

If we were the five then there was no decision to be made, added to which, only six of us had turned up to the audition, for God's sake! Had there been a massive sieve of thousands of potential candidates before we all met? Was today the culmination of months and months of sorting through CVs and demo tapes? Somehow I didn't think so. If you were to ask Nigel he might well tell you how he searched all over Britain, seeing thousands of hopefuls, before scientifically putting together the superband of the nineties. Television is now full of prime-time shows based around the process, out of which supposed stars are born. Then again, could it be that by chance Nigel had taken Jason and me to the audition as definites, invited Robert as a nearly definite – as he'd already met him and liked him – and asked Mark and Howard just because they were on his books at the model agency? I guess I'll never know the answer to that one.

It feels amazing to me now that it was us five. Of all the random people he could have picked, he picked us. When we're on stage I think we have something so special. What were the chances that we would gel and have that sparkle?

A few days later I got a phone call telling me I was in, and so were Howard, Jason, Mark and Robert. We were to be Nigel's band – the famous five in waiting. The first thing Nigel made us do was go and see a lawyer. He recommended that we should use Steven Lea who would act for all of us in our dealings with him. Not that we took a lot of notice of the detail of the contract – who does at the point when their career is about to take off? When we went to Steven's office he drew our attention to one unusual aspect of the contract – Nigel was asking for 25 per cent of everything we were hypothetically going to earn.

'It's normal for a manager to take 20 per cent, which in your case means he'll be earning more than you boys individually,' said Steven. No one dared to suggest to Nigel that in fact 20 per cent would be a more appropriate figure.

'Take it or leave it,' Nigel would have said. 'I can find another five lads.'

Needless to say we took it. To be fair to Nigel, he came to us around the time of our third hit and said he was dropping his commission to 20 per cent, as it seemed fairer to him. Not long after our meeting with the lawyer, Nigel called us all into his office to go through what we would be doing over the coming weeks and months. As he finished outlining his plans he said, 'In five years' time we'll probably hate each other, *but* we'll be rich.' That was how confident he was. Cynics would say it was all talk, but I truly believe he believed. That's the power of dreams.

With the contract signed and plans still up in the air, Mark went back to working in the bank, Howard went back to spraying cars, Jason to painting and decorating and Robbie to school to finish his O-levels. Life as usual. I didn't give up working the clubs just yet as I thought it might be useful to save some money to keep me going until we began to work seriously as a band. Not that I knew what to expect, maybe it was just a gut feeling that things might take a little while. Not long before I met Nigel I had found a way of making some extra cash – I started my own little merchandising business. Not T-shirts or caps or badges, just tapes of me singing which I sold at my gigs. One day I went down to Dixons and bought a box of ten TDK cassettes for £7.99. I recorded ten of my songs on each one and took them to my next gig. I included 'Love Changes Everything', 'Feelings', 'Love On The Rocks' and seven other songs. I cut out my picture, stuck it on the cassette box and included my little business card. On the way to the gig I thought, how much am I going to sell these for? I settled on £3 each. My logic was simple: two pints of lager and a packet of crisps!

'Ladies and gentlemen, just in case you're interested, I have some tapes for sale. If you'd like one, see me afterwards.' All ten tapes went immediately. The next day I went to Dixons and bought thirty tapes; at my next gig they all sold. It got to the point where I would leave my dad boxes of blank cassettes for him to tape when he got home from work. I ended up selling between fifty and seventy at each show – I was coining it. I managed to save about £4,500, which is what I lived off until we were signed.

Nowadays you don't even put a band together until you've worked out how they're going to sound, who they'll appeal to and how they're going to look – there's a whole load of boxes you have to tick. We hadn't ticked one. Well, no, we had – five boys in a group, tick. Nigel's next plan was to create an image for us, and he especially wanted to see what we'd look like in photographs. Before our first photo shoot he sent us all to Pierre Alexander, Manchester's celebrity hairdresser, who had a salon across the road from Nigel's office – he had agreed to do our hair for free in exchange for a credit on our record sleeves. Pierre, who seemed at least 190 years old, was the gayest man I or any of the others had ever met. The first thing he did was cut my hair off. It was quite long at the time and he made it even more spiky than it had been a few years before. He dyed Mark's yellow blond, which looked bloody awful, and Jason's jet black as well as clipping on a funny hair piece to the front of his hair for 'dramatic effect'. Rob and Howard escaped relatively lightly. Best of all, we were treated like royalty; I'd never had a cup of coffee in a hairdresser's before. We even got Jammy Dodgers – it was brilliant, a whole new world.

For the photo shoot Nigel took us out to Audenshaw, on the east side of Greater Manchester, to a company called Picture House, where we met a photographer named Philip Ollerenshaw. As soon as we walked up the stairs and into the studio, I knew straight away which one was the photographer. Philip was a large man with a George Michael-style hairdo, and while Nigel was gay and Pierre gayer, this guy took the biscuit. It wasn't just his hairstyle, it was his clothes and mannerisms – his voice was the epitome of high camp. As you can imagine Philip loved having us five 'boys' in his studio. There was also a make-up artist called Mark Cook, who, I soon learned, was Nigel's ex-boyfriend. Mark was a very good-looking guy, very tanned and fit and extremely camp. And one final twist, Nigel was Mark Cook's agent. We were being well and truly introduced to the gay mafia that would soon surround us. As Nigel was quick to point out, 'Don't fuck with the fairies!'

Nigel had told us to bring some of our own clothes with us for the shoot. After a lot of rummaging around at home I'd settled on some Burton's cords, a glittery shirt that I often wore for gigs, and my much-loved white shirt with black stars on it. Oh dear. When I saw what the others had brought with them I realised that I was about to redefine 'fashion disaster'. I looked like the guy from the local Ritzy.

As luck would have it, Jason had brought along some of his *Hitman and Her* uniforms, mostly coloured cycling shorts, vests and other fairly skimpy outfits; it says something about how worried I was feeling that I fell upon them as my salvation from the jaws of a fashion meltdown. I wasn't the only one who was happy he'd brought along the outfits – Philip, Nigel and Mark all seemed very excited by what they saw.

Phase two of Nigel's strategy came a few days later. He announced that we were to be at Peaches dance studio in Manchester at 9.30 a.m. sharp. Here we met Paul Walsh, a choreographer who immediately had us doing press-ups, sit-ups and other forms of torture until seven in the evening. Nigel wanted us whipped into shape before our first public appearance. Boot camp was one thing, but when we graduated from fitness training to routines, we were less than impressed. Jason and Howard, with their skill and experience, led the rubbishing of the routines. We went to Nigel: could we be allowed to choreograph a number to show him that we could do it better? He eventually agreed, but it was a short-lived victory. After working up a routine for one of the songs, we showed Nigel what we'd done; he hated it. With hindsight, it was inevitable that he would reject whatever we came up with – he was teaching us lesson one: this was *his* vision, *his* presentation and we were *his* band.

It proved to be the opening salvo in the rift between Jason and Nigel, something that would become a recurring theme throughout Take That's existence. Afterwards, while Nigel was giving us the full dressing down, Jay started arguing over a small point and Nigel stormed off in a petulant hissy fit. This tiny crack in their relationship would become a chasm as the years went by. It's hard to say what was behind it. Certainly Nigel fancied Jason and made it very obvious. They were more than a match for each other intellectually, but I wonder if it wasn't about control as much as anything. Jay likes to be in control of his life and we were entering a phase where our lives literally weren't our own – from now on we were Nigel's puppets.

Obviously, to do personal appearances we needed music to perform, tracks that were a step up from my homemade demos;

they would also be helpful in trying to secure a record deal. My music was about the only input we were allowed in those early days. Nigel booked a studio in Cheadle Hulme and we all went over there for our first day as a recording band. From the outside Revolution Studios on Church Road looked more like a normal detached house. Someone brought a bottle of champagne and we were all very excited.

There were two young guys working there and we spent ages putting down all the vocal parts for 'Girl' and 'Waitin' Around'. When I say we, it was actually just me and a guy called Ian Wilson, who was in the band Sad Café who had a big hit with 'Every Day Hurts'. It took us hours to get all the vocals done, and while we worked the others sat around, understandably getting more and more pissed off the longer we took.

To help the boys prepare for recording I had spent some time teaching them mic technique round at my house. Because they weren't used to using one they had no idea how to make it work for them – Rob and Mark wanted to hold it with the bottom of the mic pointing up, like a rapper does, but I kept reminding them that it's got to rest on your chin so you sing across the top and your voice goes into it. But by the time we got to their parts, it was past midnight and there was only time for one run-through. It was like a rerun of the audition: Howard, Jay and Mark were OK, but it was Rob who made me think, there's my other vocalist. Then the lads went back downstairs and the engineer soloed the vocals; it sounded pretty bad. I felt it was my fault – no one had been given a chance to do a proper job. Ian had left at about 10 p.m. and I'd spent the last two hours of his time doing my lead vocal. Not surprisingly, when we left the studio there was a bit of an atmosphere – mostly aimed at Nigel I think. When we stopped to get some petrol Jay said,

'That wasn't very fair, I didn't really get a chance to sing.'

Nigel's reply didn't bother to spare Jay's feelings. From that point on Jay took something of a dislike to singing and the studio, something that lasted the whole way through the band.

We had the publicity shots, we had a single of sorts, now we just needed a name. We were sitting around Nigel's office one day talking about ideas when he came up with Kick It. We tried to tell him it was terrible, although of course we didn't actually put it that way – in those days we were all scared of Nigel and desperate for his approval, so we just said we didn't like it. We went through others, but all of them were pretty dumb. Take That was the worst of a bad bunch! Then Nigel gave us another little lecture on how people thought the Pet Shop Boys' name was daft when they first came out.

'Once you're famous it doesn't matter what you're called,' he said. And d'you know what? He was right.

4

Manchester Mogul

Everyone always says I was Nigel's favourite, but Howard was a close second; the distance between us and the other three was enormous. Nigel managed all of us differently but it was true that at the start the focus was on me. I was the one in the studio, it was my songs we were singing and Nigel seemed to respect my talent. As soon as we signed with him, Nigel took on the role of my manager. He was keen to keep me working in the clubs while we waited for the band to take off, and he had flyers printed offering some dates in early 1991.

One night in September 1990 Nigel came with me to a gig at Henry Africa's in Oldham and on the way back in the car I was joking with him and said, 'When I become a star I want to go to America.' So, because he was going to see a friend in Florida in November, he took me along with him. It never occurred to me that there might be anything more to it. We left Nigel's house, where he lived with his boyfriend, climbed in the car, got on the plane, reached Orlando, checked in, and it was only when we got to the room that I thought, thank God for that, it's got two beds!

I remember finding a letter in the back pocket of my jeans. It was from my mum. She's never done anything like that, either before or since: my family are not the type to open up. She wanted me to know that she and my dad had wanted to take me to Disneyland one day, but they'd never had the money. Now Nigel was going to be the one to make my dreams come true.

I wish I'd kept that letter. It was a good letter and I'd have enjoyed reading it even more now than I did then, especially now that I'm a dad and can appreciate how much you want to give your kids everything. At the time I'm not sure I knew what to make of it, but she'd obviously thought very deeply about the trip, and about all the new developments in my life and what they meant for me. To this day she still gives me a roasting if I say a word against Nigel.

That week, Nigel was incredibly generous and let me do anything I wanted. Once we got there I just took over. I drove the hire car, I found the maps, I worked out the places to go. We did everything: Disney World, Universal Studios, Wet and Wild, Sea World, Epcot – we walked and walked and walked. By the end of the week Nigel was knackered and stopped accompanying me on days out. I had an amazing time, and if I was getting special treatment I wasn't aware of it – we didn't feel like a band yet. But it had repercussions. Years later I found out that Robbie was still jealous of that trip. And even now the lads make jokes about it. The other day when we were recording and the producer said, 'Can I have Gary first?' Howard, who's got a long memory and a gentle sense of humour, said, 'Yeah, he always goes first. He went to America with Nigel, you know.'

Even if we didn't yet feel like it, we were a band, and Nigel was anxious to get us our first gig. One day at his office he told us that he had booked us into a few places. Just as things were winding up he said in a serious voice, 'Listen, lads, I have something to tell you all.'

My heart sank and I bet the others' did too – even this early on we'd come to dread a Nigel announcement.

'I'm gay. Has anyone got a problem with that?'

Why did he feel he had to tell us? We all knew by this stage –

how could we not? – and had made the odd joke about it. In the same way that pretty girls use their beauty to get their way, I think we'd all started to realise that we could manage Nigel a little if we played up to him. Giving him the odd kiss, hug or bit of attention would give us some leverage.

I think Nigel felt he had to say something because gay clubs were such a key component of plan for Take That's world domination. I for one had never even considered who our audience was going to be – if asked I would probably have said people our age and younger. We didn't care who they were – gay, black, straight, bisexual or whatever – just as long as we had a following. Nigel's route into the music scene was through the gay clubs – even now he owns two clubs and is out clubbing several nights a week; it's his world. In one sense it was a mad approach; the gay market has its limitations and I know now that there's a big difference between a club record and a radio dance record. Singles go into the clubs on anonymous white labels that the DJs play; the clubs are simply the longest way round to get a hit. But there was another reason why we played the gay clubs: they paid us. From the outset Nigel would only book us into places that would pay, and although it was only £60 or £80 a night, it was better than nothing. Today an unsigned band would be lucky to get five pence from anyone.

We'd have tried anything, we were so full of enthusiasm, fuelled by what Nigel was telling us – you've never seen ambition like it. Our first proper paying gig was at Flicks in Huddersfield. We drove there in Nigel's XR3i and my Ford Orion, raring to go. Flicks was your standard Ritzy nightclub, with lots of chrome, a high stage, too-bright lights and the obligatory crap sound system. It actually wasn't a gay club but maybe it would have been easier if it was. Our set list was 'Waitin' Around', 'Girl' and 'A Million Love Songs' from my original demo tape, plus a couple of covers. At Nigel's suggestion we'd learned the Rolling Stones, 'Get Off Of My Cloud' – now that was a strange choice for a boy band – and the Village People's 'Can't Stop the Music' – I'm just glad it wasn't 'YMCA'. We were on for less than half an hour, but it felt like two. Backstage afterwards there was no big buzz, no hugging each other, no punching the air – it didn't feel that good. For me it probably felt worse than for the others, because I knew what an appreciative audience felt like.

Nigel used the recordings we'd made in Cheadle Hulme to start shopping us around. London was the only place to make things happen and he made frequent trips down south, often taking me with him – Nigel's never felt that comfortable outside Manchester. When I'd first sat in Nigel's office and looked at the gold disc on his wall I had assumed he must be a man with connections; in reality he had a few, but mostly on the periphery of the outskirts of the music business. One of the A&R people that Nigel and I met was Simon Cowell, who was just a younger version of the man everyone knows today. As soon as I walked in I thought, this is good, those two seem to be getting along like a house on fire. Perhaps we've struck it lucky at last. But when Simon heard our demo tape, which included 'A Million Love Songs', he said, 'Well, the band are good-looking, but I can't hear any songs.' Subsequently Simon has been quoted as saying, 'Fire the fat one and I'll sign the band' – and I wasn't even fat then! He's also been quoted as saying that he felt 'physically sick' every time we had a number one and he knew he'd let us slip through his fingers. It's an everyday story of A&R.

Jive, the label that had released Damian's 'Time Warp', which won Nigel that all-important gold disc, was the only label to show a hint of interest. But polite notice was as far as it went. I have no idea how many labels turned us down, but there's no question it was a lot.

Where Nigel seemed to come into his own was publicity, even if it was sometimes for himself. He told a local Manchester paper that there were three companies trying to sign us in a 'duel by cheque-book', adding for good measure that they were prepared to spend up to £250,000 on making us stars. *Look North West*, our local TV news programme, did a feature on us, but it mostly featured the manager, 'Nigel Martin-Smith – Manchester Mogul'. Throughout Take That, the minute he saw us off on a long-haul flight Nigel would be on to the local papers. He thought we'd never hear about it, but of course we came home to find our mums saying, 'Nigel's been in the papers again.'

We were playing odd gigs here and there, but appeared to be going nowhere fast. We would sometimes play a club on a Thursday and maybe a gay club on a Monday, but gigs were sporadic. I remember driving to rehearsals with Howard in his Fiesta one day when we stopped at the petrol station. No sooner was he out of the car than he was back in again.

'I thought you were putting petrol in the car.' I said.

'I did, I put in £2 worth. That'll last me two weeks that will.'

Back then £2 was a lot of money to Howard.

Conversations that revolved around our lack of progress usually ended with one or other of us saying, 'Fucking hell, let's not bother.' But to Nigel's credit he just kept saying, 'No, no, we're going to make it.'

One afternoon we drove over to a club in Hull called Lexington Avenue. On the way there we were asking each other, 'Why are we playing at six o'clock? Who's going to be there then?' We soon found out. it was wall-to-wall teenage girls, mostly aged eleven to fifteen. That's when we decided to wear more clothes – jackets and lycra shorts – than we did at the gay clubs; if we hadn't we would probably have been arrested. When we went on stage, it was like being Bros. They just went bananas. They were all reaching out, running on to the stage and trying to hug us; there were girls climbing over the crowd at the back. It was pandemonium. They wouldn't let us off the stage and there was a queue outside our dressing room. I ended up with fifteen phone numbers in my back pocket as we fought our way back to the car to complete our getaway. They loved us and we loved it. This was more like it!

'We've got to call Nigel and tell him.'

We stopped at a garage and reached in my bag for my mobile phone – always the first with a new gadget, it was one of the early ones and weighed a ton; it practically took two of us to lift it out. 'Nige, we've found the place for us to play, you've got to book us into every under-eighteens club around Manchester, or within an easy drive.'

We were buzzing, and not just because it was girls reacting that way rather than gay guys. They were just so much more enthusiastic. Nigel came with us to the next under-eighteen club night and he couldn't believe his eyes. We had found our calling.

There was only one downside. We would often squash into Nigel's XR3i to go to gigs, but we'd come out to find messages all over it.

'Ah. Sorry, Nigel. Sorry about the lipstick on the car again.'

'Lads, you've got to be more careful.'

'Well, I don't see how we can be, Nige,' I said, 'because the only alternative is for one of us to watch the car while the rest of us are on stage, and that buggers up the routines.'

'Very funny, Gary. Next time you can take your car and see how you like it.'

Soon we were travelling further for our appearances, including our first London gig. It was for *Fast Forward* magazine at Hammersmith Palais with Phillip Schofield; they took our pictures, which made us feel like something tangible was happening. We also started appearing in *No. 1* magazine; although ours was usually the smallest picture. At that first gig Nigel told us, 'Lads, over there is the editor, go and make a fuss of her.'

We went over and put our arms around her and started chatting to her. Her reaction was great. 'I'd like to do a photo shoot with you next week,' she said.

It was a tactic we employed from then on, be nice to magazine people and they'll be nice to you. Nigel intuitively knew what to do.

We were an unsigned band with no deal, and yet we were starting to be featured in all the teen magazines, that had to mean something. Jason was quoted in one of them as saying, 'We are sex gods', which certainly helped. At the same time it seemed like every time Nigel talked to the media he gave our story a different twist. He told one magazine that he had appealed through the pages of the *Sun* and 800 wannabes turned up to audition, but it was the five of us that had been 'allowed to join the exclusive world of pop (show) business'. But it wasn't all Nigel, the magazines were just as quick to go over the top. On the front cover of *My Guy* they billed us as 'The Sexiest Band on the Planet' – surely the labels would have to take notice now?

We needed a record to get things moving. Nigel put us together with a guy named Ray Hedges, who would later work with Westlife, Boyzone, Ronan Keating, B*Witched and Emma Bunton. At the time he was still on the brink of success, so he was prepared to work with us. Nigel, Howard and I went to Ray's studio in London for a two-day session; Howard has a great ear for harmony, so he was the only one that was needed to help with the vocals. He was also nursing a bad cold and when we got there Ray took Nigel to one side and said, 'I'm really busy at the moment and I can't afford to get a cold myself, so I'm afraid I'm going to have to ask you to take Howard back to the hotel.' It was just me again.

Ray and I worked all day on a track and come five o'clock he suggested I take a tape back to the hotel where I could work on the lyrics some more. When I got back I played it to Nigel, who immediately said,

'Right, I've got it in my head.'

For the next fifteen minutes he sat at the table writing furiously.

I sat there thinking, what's he up to? Finally I said, 'What are you doing, Nigel, changing my lyrics?'

'Gary, I've written two verses.'

I've seen some dodgy lyrics over the years, but these were something else. One line said, 'Your love is like an Emmy.'

'What's an Emmy?' I asked.

'It's an award in America, these lyrics will help the song sell there. And Gary, don't worry these are a gift from me; I won't want any royalties.'

I thought, there's no chance of us fucking getting any, Nige.

Next day at the studio I said to Ray, 'I don't think this song is happening.' I had come to the conclusion that the only way to get out of using Nigel's lyrics was to not finish the song. 'I've got a new piano riff, Ray, tell me what you think.'

Fortunately he liked it, and I rushed us along and by five we'd come up with 'Do What U Like'.

Nigel more than liked it. He was convinced that 'Do What U Like' was a huge hit, so sure, in fact, that he decided there was no point in wasting any more time on London-based record companies. 'I'm going to release it on my own label,' he announced. This implies that Nigel had his own label, which wouldn't be entirely true. He started the Dance UK label especially for our single, and initially he only printed up a couple of hundred records in order to send them to radio stations so we had something more to show any of the majors who were interested. To give you an idea of how convinced Nigel was that we had a hit on our hands, as well as the potential to go all the way, he remortgaged his parents' house to get the money to start his own label.

Nigel was now in his element. He was coming up with ideas all the time, some of them good and some of them very bad. The video was where it really got moving. This wasn't going to be a video like any other up-and-coming band's, oh no. Nigel had met a girl who worked on a TV show, and either he'd convinced her or she'd convinced him that she was the one to produce it. He'd allocated her a £5,000 budget – our latest video had a budget of £500,000. We were to shoot the video at Vector TV in Manchester on 21 June 1991 and Nigel had invited a researcher from a Saturday morning TV show, *8.15 From Manchester*, to come along to the shoot. Everyone else seemed to be a friend of Nigel's, working for free.

We'd gone down to Affleck's Palace in Manchester to choose our new costumes, and once we got there a kind of clone zone version of Nigel's taste had rubbed off on everyone. The boys had gone mad, pulling out bondage gear and all sorts, going, 'Will you look at this!' and 'what about this?' I think the idea of the costumes was to shock people, but it wasn't meant to shock the band members as well. They were ridiculous. So there we were all ready to go in codpieces, studded leather jackets and enormous bloody Motorhead pass-me-down boots – they stayed with us for years.

Beforehand Nigel got us all together to reveal an amendment to the masterplan.

'Lads, we've got to get the video banned.'

How in the hell were we going to do that?

That's when the jelly arrived. There were buckets and buckets of it. Red jelly, yellow jelly, orange jelly, the models were throwing it at us, we were throwing it back, it was like a huge food fight, and by now a couple of lads – I think it was Robbie and Howard – were down to their undies. Soon everyone else starts stripping down, I think I was the only one fully clothed at this point – well, if you were stood next to the rest of them you'd keep your clothes on too.

Nigel was yelling, 'Come on, lads, I want this banned!' So soon we were all lying face down, butt naked, with the models slinging jelly up our bums with a broom. I'm just glad he didn't take the songs lyrics too literally, otherwise there would have been cherry pie and jam along with the jelly.

I have to admit that we loved the finished version, not that anyone ever saw it. To get something banned a TV station has to want to play it, and none of them even considered the unedited version. All we could get played, and then rarely, was the clean version.

After it was made Nigel said, 'Right, lads, if you want one of the videos it's a tenner a copy.'

And like mugs we all bought one. Can you imagine paying money to watch your own video?

Next stop: local radio station road shows. Nigel was on to it. The first one was a Key 103 Rave in the afternoon of Sunday 23 June at Manchester Academy. Pretty soon we were on the Independent Local Radio circuit with other acts just like us, although most of them had had hit records. Curiosity Killed the Cat, Dannii Minogue and Chesney Hawkes were regulars, and we were the only band without a record deal. Playing the radio station gig circuit around the north of England gave us great exposure and we also got to know the DJs, which did us no harm later on. Some of them even put us up at their houses for the night.

Just before our single came out, we got on to the Nescafé Network Chart Show live tour with David Jensen. It helped get us gigs in places further afield, and meant we didn't have the hassle of having to find them ourselves. We went to Ayr, Telford, Liverpool and Leeds, among other places. On 10 July, Jay's twenty-first birthday, we did a show in Essex, where there were no more than fifteen people watching us. We had driven down from Manchester, done the gig and then driven straight home, that's how bloody determined and dedicated we were. At that stage we travelled between gigs in a yellow Salford Van Hire Transit; we'd all be racketting around in the back of it, our feet up on the seats, chatting, laughing and smoking Rob's fags. It felt like we were in there for days, chucking our sandwich wrappers wherever. I swear there were new species of flora and fauna growing on the floor of that van. Nigel came everywhere with us, he watched us, saw who we talked to – it was like he had five pairs of eyes.

Take That's story continued to evolve, in ways that had little to do with the truth. In his attempts to make the band saleable, Nigel changed Howard's age, knocking a couple of years off, he also made Mark two years younger and invented a story that Mark and I had been working together in a band called Cutest Rush – has there ever been a gayer-sounding band? Nigel claimed that we had met at Strawberry Studios, where Mark had worked as a tea boy, and he just transformed my lost single as Kurtis Rush into Cutest Rush. I suppose it was just reinventing our history to make us sound more interesting.

It was around this point that we started to split into two camps – there was me, Howard and Jay, and there was Bob Double, as we sometimes called Rob – although I can't remember why – and Mark. It was probably something to do with the fact that they were younger than us, Robbie in particular – four years doesn't sound like a lot, but when you're in the fifth form you don't hang out with people in the first year, and that's how it felt. Robbie was always just the young one to me, and now I think it was probably hard to be on the receiving end of that. In those early days, when we had to share rooms in crappy B&Bs, it would always be Rob and Mark sharing, and Howard, Jay and I would take it in turns to share. Rob and Mark would always go out together shopping and clubbing, too.

Mark and I never really connected in a deep friendship way during our first time together as Take That. That's not to say that we didn't have fun, or that I didn't like him – far from it. Unlike myself, who has been known to have the odd bitch, Mark never has a bad word to say about anyone. Mark seemed happy to stay in the background, whereas I was something of a team leader, and was always the first to voice an opinion.

Some of it was to do with the fact that Mark and I love different things. Mark is very fashion-conscious, and it's clear for all to see that I'm not that bothered – in fact, Mark always used to find me something to wear at shoots; he still does now! I love going out for dinner, Mark definitely doesn't. When we went out as a band, Howard and I always wanted to sit around and have a coffee after dinner – for some reason we called it a cream key.

'Come on, Mark, let's go for dinner tonight.'

'No, no, I can't be sat in a chair all night eating.'

'If we don't have a cream key will you come?'

'Oh, OK, I might come then.'

It was as though that last fifteen minutes of the meal was just too much for him.

To boost our chances with the single Nigel recruited two promo girls he had worked with when he had his hit with Damian. Carolyn and Judy had plenty of contacts; one of them did press and the other did radio, which was something we had no chance of making happen ourselves. Those two absolutely worked their arses off for us, and even got us on a warm-up gig for the Radio One road show, which was great news. The bad news was that it was in Falmouth. We were probably the only act prepared to drive that far; we'd have gone anywhere to get on a Radio One show. According to Nigel we were on our way.

'Well, that's it. Lads, I'm telling you, if you get a play on Radio One that's 3,000 sales right there.' Nigel would equate a TV appearance to 5,000 sales and over the next few weeks we did enough to have got ourselves a good chart placing. In reality when 'Do What U Like' came out on 22 July 1991 Nigel's maths didn't quite add up. We only made No. 91 which probably meant we'd sold just a few hundred records.

By this time Ying, who I met the first time I went to Nigel's office, had started travelling with us. Although she was a casting agent, Nigel would sometimes send her along to look after and keep an eye on us. We also toured with a big red and yellow box that would have looked more at home in a circus – it was just another one of Nigel's big ideas. The thinking behind it was not so daft. Nigel had cards printed up, which we would chuck out into the crowd at gigs.

'Put your name and address in the box and we'll post out details of our gigs and records.'

Collecting names and addresses in this way was an example of just how ahead of the record labels Nigel was. It would be years before they started doing that type of thing, something that is taken for granted now.

It's hard to write about Nigel, because so much of what he did was good and so much wasn't. When I used to phone his office, I'd get a little knot of nervousness in my stomach every time, and I know the other lads felt the same. Even if he called me now I'd feel a bit like that, and why should I? I think he thought he'd given us a massive opportunity, and that we owed him big time. If you disagreed with him he'd be quick to cut you down to size.

'If you don't want to do it, I'll get someone else from Oldham who's small and blond and cute,' he'd tell Mark. Or, 'I can always get another lad in from Stoke,' to Robbie.

He never said that to me, but then I played his game by always making him feel like I was completely on his side.

Nigel probably had us scared to death because we were still so young. He was always on at us to behave impeccably – his worst nightmare was that something might appear about us in the press. What if the press found out one of us had a girlfriend? What would our fans of either sex make of that?

He never let us out of his sight until, unbelievably, he let us do a tour on our own – well, not so much a tour as PAs in clubs around Scotland. Most of the gigs were in Glasgow and Edinburgh; we did an under-eighteens club at six o'clock, an over-eighteens at nine o'clock, a gay club at midnight and another at 1 a.m. Gary Wilson, who now manages Liberty X, looked after us, and he did a brilliant job during those six days in Scotland. The first thing we did was check him out to see if he was going to report back to Nigel. He wasn't, which was a cue for us all to go wild, or at least to be ourselves. We stayed up late, had holiday romances, drank too much and, overexcited by the fact that the Swallow Hotel in Glasgow had an indoor pool, took photographs of ourselves in it doing moonies. It was during this trip that we started to feel like a band, as we were finally allowed to be mates. We took the pictures back to show Nigel and he went mad: 'If that girl in Boots had been a fan, these would have been all over the papers by now. Your careers could have been ruined!'

Nigel's idea of fame came from the eighties, when showbiz was very smoke and mirrors. You didn't really know who stars were – they were other beings, not like normal mortals, and their success depended on preserving a bit of mystery. After the nineties I think things changed. People want their celebrities real and fallible now, they want to see the cracks and the stresses; it's all reality TV with nothing hidden. Nigel wanted us to be cleaner than clean. I'd come out of interviews and realise I'd not said a word of truth. We were told particularly never to mention girlfriends, or any girls at all in fact – it seemed ludicrous and made us look daft.

An accumulation of small triumphs was slowly beginning to make us feel like we were cracking it. We went over to Newcastle, where Metro FM was holding a road show in a big park. Because we weren't actually booked to appear on the stage, we set up a little PA system in another part of the park and did our act there. Eventually we attracted so much attention that they let us on the main stage.

In early August, following an evening spent schmoozing the researcher after the video, we appeared on *8.15 From Manchester*. There were loads of fans outside the studio; more than when Bros appeared, so we were told – bloody hell! The only problem was getting the producer of the show to play the video for 'Do What U Like'. He insisted on three lots of cuts to the clean version before it was acceptable for Saturday morning viewing. It was another one of those important milestones in our career. It wasn't just the teen magazines that featured us; now TV was taking notice. But why weren't the labels?

Another person who spotted us was Linda Duff, the pop columnist from the *Daily Star*. She was the first person at a national newspaper to write about us, and I have to say she was both very generous and very nice to us. In her article at the time of our appearance on *8.15 From Manchester*, she devoted a whole page to us under the headline CHIP OFF THE NEW BLOCK. It was exactly the angle Nigel was going for.

Linda invited us to play at the *Daily Star* party, at a club in Wardour Street. It was a three-floor club and we were on the floor with virtually no one on it. There were just a few bored hacks and us doing our back-flips and singing our pop-y tracks in a dark corner. We'd travelled down thinking this was a big night for us so it was a horrible anti-climax. We dreaded reading the newspaper write-up the next day. We needn't have worried. 'The crowd went wild,' wrote Linda, 'as bright new hopes Take That . . . performed a stunning routine . . .'

A week later *Music Week*, the industry's weekly trade magazine, ran a story about us, and as usual Nigel talked us up. Whether it was because he was talking to *Music Week*, or just because he forgot, he didn't tell them the Cutest Rush story, but instead told them the truth: that I had been playing the club circuit in the north. But he also said it was going to cost a major label a lot of money to sign us because he had spent £40,000 on 'the campaign to date'.

Take That's imaginary history crystallised when *The Word*, Channel 4's pop programme, were looking for a new presenter and somehow we ended up helping with the auditions. They wanted a band that their would-be presenters could interview for a screen test and of course no successful band would have touched it. We, or rather Nigel, jumped at the chance. To be sure that we were all on message Nigel typed out the Take That story, gave us each a copy and told us to learn it.

'Lads, this is the story. One it makes you look younger, and two it gives you credibility. And remember, you are not a pop act, you're a dance pop act.'

In Nigel's mind a 'dance pop act' represented the pinnacle of credibility. One of the wannabe presenters was Davina McCall, well before she got the gig on MTV and went on to even better things; she was pretty and comparatively nice. Katie Puckrik, who got the job, was mercilessly sarcastic.

Whatever we were asked to do, we'd do it. If the editor of *Smash Hits* wanted us photographed with pineapples on our heads, no problem. On one of these shoots, a front cover for *My Guy*, we almost became a four-piece. We were booked to do the photo shoot in London, which meant leaving Manchester at about six in the morning. We were all in the van, including Nigel, and we went to collect Jay on our way out of the city. But when we got to the pick-up spot, there was no sign of him. Nigel went mental and got straight on his mobile:

'Jason, where are you?' asked Nige in his softest, most chilling voice.

Jay apparently said he was going to be two minutes.

'WELL IT'S JUST NOT GOOD ENOUGH!' shouted Nige and put the phone down.

This, I thought, is not good. Jay arrived at the van in a right state; he apologised but Nigel still looked like thunder. We set off quickly but just before we reached the M6, Nigel said, 'Turn the van round.'

We got all the way back to Wythenshaw, where Jay lived, and Nigel said, 'Jason, get out.'

Jay picked up his bag and got out, and we turned the van around and set off again for London. No one said a word until we got to the bottom of the M6 an hour or more later.

'Nigel, what's happening?' I finally asked.

'Right, we're going to do this photo shoot and we're going to say that you were a five-piece but you're now a four-piece.' No sooner had Nigel said that than Rob was trying on Jason's 'Do What U Like' gear and deciding he wanted to wear it for the shoot.

We got through the shoot and the interview, and on the way back we stopped for a curry on the Edgware Road.

I asked Nigel, 'Is this really it for Jay? Surely we can't go down to a four-piece just for that?'

By the time we reached Manchester that evening Nigel had mellowed. He was never very good in the morning; he didn't usually get up until eleven. He phoned Jay to tell him he was back in. That was the easy bit. Getting the *My Guy* cover changed was not quite so simple. They wouldn't do another shoot, so on the cover of the 12 September issue there are the four of us posed in a group shot with Jay's cut-out head and shoulders coming in from the side horizontally; he looks like he's on a lollipop stick. The two-page interview on the inside has lots of comments from the four of us and just one from Jay: 'I was a painter and decorator.' Nigel had obviously fed them this; it says a lot about what he thought of Jay.

We had gigs and we even had fans – we began to notice that there were some kids following us around, and at some dates there would be a few banners with 'I Love Mark' on them, or just 'Take That'. But we still didn't have a label, apart from Nigel's. He'd gone back to Jive, where Steve Jenkins, the managing director, had suggested I work with a songwriter and producer named Graham Stack. I went to Graham's place in Twickenham right after we toured Scotland – I'm sure of the timing because a girl I'd met in Glasgow kept phoning me up all the time – and Graham and I came up with a song called 'Promises', which showed potential, although even then Jive didn't sign us.

Now, following the *Music Week* article and other press coverage, Nigel got some serious interest from a label, and not just a small label like Jive, but RCA, the Radio Corporation of America, one of the oldest and largest record labels in the world. RCA had been bought by the German company Bertelsmann Music, and was in the throes of becoming BMG.

The guy at RCA/BMG who showed some interest in us was Nick Raymonde, a junior A&R man. Nick later told me that he was far more interested in urban acts and wasn't really into pop – listening to daytime radio was a bit of a culture shock for him as he thought it was all Aussie soapstars and no home-grown talent. But one day Dave Donald, a promo guy at the label, walked into Nick's office with a VHS of us which had been shot in a shopping centre. Coincidentally, Nicki Chapman, one of their TV promotion girls, had pinned a picture of us from *No. 1* magazine on the door of his office. The photo showed us wearing nothing but underpants, with 'Take That' written on our arses.

Nicki had been tipped off about the buzz the teen magazines were creating around us when she went to see Cathy Gilbey, the producer of TV's *Going Live!* Cathy, who was the goddess of pop TV, had told her, 'You need to sign a band like this. We're fed up with these faceless dance acts who are absolutely no good on TV; we need a band with personality.'

It was true, pop was in the doldrums. *Smash Hits* was struggling to make pop music matter for the first time in the twelve years since it was published. There was nothing exciting happening and no one to put on their cover. '(Everything I Do) I Do It For You' by Bryan Adams had been No. 1 for months. The rest of the charts were overrun by the faceless ones – Bomb the Bass, C & C Music Factory, Technotronic, and Heavy D. & the Boys; not forgetting Right Said Fred's 'I'm Too Sexy'.

Events collided enough for Nick Raymonde to call Nigel and suggest they meet, but not before he had been to see us at an under-eighteens club in Slough, where we were supporting Right Said

Fred. When they met he told Nigel that we were, 'Such fun, they are trashy and flashy and sexy and camp all rolled into one heaving mass of pop hysteria.' He had fallen in love with our image.

Next thing we knew we were flying to London, not driving ourselves in our usual yellow Transit. We landed at Heathrow, and when we reached the terminal building there was a man in a peaked cap waiting to meet us – he was even holding a sign saying 'Take That'. The five of us – Nigel was already in London – piled into the limo and the driver took off his hat.

''Scuse me, mate, would you mind putting your hat back on?'

We were loving it and wanted to savour the full treatment.

We first went to RCA on 19 September, and met Nick Raymonde, Nicki Chapman, Nick Godwin, the Head of Promotion, and Joe Cokell, the Head of Marketing; they were a really nice bunch of people. We signed for £75,000, which may sound like a lot but after Nigel had taken his 25 per cent and expenses, it didn't leave much to split five ways. During, the months we had been working with Nigel, if he had spent money on us, for example taking us out to dinner, he would say, 'I'll put that on your account,' and now our account was called into reckoning. But then again, we didn't need much; from that point on the label paid for everything.

At last we were a signed band. It was a major step up for us, not least because now people were being paid to get us coverage and to promote the hell out of us. We decided that BMG stood for 'Big Money Galore', although later we changed our minds and decided it meant 'Bloody Mean Germans'! The night we signed Nigel took us out for dinner in Chinatown – on his account.

The day after we signed our deal Nigel told me a music publisher wanted to sign me, and to be honest I didn't fully understand what that meant. We met Mike McCormack at Virgin Music

Publishing four days after the RCA deal, and a month later I signed a £150,000 publishing advance for my songwriting, which absolutely amazed me. But there was an added complication: apparently Mike McCormack's boss had said that if he was going to sign me he wanted to sign all the other members of Take That. So when I signed the deal, the others had to sign to the publishing company, too. But they didn't get an advance, which in hindsight was not good for band dynamics. Initially everyone accepted that I was the songwriter, and we weren't yet making much money so didn't seem to matter too much, but later, when the royalty cheques started to roll in and I was doing considerably better financially, I'm sure it rankled.

I had thought I'd been doing pretty well playing the clubs but this put things on a whole different level. Not only had 1991 seen us go on Radio One and TV and sign to a major label but this publishing deal meant I had more money than I had ever imagined. In my naivety I thought I could live off it for the rest of my life. Nigel cleverly made me put my entire advance in a NatWest Money Market account and wouldn't let me touch any of it – in fact, to draw money out I needed his signature. Instead I would sometimes go to the cashpoint and put my card in just to stare at the balance.

5

Run for Cover

Four days after we signed to BMG, Nick Raymonde got us into the studio. He wanted to record 'Promises' as our first single right away. He put me together with a guy called Pete Hammond who had just split from Stock, Aitken and Waterman, and we met at Metropolis, a recording studio in West London. Having always loved the SAW sound I was so excited to be working with someone who had worked with them. I felt as if I'd finally arrived.

When I walked into the studio there was a DX7 all set up; I felt right at home. We set to work programming sounds and I think he was impressed by how well I knew my way around the synthesiser. The track took about three days to finish and just Howard and I sang on it. We used a lot of the material I had done with Graham Stack for the Jive demo – too much in fact – so as a trade-off, when 'Promises' came out a few weeks later, the B-side was a remix by Graham of 'Do What U Like'.

Before we could begin promoting 'Promises' we needed a video, and this time it was in BMG's hands. They put us up in the Regency Hotel in Queensgate, where we met the video director, Willy Smax. His idea, he explained, was to film us at a gig and cut into it footage of us rehearsing, along with film of us around London and at our hotel – not one of the world's most revolutionary pop video ideas. The gig sequence was filmed at Hollywood's in Romford in the middle of October – it was one of the better places we played in London at this time and the Essex girls always went crazy for us. Then back at the hotel, Jason and Howard were filmed break dancing in the gym, Rob was shown leaping out of the jacuzzi, and I'm featured prancing around with my peroxided spiky hair. And yes, despite the fact that it was a bit cheesy, we were thrilled by it.

Before the single was released the BMG publicity machine kicked into action. They got us playing on *Wogan*, *Pebble Mill*, *Motormouth* and *Going Live! Wogan* had massive early-evening viewing figures at the time, and it beamed us straight to the heart of middle England. We had graduated from Saturday morning TV. At that stage we weren't well known enough to talk to Terry, we didn't even meet him until after the show, in the green room, which disappointingly wasn't even green. Pushing through the BBC gates afterwards, the car that Nigel and Nicki Chapman were in knocked down one of the waiting fans outside. Unharmed, and undeterred, she bounced straight back up, yelled 'Take That!' at the windscreen and ran off. What I most vividly recall about that evening is that the band all went to the Hard Rock Café for something to eat afterwards and that we didn't have to queue to get in. 'You know what? I've made it – *Wogan* and the Hard Rock on the same night!' said Rob.

'Promises' came out on 11 November. On Sunday 17 November we were staying at the Metropole Hotel, right under the A40 in Paddington, to do some promo work. Nigel asked us to come to his room during the afternoon.

'Right, lads, let's listen to *Pick of the Pops* and hear if we're in the charts.'

He'd already been primed by a call from BMG. We had gone in at number thirty-eight.

We hit the roof. It was so exciting. We were jumping around Nigel's hotel room, delirious with joy. Rob was bouncing from bed to bed when all of a sudden – boof! – he went straight through one of them. It was bloody brilliant – we were in the Top 40.

When we finally signed to a label and released our first album, there was a part of me that thought, yeah, I deserve this. It had been such a long haul for me – all those years working the clubs and sitting at home writing songs, I thought it was payback time. It was confidence as well as cockiness, but I don't think that made me easier to be with in the band. I think for the first two years I was quite a loner. I felt the musical direction of the band was all up to me. I'd done it on my own for so long that it was hard for me to involve other people creatively.

Nor did I have any idea quite how many people would have to be involved, or how many people I had to please. 'Promises' had been comparatively straightforward, but the follow-up single – and BMG were keen to get it out as soon as possible to make up for the fact that 'Promises' spent a mere fortnight in the charts – was much more complicated. The track was no problem – Nick Raymonde liked a song of mine called 'Once You've Tasted Love' – but what I didn't know at the time was that he was having trouble getting anyone to produce us. His first choice for producer was a guy named Alan Tarney, who he respected for having made some of the best pop records in the eighties. But Alan wasn't keen and Nick wanted something to happen quickly to capitalise on the momentum created by all our publicity. We were appearing somewhere almost every day at this point, in clubs the length and breadth of Britain.

He finally settled on Duncan Bridgeman, a talented guy who had worked with Transvision Vamp, among others. Whereas Pete would say, 'I know what to do here,' and all of a sudden there would be a drum pattern that showed everyone where the song was going, with Duncan it was all about programming. My overriding memory of working with him was that I seemed to be in the vocal booth for days on end. He obviously had a system he liked to work through, but sometimes it felt more like a process of elimination.

To be close to Duncan I stayed on my own for three weeks at La Reserve Hotel next to Chelsea's football ground. Tall, thin and hollow-eyed from lack of sleep, Duncan was a bit of a spliffer who liked to work until four or five a.m. Every day I left the hotel at ten in the morning and returned in the early hours of the following morning. One day at the studio I got a call from Nigel saying, 'Gary, Nicki Chapman has called me and said if you want to go out to dinner she'll be happy to take you. If you want to do that I'll call her back and say yes.' It was an early sign of Nigel's possessiveness of the band – if Nicki had called me without going through Nigel he would have demanded the label sack her. I was just happy to have a night off from the studio. Nicki took me to My Old Dutch on the King's Road, and it felt like being on day release. From that night on, Nicki, who must have accompanied us to more than sixty-six *Top of the Pops* over the years, and who's since been good cop to Simon Cowell's bad cop on *Pop Idol*, was always Nicki C. to me.

Halfway through the last week the boys arrived and did some vocals. Rob did a rap on the track; he was really into rap and quick at writing little pieces. Duncan put it through a thousand boxes and electronic gizmos and, though it made it sound like Metal Mickey, it finished the song off nicely. Later Nick Raymonde came up to me and said,

'Robbie's been asking whether he'll be credited for his rap piece.'

'Well, if he wants a credit, let's just take it off the song.'

I wanted the sleeve notes to read 'Words and music by Gary Barlow'; I wasn't ready to share the glory. For me, at that stage, so ambitious to make my name, Rob's contribution seemed like an afterthought. But he should have had a credit, and I should have talked it through with him. As it was Rob never mentioned it to me, but he stored it up.

When he'd finished, Duncan sent his mix in to BMG for their approval. The reaction was the opposite of what was anticipated.

'This is awful,' said a worried-looking Nick Raymonde into the silence that followed. 'I don't think we've got a single any more.' Nick suggested Trevor Horn remix it, but he was either too busy or not up for it, so Duncan suggested using Spike Stent. Spike was only known to a few at that point, having recently come to prominence working with the KLF. Today, however, he has worked with everyone from the Spice Girls to U2, Oasis and Madonna, and there's no one in the business who hasn't heard of him. One evening I went with Nigel to Olympic Studios to hear what Spike had made of it – it was a do-or-die moment for my track. Oh man, it sounded brilliant. Spike had done an amazing job, but it also had me a little worried as, 'Once You've Tasted Love' sounded *so* different from 'Promises'. To me there was no continuity at all, they sounded like two separate bands had made them. It turned out to be a taster of the mish-mash of styles our first album contained.

We stuck with Duncan for the album tracks. The Christmas after 'Promises' came out, he came up to a studio in Bury, near Manchester, so that we could begin work straightaway. We did 'Satisfied', 'I Can Make It', 'Never Want To Let You Go', 'Why Can't I Wake Up With You' and 'Give Good Feeling' with Duncan painstakingly recording each of the lads to give us the opportunity to achieve the vocals he needed. He brought piles of records with him and we critiqued them together. I was used to finishing a note in a particular way, whereas a good chart singer would carry the note on in different ways – one artist he used to demonstrate the right approach was Kenny Thomas. After years in the clubs, I was all vibrato and very cabaret. Duncan spent hours knocking it out of me – he literally made me into a pop singer, so I owe him a huge debt of gratitude.

After so long playing about with my demos at home, I found it fascinating to watch a producer work, and a real learning curve. I wanted to be there, at every step of the way, doing track after track and take after take. I was like a sponge; I just soaked it all up. And before anyone thinks I'm weird, I have to say that this obsessiveness is pretty typical of musicians and the industry. I know friends of mine now who will work from eleven in the morning until five the next morning for an entire week, Monday to Sunday, making records, and they love it.

Even though 'Once You've Tasted Love' sounded great, after it came out it felt like we shifted down a gear from the TV frenzy of 'Promises'. I think maybe it was down to inexperience: BMG were still grappling with how to break a boy band. The video, made by a guy called James LeBon, was just a straightforward performance video of us doing a dance routine and was far from sensational. I think the single got a couple of plays on Radio One and Gary Davies, who hosted a weekly show called *Round Table*, gave us a good review saying, 'I think this could be the record for them, it's great,' but we didn't get nearly enough airplay. It lacked the intensity of the campaign surrounding 'Promises'. Our profile was high, but I was quoted as saying, 'We're becoming the most famous group in Britain for not having a hit.'

We often went round to Nigel's place on a weekend and he would cook us one of his legendary Sunday dinners. He was quite a mother hen that way – I guess we're his surrogate children, even now. We were all there, gathered round the roast beef and Yorkshire pud when we got a phone call from the label to say that 'Once You've Tasted Love' had gone in the charts at number forty-six.

None of us could believe it. For the first time I looked at Nigel and a worm of doubt crawled into my mind. I thought, oh God, you're just like the rest of them, you're fooling us. I thought you were telling us the truth when you said we were going to make it and now I just don't know.

Nigel instantly started to bluster. He was coming out with every excuse – the real ones, like not enough airplay or TV time, and nonsense, like something being wrong with the charts.

'I'll get it checked tomorrow, lads.' I thought he was on another planet.

We were all kicking ourselves for not working harder; we agreed that having done half the number of under-eighteen clubs that we did around the time 'Promises' came out had made a difference. Nor had we done as many magazine interviews. It was as though we all thought we'd already made it. In hindsight, it was the best wake-up call we could have had.

But while the others were working out what we should have done to crack the big time, I was worrying about the music. Oh fuck, I thought, we're going to get dropped. Both singles have missed and we're definitely going the wrong way here. I didn't want to be a one-hit, two-weeks-in-the-charts flash-in-the-pan.

I was starting to feel the pressure. Instinctively, I seemed to write traditional ballads or songs that sounded like Stock, Aitken and Waterman B-sides. Songs like 'A Million Love Songs', 'I Can Make It' and 'Why Can't I Wake Up With You' had come to me with no trouble at all, but when I'd hawked my tapes around recording companies before meeting Nigel, I'd been told, 'You've got to toughen up the lyrics, they're not current.' The boys too were saying they wanted to sing something tougher, something with more attitude, something more like New Kids on the Block. I began to worry I was letting everyone down – they all seemed to want this vibe that people had been telling me to get for years and which I hadn't quite got a grasp of. When I'd been writing 'Promises' I'd been helped by Graham Stack, but I'd written 'Once You've Tasted Love' all by myself in my bedroom at home. I was really into Seal, which I think you can tell. Dragging my music into the nineties was a huge effort for me.

The person in the band who helped me most at this point was Howard. He and I had hit it off as friends from the start. He's kind of the opposite to me – very quiet and shy, and never pushes himself forward – but he was the one member of the band who was as into music as I was. Right at the beginning of Take That, I used to go and stay at his parents' house in Droylsden, where I would sleep on his bedroom floor next to his bed. And now that everybody was on at me to be more contemporary, the fact that his musical tastes were a lot hipper than mine was a huge help. He'd invite me over to spend afternoons listening to old break beat records and sampling stuff, and sometimes Nicky, who I was still seeing when the band started, and I would go to the pictures with Howard and his girlfriend Gillian.

There certainly wasn't much support forthcoming from BMG. Things within the company weren't good, the label had made about 150 employees redundant and at the same time brought in new top management, a president, Jeremy Marsh, and a savvy young marketing guy from *Sky* magazine called Hugh Goldsmith. 'The two of them are going to transform the company,' we were told. Nick Raymonde was less optimistic, saying, 'We're on shaky ground here.' Nick's boss was among those who had been fired. Brought in to replace him was Mike McCormack, the man who had signed me and the other lads to Virgin Publishing. This was a stroke of luck as he was really into the band. 'We need to do a number on this Hugh Goldsmith,' said Nick. 'He's the man with the cheque book, so we need to get him on our side.'

The seven of us hatched a plan. There was a gig in Sheffield where we would always get mobbed. We may have had two relative failures as singles but the kids in this club loved us. We invited Hugh to come and see us, and hoped we'd have our clothes torn off us – we nearly always did. We were in luck: the crowd went beserk, even beyond our expectations, and Hugh loved it. He went back to London and announced to the rest of the label at a meeting, 'I've found my first project – It's Take

That'. Great, except that, having listened to the tracks that Duncan and I had recorded, no one at BMG was hearing a hit.

'First off, the music's all wrong,' said the BMG president Jeremy Marsh when he called Nigel to explain that we were to be subject to a whole new strategy. 'What we need right now is a cover of a sure-fire hit. I've been talking to Simon Cowell, one of our other A&R men, and he thinks they should go and work with Nigel Wright.' Nigel Wright had come to prominence working with Shakatak, and sealed his reuptation working on many of Andrew Lloyd Webber's projects. It was one in the eye for Nick Raymonde – not only his boss but also another A&R man was telling him what was best for us.

The first I heard about the idea of a cover version was when Nigel and I arrived at Nigel Wright's studio in Chertsey in Surrey. Nigel Wright suggested a remake of an old Tavares record written by Dennis Lambert and Brian Potter from 1975 called, 'It Only Takes A Minute'. We sat in his beautiful studio and he played us the Tavares record. As I sat in Nigel's state-of-the-art studio that afternoon I felt crushed. I had taken a tape down with me to play to him, but I couldn't bring myself to ask him to listen to it. And anyway, between them neither of the Nigels gave me a chance. Nigel Manager was quick to say that this was what we had to do, Nigel Producer was simply acting on orders from BMG. To me, it felt like everyone had lost faith in me as a songwriter. I'd believed that we had at least partially got our record deal on the strength of my songs. We had built our hopes on my writing and in turn it had got me a publishing deal. Added to which, the man who signed me at Virgin had now joined BMG. It should have all been looking so good. Instead I kept thinking, they've advanced me money on my songs and now I'm being squeezed out. Nigel Wright finished the meeting by saying, 'You leave me to get the track together and then you guys can come back to put the vocals on it.'

In some respects we were suffering from BMG's lack of a concrete direction for the band. While their people tried to figure it out, my songs became the casualties. By the time we were back in London, someone at the label, probably Nick, had come up with the idea of using another producer, Ian Levine. Interestingly, Ian and Nigel Wright, as two of the biggest pop producers at that time, were bitter rivals.

So it was off to Ian Levine's studio, and this time Howard and Nick Raymonde came with me. Nigel Wright had at least been warm and encouraging, and said my voice was good, but Ian Levine waded in with the criticism. He listened to some of my songs but the only one he liked was 'A Million Love Songs'. 'I'll produce that one,' he growled. His background was as a DJ in Blackpool and later at Heaven, one of our regular gay gigs, so for a young band like us he was very intimidating.

Even before meeting him I'd heard that Ian was tough to work with. 'I've got an American named Billy Griffin coming to London to write some songs for you,' he told me. Billy had had a minor hit in the early eighties with 'Hold Me Tighter In The Rain'. 'Come back in a week and we'll play you what we've come up with.' Once again we were ushered out and once again I felt disillusioned and upset that my songs were not considered good enough.

I then ricocheted back to Nigel Wright's studio, this time with Howard and Rob in tow. Nigel had made the backing track for 'It Only Takes A Minute' and the three of us did the vocals very quickly. We sounded good as we listened to a rough mix on the studio console. Nigel was a sweetheart and was very positive about what we'd done. After we finished he took us to the pub for lunch; Nigel's a big guy who drinks his pints with both hands. It was a fun day and we were made to feel very welcome, which helped me get over the upset of having to do a cover, especially as I felt we had emerged with a strong potential single.

At Ian Levine's studio a few days later it couldn't have been more different. When I began producing other people, Ian

Levine was my role model for how *not* to do it. There are various kinds of producer: some are musicians, some have an engineering background, others create a vibe and a rare few can do all three. Ian, on the other hand, doesn't play an instrument, needs an engineer to work the console and treats everyone around him, including the bands he works with, like his minions.

'I want chocolate. Johnny,' he'd say to his tape op, Johnny Douglas, 'go and get me chocolate. I'll have a Twix, a Topic, a Marathon, a Mars Bar, Smarties, a Turkish Delight, a Milky Way and a mint-flavoured Aero.'

Then he'd sit there and scoff the lot. He was one greedy bastard.

Ian and Billy Griffin had written a song called 'I Found Heaven'. They played us the song and then got us to sing bits on it. We went into the vocal booth one at a time, and Billy gave Rob all the song's main lines – his first lead vocal. I was given the parts in the falsetto range, a part of my voice I'd never used before. Billy nearly always sang in falsetto and maybe I should have taken it as a compliment, but I hated singing that way.

On the way back to our hotel after the session I felt weird. I was normally so prepared for everything I did, but the way Ian worked put me on the back foot. I didn't mind that Rob had been given the lead vocal, even if I was a bit taken aback. Rob had never pushed himself forward or tried to sing over me – there was no competition between us then. But the song Ian made us sing was truly fucking awful. I still hate it to this day. In fact, we all hate it and absolutely refuse to perform it on stage. It is, by a huge margin, the worst song of Take That's or my career. At the time I said nothing because I felt I didn't have leg to stand on.

But now we had two new recordings in the bag by two producers, both desperate to have their creation as our next single. Both producers did mixes of their records, and to add to the sense of anticipation, they both used the same mix engineer, Robin

Sellars. Soon enough both records were presented to BMG and we were invited to hear the finished articles for the first time. When we listened to 'I Found Heaven' we were confused, shocked and maybe even a little amazed. Here and there an odd voice appeared – Rob's lead vocal had been replaced every now and then by someone else's. Ian Levine had brought in Alan Carvell, a well-known session singer, and recorded him to sound like Rob, dropping him in on the finished version. Alan's voice is apparently in a lot of 'Making Your Mind Up', Bucks Fizz's 1981 Eurovision hit. It was years later that I found out his name; all I knew at the time was that it wasn't Rob. We couldn't believe it, we were howling with laughter at Levine's attempt at producing the vocal. It was like he couldn't be arsed to do it properly.

Next we listened to Nigel Wright's 'It Only Takes A Minute', and it was clear which was the best record. We all had smiles on our faces just listening to it and luckily everyone at BMG agreed. 'OK, we've got the single,' Jeremy Marsh said.

'Great,' said Nigel, 'but we need one more thing. I want you to buy the boys a Toyota Previa and fill it with petrol, and keep filling it every time it runs out, so we can get on the road and ensure we have a hit.'

We weren't going to make the mistake we'd made with 'Once You've Tasted Love' again.

We played schools, we played under-eighteens clubs, we played regular clubs and we played gay clubs. We were everywhere. BMG put back the release of the record until the beginning of June, so we could generate excitement and demand for the single. We did almost three straight months of gigs, including the often talked about Safer Sex Tour for the Family Planning Association, which was really just an excuse to get us in front of an audience of ten- to sixteen-year-olds. At first we gave a little speech about how important it was to be safe and not sorry, but after a few we ditched the sermon and stuck to the songs – that's all anyone wanted to hear anyway. The Toyota Previa went the length and breadth of the country, to the point where we'd say to our driver/promo guy, 'Come on, let one of us have a go at driving, you must be tired.' I don't want to give you the impression that it wasn't fun, though, we laughed practically the whole time – private jokes were always a feature of the band.

For months Nicki C. had been pitching us to Tudor Davies, the producer of the Children's Royal Variety Show. She brought him along to a gig in a club in Kingston-upon-Thames with the tiniest of stages, where the kids went wild for us. It was a stroke of genius. Tudor turned up with a guy called Kim Gavin and his wife Helen, who were working with him on the variety show – Kim would later make more difference than almost anyone to the way we developed our live performances. I remember appearing on the Variety Show for another reason. One of the dancers on the show was Dawn, who I hadn't seen since she'd appeared on the Kurtis Rush video. I went up to her and reminded her of our shared career highlight and she went bright red and looked the other way – and that was it for another three years.

The week the record came out we started doing signings in record shops, as many as we could fit in between the school gigs and our evening club appearances. It wasn't just records we signed, we did pictures, arms, hands and scraps of paper. On Tuesday we were in Glasgow, where we spent five hours signing, on Wednesday it was Newcastle and then on Thursday, the day the midweek chart is announced, we were in Stoke-on-Trent. Nigel had brought his new cellular phone with him so he could take the call from BMG.

'Lads, you've made No. 25 on the midweek – that's great. Now we just need to keep it going to push the record higher when the end-of-week chart is announced.'

On the last Sunday in May we made it to No. 16 – we were flying.

The following Thursday we were asked to appear on *Top of*

Run for Cover

the Pops. It was the fulfilment of my dream. While I was very keyed up there was another part of me that took it all in my stride. Other artists have told me how disappointed they were with *Top of the Pops*. It was small like everyone says – just four little stages round a central area – but it still felt amazing to be there. We found out later that two or three members of the crew had bets on whether or not we would sing. In fact, I sang live but the other boys mimed because of the dancing. We were all so excited. 'Here we go' was the phrase of the day. Lionel Richie, one of my heroes, was on the show and Nicki C. took me round to his dressing room to meet him. Later, when we were on our way to the set, the five of us passed Lionel in the corridor and he smiled and said, 'Hi, Gary, how's it going?'

With a Radio One roadshow a few days later, and our first ever interview in the *Sun* – with Piers Morgan, who then edited the showbiz section, Bizarre – the single went to No. 7; it was our first top ten record and it stayed in the charts for two months.

The lesson we learned from this period was a simple one: we needed to stay in touch with our audience. Getting to know them, understand them and make that personal connection was what it was all about. Of course bands have done this since pop music began, but at the time a lot of artists starting out seemed to think the formula for success was Saturday morning T.V, a piece in *Smash Hits* and then hoping for the best. We instinctively knew what worked for us, even before we were signed, and that was playing live. And when it came to selling records, the same thing applied: get out there and make it happen.

It's difficult to describe the bubble we lived in during that time. I had gone from being a club act, with my own kit and carefully kept bookings diary, to someone who had handed my life over to Nigel and a record label. It was an aspect of our lives that had consequences I would only appreciate later.

People have often asked me what we did for money during that time, but money was never an issue. We were bought or given clothes for appearances or photo shoots, and because we were working six or seven days a week we were always fed and looked after. The BMG promo people had a credit card and we were bought food, drinks and cigarettes whenever we needed them. At this stage in our careers we hadn't recouped the small advance we had been paid by the record company but all that mattered was our collective future. Now, with success in the charts came better money for gigs. It varied a lot, depending on whether it was a club gig or radio road show. In July we played Minster FM in York for £1,000 and then a few days later the Talk of the North in Manchester, where we were paid £2,500. On the same night we also played La Cage for Nigel – he was a regular there – and got a big fat nothing!

In September 1992 we played the Fridge in Brixton, with Lily Savage as compere. We went on at two in the morning, and just before Nigel announced that we would be heading to the airport to catch a very early flight to Sweden afterwards. This was our first European promo trip organised by the label, but strangely Nigel hadn't mentioned it before.

From Sweden we went to Finland and it was on the flight home from Helsinki that Nigel found out the difference between economy and business class. Up front was Shakin' Stevens, while we were all folded up like deckchairs by the engine. Nigel was not happy.

'Right, that label is going to get it. That's the last time we fly economy,' he ranted.

It probably never occurred to him that maybe, even at this late stage in his career, Shakey was probably selling more records than we were, or that he was on a different label. Nevertheless, from that day on we never travelled anything but business or first class.

Now that we were constantly on the promo circuit it felt very strange going home to Frodsham and my family. I didn't fit in any more. It wasn't that home was empty – my brother Ian was still living there – it was that I had changed. I'd call up Graham and play a game of badminton with him, and it was great to catch up, but I couldn't talk about where I'd been or what I'd seen. At home I couldn't relax, I just went up to my room and started working on songs, the way I'd always done. I needed a home of my own.

With the money from my Virgin publishing deal, and with some encouragement from Nigel, I bought a three-bedroom bungalow in Bexton Road, Knutsford. It was originally a postwar prefab and a long way from most people's idea of a pop star's 'des res' but Ian set about putting a brick shell around the prefab, which improved not only its value but also its looks. Not long after I moved in the bungalow became a fortress as our fans found out where I lived and surrounded the place.

BMG confirmed that the Levine classic, 'I Found Heaven', was to be the follow-up to 'It Only Takes A Minute' – at this point they considered it the only option. We obviously needed a video to go with it and Willie Smax was once again chosen to do the business. It was filmed in the middle of July, and in honour of our worst single, Willie did a video to match. His idea was to shoot a beach party video, but whereas other bands were taken to exotic Caribbean islands or a deserted beach somewhere in Europe, we went to the Isle of Wight. Fortunately the sun shone, but the whole thing looked cheap, and while we did our best to look like we were having a good time, it had something of a chilly British feel about it.

'I Found Heaven' came out in early August and only made No. 15 in the charts. That's about all it deserved, and our fans obviously felt the same way. We were gutted not to make the top ten, but we cheered up when midway through 'I Found Heaven's chart run our first album was released. It came out on the same day as my bedroom furniture was delivered from MFI –

could life get any better? *Take That and Party* went straight into the album chart at No. 5, the highest chart position we had achieved with any of our releases. Yet again we helped our chart placing by doing more in-store signings around the country. In Glasgow 2,000 people turned up, there were 3,000 in London and 5,000 in Manchester, where we had to be smuggled out of HMV – the remaining signings all had to be cancelled for safety reasons.

It was another huge step forward for us, and proof that we had a fantastic fan base. But the next week's album chart proved something else: our loyal fans may have rushed out and bought the album, but once they had, there wasn't enough crossover appeal to a wider audience. The album dropped to No. 19 on its second week in the chart. Two weeks later we were outside the Top 50.

I was desperate to have another crack at one of my songs and was *sure* that 'A Million Love Songs' could be a hit. For God's sake, even Ian Levine had liked it. There was still talk of releasing another cover, this time produced by Ian, and in the end we recorded both a cover of Barry Manilow's adaptation of Chopin's 'Prelude in C minor', which he called 'Could It Be Magic' and 'A Million Love Songs' over the summer, although when I say we, again it was only Rob and me that appeared on both tracks. Once again, Ian got Billy Griffin to do the backing vocals. We couldn't deny that Billy was a great singer with a wicked voice.

I came to hate the way Ian Levine worked more and more. Whereas Duncan helped my confidence in the studio, Ian did the opposite, talking a great fight and then not delivering. When we recorded 'A Million Love Songs' I remember Ian setting up my vocal slot by yelling at me, 'Right! This song needs a flawless vocal, you've got to nail it. There can be no mistakes, there will be no chance of you getting away with anything, and any mistake on a ballad like this will be exposed. So NAIL IT!'

Bloody hell, I was scared shitless as I went into the vocal booth. I did a warm-up vocal of the song, and as I finished Ian flicked the switch on the talkback from the console room to the booth and said, 'Flawless. Come on out, that was flawless.'

I could have done a much better vocal, but Ian didn't seem to take the whole thing seriously. In any event, that's how the vocal on 'A Million Love Songs' was recorded.

One day Nick Raymonde said to the engineer who worked with Ian, 'When does Ian go home? I want to mix this record without him being there. I'll pay you extra for staying behind, but I need to mix it while he's not around because he can't seem to get it right.'

Unlike Duncan, Ian was always out the door by six. 'If you come back in at 8 p.m. he'll be gone and I'll do it for you,' said the engineer.

At eight o'clock Howard, Nick Raymonde, the engineer and myself crept back in; there was no sign of Ian. We got straight down to business and were soon getting a pretty good mix together when the door to the studio fire escape burst open with a crash. We all looked up to see Ian Levine, all twenty-three stone of it. He came flying in and dived on to the desk like a fucking aeroplane doing a belly-flop.

'Get out of my studio. Get OUT of my studio!' he screamed.

There was no doubt that we had offended him.

'Get out, you nasty piece of work, Nick Raymonde.'

'Just calm down, Ian,' said Nick

This is my studio. Get out. GET OUT!'

With that we grabbed our stuff and left. We never worked with Ian again.

Despite the year's highs, I found myself thinking that everything had been a battle. Nigel had worked tirelessly on our behalf, always trying to get the best for us, but even he didn't seem to know the ropes. And I can see now that Nick Raymonde and

My Take

BMG were not altogether clear about what they should do with Take That. Like every other band that signs to a major label, we assumed our problems were over, but in many ways they were just beginning. Nothing can prepare you for what it's like once you get on the rollercoaster.

6

Bees on Heat

BMG released 'A Million Love Songs' on 28 September 1992, rushing it through so as not to lose momentum. From that moment on Take That seemed to acquire its own velocity. The song received huge airplay, going in at No. 7 in the charts. The week after 'Love Songs' entered the charts it pushed our album back up into the Top 50.

For me it felt especially sweet. After so much pushing and pulling over our cover versions, to have a top ten hit with one of my own songs was fantastic. Even after working on the recording with Ian Levine over the summer, the finished song was hardly any different from my homemade demo. There was one particularly lovely moment. After entering the charts at No. 7, 'Love Songs' slipped a couple of places the next week before going back up to No. 7. The week that happened Nan Bo, who had just turned eighty, was at my mum and dad's house with me. We were all listening to *Pick of the Pops* on Radio One, and for some reason Simon Bates was doing the show that week. 'And can you believe this,' he said, '"A Million Love Songs" has gone back to No. 7. This is a testament to the songwriting talent of Gary Barlow.' My mum and nan were almost in tears.

It was time to do a proper tour. Despite our relentless publicity, as a band we were still novices at playing live. It's one thing doing a few numbers, sometimes mimed, but it's quite another doing a whole show. Somehow we knew we were capable of something bigger. I'm not sure that even we realised how much the shows would become part of our identity, though, or how they would transform us as a band.

We were far too inexperienced to spot how flaky much of the tour organisation was. As usual, with a combination of Nigel's touring inexperience and our naivety, we threw ourselves in at the deep end. Twelve theatre dates were set up, and whereas most bands give themselves a night off after four or five shows, we did them all back to back. It was madness.

It wasn't so much the audiences but the logistics that were new. With this longer show we needed a band, soundmen, lighting men, catering and a whole crew of people. We'd outgrown the Transit and the Toyota Previa – now we had our own bus. Working with real musicians, rather than backing tapes, was a very different experience, too, and I was the only one with any frame of reference. The musicians were the remnants of Gary Glitter's Glitter Band – minus Gary Glitter, although he turned up during rehearsals once at Brixton Academy. They were a typical bunch of old rock 'n' rollers, but they did the business and were fine for us at that point in our career. Even if anyone had bothered to ask us our opinion about which musicians to use for the tour we wouldn't have had a clue, and Nigel didn't know any more than we did.

There was one thing we did decide on: we all felt that Kim Gavin, the theatrical producer we'd met at the Children's Royal Variety Show, would be great to work with. From our very first meeting with him and his wife Helen, he was on 'our page', partly because he was big on dance, having trained as a ballet dancer and choreographer, and partly because he was used to big productions with huge casts. Kim was the first person to let Howard and Jason make up their own dance routines. He's a great leader – he'll change a few things, but he was one of the first people we worked with who gave us enough scope to feel like the show was our own. We just clicked with Kim, he would even finish our sentences for us, and from that moment on he became a pivotal part of every Take That live show. Ideally you need a band member looking at the stage to tell you what you need to do with lights, stage sets, backdrops and moves, and he is ours.

We heard just before the tour opened that it was sold out, but nothing could have prepared us for the first show of the *Take That and Party* tour in Newcastle on 2 November 1992. It was a Monday night, but the noise was deafening, even from the dressing room. It was full-on from the moment we got on stage at City Hall. There were 2,000 kids chanting 'Take That', and when we hit the stage, impossibly, the noise level rose even further. We couldn't even hear each other let alone the band. I knew what keys the songs should be in, but I had no idea if we, or the band, were hitting the same notes. That aside it was fantastic, all the bits we had imagined the audience would react to worked perfectly. Jay's and Howard's skill as dancers and showmen blew everyone away. It felt like our time had come.

We had a message from Piers Morgan before we went on stage, saying that he couldn't get up to Newcastle that night but Matthew Wright, his sidekick, would be there instead, so we arranged to meet him in the bar afterwards. We were nervous because we all wanted a great review from the *Sun*. 'It was unbelievable; it's set a new standard for shows,' Matthew told us that night. The next morning, as we were waiting to leave for Bradford at eight o'clock, we found out that every tabloid had said good things about us. We couldn't have written more glowing reviews ourselves.

While I was more or less keeping pace with the routines, the others were coping with singing live for the first time. The majority of the lead vocals were down to me, but Rob sang 'Could It Be Magic', we shared 'I Found Heaven', and the others did their bit with the harmonies. The back-to-back shows not only killed our voices, they also knackered us physically. Rob struggled with his lead vocal – he was hoarse almost the entire tour – and while I had the vocal stamina, the dancing was another story. In fact, we all struggled because it was non-stop for over an hour, with all of us dancing around like bees on heat.

My mum and dad came to the show at the Manchester Apollo and I don't think they heard a thing for about a week afterwards. They were totally unprepared for what they saw and heard and I'm pretty sure they didn't enjoy it much. Even before they went in to see the show there were hassles as there was a mix-up at the box office and they didn't get the proper seats. It was another example of our ignorance of touring on that scale. Neither I, nor any of the others, knew how to sort out tickets and backstage passes, so it was a bit of a shambles – no, it was complete and utter chaos – on a nightly basis. During the show there were girls trying to get on stage, pushing and shoving, sometimes stopping just short of a fight. The organisation around us was almost overwhelmed. Nigel had hired two guys he'd met through the Radio One Road Show as security, Jerry Judge and James Gentles. The support act on the tour was a lovely guy called Cicero, who was signed to the Pet Shop Boys' company, and it was Denton, his security guy, who ended up helping out Jerry and James. Denton had scars all over his head and was a great guy – without him Jerry and James, who both knew their stuff, would really have struggled.

The tour, with all its craziness, brought us even closer as a band. People would notice that we were very tactile with each other, hugging and so on. It was a sign of our friendship, as well as the buzz we felt from what we were achieving. Although we had done plenty of gigs, touring gave us a natural high that couldn't be beaten. Fear and nerves didn't play a part, we just loved being up there. The audience were there for a great time, and so were we;

it was a mutually beneficial scene. To perform, and especially to perform well, you have to believe that the audience is happy for you to be there – they have to want you, and when they do it gives you a rush like nothing else.

To look after us on the road, instead of a BMG promo guy, we hired a tour manager called Gus Douglas. At times Gus was a miserable git, but I think a lot of it was front. He was always complaining; sometimes he did it for a laugh, but sometimes it was offensive. Perhaps he was worried about our egos getting too big? 'I can't wait to get you fuckers on stage so I can go and listen to Radio Five,' would be his standard taunt. We would be in the middle of our last number and I would catch a glimpse of Gus standing in the wings, tapping his watch to indicate he wanted us off and on our way. He was a typical old-school tour manager, whose job it was to get us on stage at the appointed time and make sure there were no disasters – not always an easy job with five overexcitable lads. Rob and Mark particularly were thick as thieves. They would turn up smirking about something or disappear two minutes before going on stage – security would be frantic trying to find them – just to wind us all up.

Gus carried on working with us for a while afterwards, but one day in a meeting with Nigel we were talking about him and someone said what a good job he did. Nigel's ears seemed to prick up and within an hour he had torn Gus off a strip and put him in his place. It seemed that Nigel's big anxiety was that we would become too independent or get close to someone other than him. He kept close tabs on all of us; I suppose we were like five monkeys in a cage all going off in different directions. If so, he was the ringmaster. He kept it all together, and it's amazing he managed for as long as he did. I can't credit him for all of it, though, because by now we were very strong and close as a team.

Shortly after that first tour we did a promotional trip to Amsterdam – what an appropriate place for the floodgates to open. It was the first time I had ever had a one-night stand. While the others had got up to things with girls while we were on the road, they were very discreet about it. Everyone was terrified that Nigel would find out and even more scared of what he might do. It was as if we had been given an unwritten rule: 'The Management has decreed that the boy band will not have any relationships with girls.' In Amsterdam it was different: Nigel wasn't there and neither were any of his spies.

After the TV show we went back to the American Hotel and sat in the bar. Ying was with us, and at this point we didn't know that she didn't tell tales to Nigel, so we all waited for her to go to bed before we got down to business. That night each of us pulled a girl and we were all in it together. They were the ugliest bunch of birds – mine was big, buxom and very Dutch. The following evening the same girls were waiting for us, but instead we pulled five different girls, which obviously didn't please the first lot. It felt naughty, but it felt *great*! And for me, Mr Bloody Sensible, it was the first taste of poison, and it tasted really sweet.

From that point on Take That and girls on the road never stopped. The only time it didn't happen who was when Nigel was around. When he decided to join us we would revert to being the good boys Nigel wanted us to be. Besides, he would have been jealous. The amazing thing about it was that Nigel was the only one who didn't know what was happening. As time went by we worked out who could be trusted and who our confidants were. We gathered our own inner circle around the band and it was virtually impenetrable.

At this point I was twenty-one years old, Mark was twenty, Howard twenty-three, Jay was twenty-two and Rob was eighteen. For boys of our age it was a dream come true: girls on tap. There would be nights when only four of us would go out and someone would stay behind at the hotel saying, 'I can't be bothered to go out tonight, could you bring us one back?'

And we would. Now I can't remember what I'd say to get them to come back with us, but they would; it was crazy. Other times we would be out and the whole thing would turn into a laugh. Any one of us could point to a girl and next thing they'd be upstairs in our room. We weren't allowed to leave until everyone was sorted out with a girl for the right. The next day, of course, there was all the chat.

'I didn't think much of yours.'

'What an earth was she all about?'

We were just a bunch of lads let loose in the sweet shop.

Throughout all this time I had a girlfriend at home in Frodsham. Nicky and I split up not long after the band got going – she was quite competitive and I think my ambition put paid to that one – and I started seeing another local girl, Rachel, soon after 'Once You've Tasted Love' came out. Amazingly Rachel and I were together, if you could call it that, until January 1995. To begin with it was great and I would rush home from tours to see her. She was nice, quiet and very, very pretty in a girl next door way – she felt like stability and normality after touring in the van with Nigel and the boys. But as I got more busy she made her own life. She was bright, and went off to do a degree at the local university, and increasingly she found the band, and the life that went with it, odd. To her our gigs were embarrassing and when I showed her our videos she'd just laugh. 'What are you looking at the camera like that for?' she'd say, 'you're not even singing!' When I came home she didn't understand that we couldn't just go out like any normal couple, I'd have been mobbed. She was never the type to go to gigs and idolise people so she didn't get the fan mentality.

To me, in my Take That bubble, her life was just as strange. She smuggled me into her halls of residence a couple of times, but she could never introduce me to her friends – she'd either have had people wanting to be her friend for the wrong reasons, or taking the piss. And as the band grew, and I became embroiled in the industry, I was completely and utterly unfaithful to her – and it was blatantly obvious. I'd see her when we came home from touring, but she put up with more than any girl should have to. I was just enjoying the on the road lifestyle and couldn't take a relationship seriously.

It must have been around this time that I was at home in my little bungalow in Knutsford, working on a track called 'Lady Tonight' that I thought could benefit from Rob's input. I was less territorial now and thought it would be nice to share a bit of it around. I called him up: 'Hey Rob, any chance that you could come over? I've got this song that needs a rap.'

It was nine o'clock on a Friday night but, typical Rob, he was up for it. 'I haven't got any wheels but if you come and get me I'll come and do it no problem,' he said.

So I got in the car, drove down to Stoke and picked him up. I had the tape in the car and Rob started writing something for it right away. When we got him home I stuck him in the bathroom with a mic – the acoustics were better in there– and we started recording. It sounded great. When the track went off everyone loved it and the rap stayed on. Rob said to me, 'Hey, will I get a credit for this?' and I said, 'Of course you will.'

A few weeks later, when Nigel and I were going through the credits for the album, I said, 'When you're doing the splits, don't forget that Rob did the rap on that track – make sure to credit him.' But when the album came in a while later there was no credit, just 'words and music by Gary Barlow' again. I was angry that I hadn't been listened to, and cross and disappointed for Rob as I knew how important it was to him.

Before things like that happened, Rob was more enthusiastic. Not long after our recording session in my Knutsford bathroom, he rang me up with an idea for a song – he sang it to me down the phone. I said, 'Rob, it's great but it's not really us. It sounds like Nirvana.' If he'd sung it to me now, I could have done something with it, I've learned to make a song from the smallest seed. Then I was much less flexible, a combination of being pigeonholed by pop and cursed by my old-before-my-time training in the clubs.

Our fan base was increasing by this point and the obvious thing to do was start a fan club. It was another of Nigel's big ideas, and as usual there was a sting in the tail. He thought we should run it ourselves, or should I say, he would run it on our behalf. 'Now, lads, I'm not having some other bugger making money off us. Anyway, how are we to know how many members there are in the club unless we run it?' was how he put it at the time. Of course it was a nightmare. There's always someone who's unhappy and you end up feeling responsible. Nigel brought in his sister, Valerie, to run the club, but things got complicated when Rob's sister Sally became involved. The breakdown between Sally and Valerie came when Sally discovered that Nigel was paying Valerie £2.50 for every new member recruited, which was more than we were making. Sally found out and told Rob, who in turn told us. Somehow that didn't seem right to any of us, and it certainly got up Rob's nose.

Running our own fan club wasn't just a mistake administratively, it was classic Nigel. He wanted to seize every opportunity, but he couldn't let go enough to allow things to flourish. It was the same with us, and the same with the label. Sometimes he made us feel like he wasn't on our side, yet he most clearly was. He protected us, he cared a lot, but because he was always beating up the label we missed out on a lot of love – he just wouldn't let them get close to us. The atmosphere changed when he was around and everybody was on edge. Even now there are people in the industry who talk about Nigel as the demon manager.

Without Nigel Take That wouldn't have happened. He made some stunning moves on our behalf, and to a huge degree he made it all possible. But now that I've experienced different styles of management, I've come to think that great managers are good facilitators and good nurturers. Nigel, however, was from the dictatorial school of pop Svengalis.

To keep in with him, you found yourself playing his game. For me that meant taking on some of his character traits, and I'm afraid they weren't always the good ones. Nigel was forever gossiping, and he encouraged that in me, too; he was quick to talk to me about the other boys behind their backs and I went along with it. I also became very good at befriending people from the label just to keep up with what was going on that we hadn't been told about. And while Nigel was alway ringing us up individually and telling each of us the same information from a different slant, I've lost count of the times that I've sat on the end of the phone with Nigel telling me something I totally disagree with saying, 'I know, Nigel, you are *so* right.'

Why is it I can be honest with everyone but him?

One upside to running your own fan club was that we got to see the amount of fan mail that arrived on a daily basis. I'd go into the office and be stunned by the piles of letters and cards. Take That was definitely on the way to becoming massive. Jason and Howard's piles were around sock height, mine was just below the knee, Rob's was waist high, and Mark's was shoulder high – who can resist that smile?

Among the fan letters were a lot of naked pictures, but some were more off-beat. I had one fan, Ilona in Germany, who was a policewoman. She used to send me pictures of herself taking part in riots. She'd be all dressed up in combat gear, complete with truncheon, hitting people – that freaked me out.

In the first week of December we swept the boards at the *Smash Hits* Pollwinners Party. Back then it was such an important magazine – the barometer of teenage taste – and we won seven awards including Best Band In The World, Best Single and Best Album.

The week after the *Smash Hits* awards we released 'Could It Be

Magic', and although it was Ian Levine's idea to cover it, the version that came out was a completely different mix to his. Nick Raymonde had brought in two Italian guys, the Rapino Brothers, to remix the song.

'Marco,' one remix maestro had said to the other, 'Wadda we do with this remix? I know wadda the English want. They lova da Motown; they lova Motown right? So "Could Ita Be Magic" ita will be Motown.'

Levine's original version was a disco mix, whereas the Rapino Brothers' was just brilliant. Grazia Mallozzi and Marco Sabiu turned it on its head and we all loved their mix – it was them that made it into a hit.

Between the *Smash Hits* awards and Christmas we went to Holland, Spain, did *Going Live*, a German magazine photo shoot and, on 22 December, a Signal Radio road show. In between that we found time to go into the studio to record our new single. Our growing success was reflected in how much we were paid to do gigs; Aire FM in Leeds coughed up £7,500 for a New Year's Day show. After the holidays, with 'Magic' still riding high in the charts, the first thing we did was head off to France to make the video for our next single in a chateau near Paris. I was pleased that BMG had decided to go with another one of my songs as the follow-up, but it was a very different version of 'Why Can't I Wake Up With You' from the one on our first album. I met with Nigel and Nick Raymonde in early December and the pair of them sat me down.

'You play it to him,' Nick said to Nigel.

'No, you play it to him.'

'No, you, I'm not doing it.'

When this pantomime finished they played me a funky remix of the song. 'I love it, it's brilliant,' I said. 'But there's one problem: we're going to have to redo the vocals. We can't leave the original vocals, it needs a totally new approach.'

The remix was by Steve Jervier and his brother Paul and when we went to their studio to redo the vocals a number of things clicked. Steve was a classic black producer – there were hundreds of people, or so it seemed, just hanging around. Paul did the control line stuff and Steve was like a DJ producer. Working with them was this little guy called Mark Beswick – he was the vocal part of the production team. Mark took us into the studio to warm up and then started us singing. It was at this moment that the Take That 'answer' thing kicked in. This is when I sing the line and it's answered by the background vocals and it was Mark Beswick's idea. It was brilliant – for the first time we were in the studio as a group, singing together. When we finished we couldn't wait to get back into the control room and hear the playback. As we stood and listened we couldn't believe it: for the first time we sounded good as a group. Mark and Steve set us on the right road and showed us what we could achieve.

We were all convinced that having done so well with 'Magic', 'Why Can't I Wake Up With You' would be our first No. 1. But rather than stay at home to promote the new record, BMG flew us to Germany and Sweden for promo work as part of a concentrated European campaign that eventually saw us make it very big in Germany, Holland and Scandinavia. After that they set their sights on America and the Far East.

We had very little control over any of it. You'd be at home making a cup of coffee and a car would arrive to pick you up. You'd grab your coat and keys and next thing you knew you were on a plane. The planning, the costumes, the travel arrangements – every detail was taken care of.

On the morning before we left for our first Take That trip to America we did Saturday morning TV, *Live and Kicking*. Unfortunately Nigel arrived at the studio absolutely off his head. Everyone, including us, stared at him in amazement, and Howard whispered to me, 'He's had an E or something.'

Whatever it was I reckoned he'd been on an all-night bender and probably hadn't even been to bed. I was shocked because I'd never seen Nigel, or anyone for that matter, behaving so strangely. He was walking around the studio saying, 'Kylie Minogue and baked beans, Kylie Minogue and baked beans', over and over, like a mantra. We decided that someone in America must have asked Nigel to bring both things over with him, presumably the CD rather than Kylie herself. I spent the morning following him around apologising, which is typical of me.

Things weren't much better when we reached New York. A guy from RCA in America met us at the Marriott Marquis on Times Square. He was the usual upbeat American promo guy, but for some reason or another the hotel billing had been arranged incorrectly, which resulted in Nigel having to use his credit card. He went ballistic at the poor promo guy, whose only crime was to have given up his Saturday evening to come and meet us. Nigel shouted at him, made a scene in the foyer and generally embarrassed us all. It was as if the further Nigel ventured from Manchester and his sphere of influence, the bigger the tantrums he threw.

The next day the guy from the label arrived to take us around the sights of New York. Before we went we wanted to find out our chart position in the UK. Having been No. 1 in the midweek charts we were confident we would stay there, but we needed proof. Jerry Judge was our security guy and he knew Bruno Brookes, so he called the studio at Radio One to find out our chart position. We couldn't believe it, 'Why Can't I Wake Up With You' had slipped to No. 2. We had been pipped to the post by 2 Unlimited, the Dutch Eurodance group. Nigel decided not to hang around and left after a meeting with the label the following day, giving Jerry strict instructions that we were to stay out no later than 1 a.m.

We were at the start of what would be our first taste of the gruelling slog that is long-haul promo work. From New York we went to Canada, then down to Miami – Howard and I squeezed in a quick trip home to see our girlfriends – then Dallas and on to

Los Angeles from where we flew to Japan. From Tokyo just Ying and Chrissie Harwood from BMG's International Division accompanied us to our final destination, Taipei in Taiwan. When we got there, after flying for what seemed like for ever, we were arrested. We had been given the wrong type of visas and at first they weren't going to let us into the country. Eventually the police escorted us to our hotel, where they then stood guard outside our doors. Thankfully, the next day the mess was sorted out and we got down to business, which was the usual round of promo work.

Except that none of us had any idea what to expect from promo work so far away from home. Two days later, on landing in Tokyo, we were each given a huge bound book of our itinerary. It started at 7.01 a.m. each morning and didn't stop until midnight, with each and every minute filled. If one of us so much as went to the toilet it ruined the whole day's schedule. Later we learned that if we wanted to breathe we had to get the Japanese to send over the itinerary before we arrived so we could say no, no, no, no, yes, we'll do that one. This time, though, we were bloody exhausted.

Another challenge was the food. One night we were taken out to dinner and it turned into a bit of a culinary voyage. We were seated at a counter watching the chef prepare the food when a bowl of prawns arrived. I and the others immediately noticed that they were still alive. Next thing they were popped on the griddle and cooked. I noticed Rob looking a little perplexed.

'What's up, mate?' I asked

'I ordered the beef!' said Rob.

It got worse. When you mistake miso soup for a finger bowl and notice that everyone else is drinking theirs while you have your fingers dipped in yours it's hard to look cool.

But Japan was the start of a passion. At home we'd always had very plain food, everything came with chips and you'd have a particular dish on a particular night, like in *Shirley Valentine*.

Tuesday night, egg and chips, Wednesday night, bangers and mash, and so on. Being in the band and discovering restaurants and different cuisines was the beginning of a love affair. I'm crazy about food and love eating out, so it's been a battle ever since. The dance routines kept my weight down at the time, but there was no doubting the fact that I was the fat white one. I'd be the last band member the stylist would tackle and even then Nigel would say, 'Will someone find Gary a top? He looks like he's from Frodsham.'

All this travelling posed a particular problem for me as I needed to get on with writing our second album and being away from home made that almost impossible. While the rest of the band went with the flow, I was constantly haunted by what Bob Howes said to me about having years to write the first album and then, if you're successful, weeks to write the second. To alleviate the problem I bought an Apple laptop in America. It was a big dark grey machine that weighed a ton, but at least it was portable. I put Cubase, a recording and editing tool on it, and lugged it all the way to Japan. Prior to our arrival the label contacted Yamaha in Japan and asked if I could borrow a keyboard during my stay. When we arrived at the Capitol Hotel there was not just one keyboard in my room but five. When we came back late at night from the promotional rounds I'd get on with writing. I'd order bread from room service, and use the toaster in my room to keep me going with peanut butter on toast. That's how most of our second album got written.

Before we left England, Nigel had said to me, 'I think it's really important for Mark to have a song on the album. He gets the most mail and he's never had a track to sing.' It was in Japan that I started work on 'Babe'. Besides being Mark's song, 'Babe' was an important song in the history of the band for another reason – it was the song that got Jason into playing the guitar. Jay had always felt that musically he didn't contribute to the band like the rest of us, which is what prompted him to take up the guitar. Not that the rest of the band felt Jay didn't add a great deal to our success: he was a brilliant dancer and an integral part of everything we did. Once Jay decided to take up the guitar he showed amazing dedication and would play until his fingers bled. He started learning 'Babe' while we were in Tokyo – I taught Mark the vocals and Jay the chords and he went away and practised non-stop. The three of us would sit there with Jay playing the guitar and Mark singing along even before the song was finished – I hadn't written a middle eight, only the chorus. Eventually Mark, whose voice was getting better, and Jay, who had totally cracked the chords for the chorus, had the song down pat; it was time for the middle eight. The trouble was I didn't want Jay to have to learn any more chords, so I wrote the rest of the song around the ones he already knew. There was one other complication in that Mark was at the top of his range, so it couldn't go any higher. It's a hell of a way to write a hit.

In early April 1993 BMG had us travelling extensively to Spain, Belgium, Germany, Norway, Finland and Holland. Nigel came on very few of these trips, but he did come with us to Amsterdam, and as usual we went to the Bulldog to pick up a bag of grass. If Nigel was worried some bad press might follow, he was even more worried when he saw how bad we looked standing in the lobby the next morning. We'd gone on to an Indian restaurant, and from there to some karaoke bar until the early hours of the morning. Despite encouragement from the others, I was feeling much too ill to sing, so Rob said, 'I'll do it.'

I remember Nigel looking at me quizzically and saying, 'What's he going to fucking do?' Rob sang 'Mack The Knife' and it was absolutely brilliant – the whole place was cheering when he finished. I was as amazed as everyone else.

'Fucking hell! Where did that come from?' said Nigel, but afterwards Rob just returned to his shell.

7

Mini Elton

The G-Mex arena, 22 July 1993. I'll never forget how it felt to come on stage. It was the first gig of a short tour that coincided with the release of 'Pray' and we had raised our game yet again. Looking back, it felt like this was the moment the five of us became Take That the phenomenon.

There were 18,000 in the audience and every one of them was screaming their head off; the noise was the highest-pitched sound you've ever heard – pure hysteria. Looking out, the whole audience was a mass of signs and banners: 'Let me mother you, Mark', 'Go deep with me, Jason', 'Gary, we love your music'. The stage had had to be shovelled clear of teddy bears, chocolate, pictures of Kylie or whatever we'd said we liked best in last week's *Smash Hits*; they'd go into a huge bucket which went to charity. This time we had a brilliant band behind us – gone was the Glitter Band and in came a fantastically slick operation put together by Jonathan Wales. He brought in keyboard player Mike Stevens and guitarist Milton Macdonald, both brilliant and both still playing with us today. We had curtains and kabuki drops and the whole show was far more technically advanced. The theatre tour was an expanded version of our club appearances, but this time Kim Gavin had taken us off to a farmhouse in Wales to drill some order into our chaos. We'd spent five weeks in the middle of nowhere rehearsing solidly from ten till the stroke of six every day. We were bored out of our minds, but Nigel loved us being miles away from trouble or distractions. Together we'd come up with a new tack on everything from lights to staging to routines. The lads had all had great ideas and that was when we developed the Motown medley, Apache and rethought the order the songs were sung in – that part was always my speciality. Rob had bought a baby's dummy when we were in Blackpool, and playing on his role as the baby of the band, he went on stage with it. It soon became his trademark and he'd sit on TV shows with the dummy round his neck, sucking it every now and again. That sort of quirky touch was part of Rob's brilliance.

What marked this show out for me, though, was the camaraderie we had on stage, the in-jokes, shared glances and words slipped in to the links here and there – things that only meant something to the five of us. For the first time we had in-ear monitors, which cut out 40 per cent of the external noise, so we could hear what the band was playing, and even better what each other was singing. In most bands the music is the integral ingredient, but with us it was always the performance. That was where the others put their focus because they knew the music was more my turf. That night, however, was different: the music felt like a band effort.

'Pray' had begun life before we left for Japan, and armed with my new laptop I continued to work on it there. Initially it had four verses: two verses, then a musical interlude and then another two verses before the chorus. It was also very long, about five and a half minutes, so when I got back to England Nick Raymonde suggested we give it to Steve Jervier to work on. It didn't seem to matter how professional my demo tapes were – and by this stage I had bought myself a forty-channel DDA Composer, a sixteen-track reel-to-reel Tascam recorder and countless other bits of kit

Our very first promo card

Congratulations
Number One

Scenes from boy band life

TUNSTALL
ASSURANC

We rehearsed constantly

Take That mania

MARK OWEN
SCOTLANDS GIRLS ♥'S ENGLANDS BOYS
HOW DID YOU like THE CURRY last night
WELCOMES
GARY

And then we were four. This image had to be reshot when Rob left the band

to make them sound more slick – every time I took something in to BMG, Nick or someone else would suggest we got so-and-so to do it. I liked Steve and I'd liked working with him, but I didn't think this song was his sort of thing, but Nick gave the demo to him before I had a chance to disagree. When we went to his studio in May to listen to what he'd done, the track had radically changed. I'd originally been inspired by Simple Minds, but Steve had altered the beat, moved the second verse to the first, cut some other verses, moved the rest around and evolved it into a new jack swing-type thing. Once again Mark Beswick came in to do his thing, and one by one we went in to record our vocals. At the end of the night I was convinced it was a monster, a massive record, and while it was still definitely my song, I have to say that Steve and his crew did a brilliant job. Two months later 'Pray' became our first No. 1 single.

'Pray' was a risky record to release at that point in our career: it's dark for a pop track, and especially so by our standards. When we trooped into Radio One for its first radio play, Simon Bates was quick to say how commercial it was and he and his producer Fergus Dudley really built it up – a great kick-start for the single and a big leap forward for us with the station; they were pivotal to a band's success and had been slow to get behind us. In the same week we went to Crystal Palace for a Capital Radio Road Show where 30,000 fans turned up. When 'Pray' made No. 1 on 17 July I was ecstatic, but if anything the others were more excited than I was; for me it was the success of 'A Million Love Songs' that gave me the biggest buzz.

We had shot a video in Acapulco in May, which was the first of several we made with director Greg Masuak. Much of it was filmed on the beach, and believe me it was a lot better than the Isle of Wight. The rest of the video was filmed in a casino which had been shut down. Apparently the Mafia had owned it and there were bullet holes in the walls – the result of a shoot-out with the police. By far the most expensive shoot we had done, it was another example of how we'd moved up a level in quality. Greg had his own make-up artist and stylist – we could feel the difference and you could certainly see it.

The fact that we were shooting the video in Acapulco was one of those lucky accidents and had nothing to do with the label wanting to send us there. It was just convenient because we had gone to New York for a series of promotional visits in high schools. An awful remix of 'It Only Takes A Minute' was on release in the USA and the astute marketing types at the label decided that this was the way to break us. We would go into morning assemblies and mime to the song, which was somehow meant to encourage kids to stay in school and at the same time sell our record. One thing's for sure, it was no way to break a British boy band in America. We didn't even make a dent. As I was to find out to my huge personal cost much later, breaking an act in America is like targeting fifty-two countries all at once, and what happens in New York has no bearing on what happens in Texas, California or even Spokane.

After the G-Mex gig, we did a show in Glasgow, another in Manchester, one in Birmingham then three nights at Wembley Arena and, true to form, they were all back-to-back. Elton John and Paula Yates both came to the last of the Wembley shows. We had first met Paula on *The Big Breakfast* in one of Paula's flirty on-the-bed interviews, though it was so early in the morning that what we said is a bit of a blur. After the Wembley show she brought Elton backstage with her and I was star-struck, but then I always am when I meet Elton – you know you're in the company of a real star.

'Why don't you come to my house for dinner after the show tomorrow?' he said. Everyone was mad keen, everyone, that is, except Nigel, who thought Elton's manager John Reid would be there, which for some reason put him off.

'Nigel, we're all going,' I announced.

We took the tour bus down to Woodside in Old Windsor on

27 July; it was a trip that was, quite literally, to change my life for the next decade or so.

As we pulled up at the gates it was as if someone had put a huge bolt of electricity through me. I looked, saw Elton's house – actually it's not a house at all, it's a bloody mansion – with its lake and fountain, and was stunned. Bear in mind that home for me was a bungalow in Knutsford. We all started cheering as we drove through the gates. Two uniformed butlers met us as we got off the bus, and so did Paula Yates, dressed to the nines and very much uninvited. Elton was not best pleased to see her. This was the start of Paula hanging around with us for quite a long period, so much so that she became part of the scenery. Paula really liked Jason, but became a good friend of mine, and also of the rest of the lads.

Elton swept us off on a guided tour of the house – it took an hour. He had hundreds and hundreds of gold discs, while at this point we had two. And there was us thinking we'd made it.

The dinner was great and naturally Nigel and John Reid ended up getting on like a house on fire. David Furnish was there, too, though he and Elton had only been seeing each other for a few months.

When dinner was over the other lads started whispering to me, 'Gaz, Gaz, look there's a piano. Go on, play a song.'

It was a typical Take That moment; the others would often say things like that. It wasn't that they wanted to sing, they just wanted me to do it. I sat at the white grand piano and Elton stood right over me so he could see what chords I was playing. I did a song of mine called 'The Party Is Over', which we all loved but for some reason have never recorded.

'If you can write songs like that you can make a living for ever,' said Elton. I was blown away. Having said that, he couldn't wait to get me off the piano – I've come to realise that Elton loves situations like this – so he could play us 'Your Song'. Being up that close was amazing.

Even more amazing was the revelation that came to me as

Elton was playing. I looked around that room, drinking in the art, the spectacular furnishings, the luxurious curtains, everything about his home, and thought, this is it. Playing the piano, composing and performing could bring me all this. Growing up in Ashton Drive, Frodsham, I had no idea that this world even existed. I had been given this amazing lucky break in life, incredible opportunities that were exposing me to so much in terms of life experience, culture, travel, lifestyles. I think you can go one of two ways: you either look and then move on, or you embrace it. I was about to embrace it wholeheartedly.

I've always had a reputation for being tight – I think it comes from the story about me making the boys pay for using my mobile phone when we were starting out. Yes, I did make them pay £1 a shot because calls were expensive then, and yes, if it was today I'd just pay the bill myself and be skint. But my responsible side is very definitely misconstrued when it comes to my personal finances, which have often verged on the shambolic. The money was rolling in now and Elton was the inspiration I needed to start spending it. It wasn't long after visiting Woodside that I bought a large house in Plumley and later Delamere Manor, my very own copy of Woodside. My spending became extreme. I would buy anything that Elton had – watches, rings, you name it. I turned into a mini Elton.

It wasn't just a case of being seduced by wealth. Elton John is the best singer-songwriter Britain has ever produced. His career has lasted far longer than that of anyone else who both writes and performs, he's been a more consistent songwriter than any of his contemporaries and has branched out into movies and stage shows – he's done it all. I just wanted to do it all and have it all, too. About the only thing I didn't do was go off women.

The other overriding memory of that night at Elton's was what he said about drugs. He had not long come out of rehab.

'After twenty-five years in the business there's one thing I can tell you: stay away from fucking cocaine. Don't go near it. I can't even begin to add up the money I've spent on that drug. It can ruin your life.' He looked at Rob a lot of the time as he spoke. In many ways they are very alike.

What interested me was that throughout dinner we were drinking and Elton was the first to say, 'Another drink anyone?' And yet he didn't touch a drop. At the end of the night he drank a non-alcoholic beer and I thought, bloody hell we've had the time of our lives here and he hasn't been able to join in. Then immediately I thought, no that's not true. He's loved it.

Elton's was a long strong lecture and I sat there and really listened – it wasn't like this was your teacher at school. I must have taken in what he said, as, for the most part, I've practised what he preached. Drugs have never featured that much in stories about me for the simple reason that they've never featured that much in my life. Yes, of course I've taken things, tried things and for a while, during a very low point in my life, I smoked far too many spliffs. But it was just for a very short period. Looking back, I've come to realise I've taken hardly any drugs at all. Drugs and me are a bit of a non story – disappointing maybe, but true.

Being in the music industry, I've been around drug taking, but again, not a lot. Take That were just not that kind of band. There's so much bullshit talked about the tortured artist and the effects of drugs on the creative process that many people just assume that 'doing drugs' goes with the territory. But for me it's never been like that. For a start, performing the kind of shows we did was knackering and we had to stay in shape, both physically and mentally. We drank a lot, went out a lot and we were young and resilient, but we couldn't push it too far. Also, I've always felt that to get into drugs seriously you have to be punishing yourself for something, and I had no bloody reason to punish myself – it was all happening for us, and I was having a ball.

Nigel goes clubbing every weekend – he now owns two of them – and around this time he was in a gay club somewhere and heard 'Relight My Fire' by Dan Hartman, which had originally come out in 1979. It gave him the idea for yet another cover and when he played it to me I knew it was an inspired choice. As a songwriter and performer you are never as excited about having to do other people's songs as you are about your own, but the great thing about having a manager like Nigel was that he didn't know the rules of the game. He was constantly trying new things and thinking outside the box.

Nigel had another idea: 'We need a really strong female vocal. Let's use Lulu to sing with you lads on the track.'

'Who's she?'

I had to ask my mum what Lulu had sung. All I knew was that she had red hair. BMG was initially reticent about using her, but what did they know?

Lulu arrived at the studio with flasks full of honey, lemon and ginger, and was totally together. Despite having already done an hour's warm-up before she got there, she then went into another room at the studio and did thirty minutes more. This was the first time we had worked with another singer and we were curious. Our standard warm-up was a few ooh ahhs and a Diet Coke. I said to Lu, 'You really go to town, don't you?'

'Of course I do, this is my instrument. I don't play guitar or piano, so I have to be sure I'm at my best.'

She went in and did a great vocal – we barely had time to warm-up our headphones. Lulu was very grounded, very motherly towards us, and we all became close to her in our different ways. I really appreciated her long experience of the industry – she'd done everything and knew everyone – we had some great chats. She used to tell me I was an old soul and that I'd been here many times before. Maybe she just meant that I was an old head on young shoulders.

The plan for 'Relight My Fire' was that Rob would sing

lead vocals as his follow-up to 'Could It Be Magic'. Rob was in the studio for two nights, but he just couldn't get his vocals right, so on the third day Nigel called me and said, 'Can you go into the studio tonight and sing it so Rob can copy your vocals?'

I did and everyone loved the voice I found. Nigel, who wasn't big on compliments, said, 'Where did you pull that from? It's one of the best you've ever done.'

'I dunno, I just did it.'

So that's how I ended up on what was supposed to be Rob's song.

'Relight' came at the end of an intense few weeks in August, during which time we recorded a lot of the album. Without Rob's vocal on 'Relight' it meant that he had no song on the album, whereas Mark had 'Babe' and Howard sang 'If This Is Love'. Nigel was worried that Rob didn't feature and told me to get on the case. I had already recorded 'Wasting My Time' with some guys in Sheffield who called themselves Five Boys Productions, which was the first time I worked with a great guy called Eliot Kennedy. Eliot and his crew were completely on my wavelength so I decided to go and see what we could come up with. They had a backing track, I had a title and we just worked on it together. When we'd finished it was a perfect three-minute pop song, all it needed was Rob to do the business. The night before I called him and said, 'Now listen, Rob, you've got to pull out all the stops on this one, mate. If you don't you're going have no lead vocal on the album and it won't work for us.'

I realised the pressure he was under, so for the first time I decided to stay away from the studio, which was a difficult thing for me to do. I left it to Eliot and his boys, which I thought was far better than me standing there with my arms crossed, staring at Rob every time he got something wrong.

It ended up a bloody marathon – nine hours in all – with take after take after take, because this was pre-auto-tune days, which meant you had to get it right, no matter how long it took. Rob is definitely in the one-take school and absolutely hated having to do that, but in the end he did a really, really great job. I forget what the album was going to be called, but the minute I heard the new song I knew it would make a great title track, and so we changed the album to *Everything Changes*.

We played our biggest gig to date in front of a huge crowd at the Chelmsford Festival at the end of August. A couple of days later we made the video for 'Relight My Fire' at London's Ministry of Sound and on 1 September we flew to Hong Kong to start a promotional tour that took in Japan. We also played our first gigs in Japan at Tokyo's Nakano Sun Plaza; this one was less frenetic as we had sight of the itinerary before we left, but it was still knackering given everything we'd done before we left. When we got back from Japan, Nicki Chapman called to say we were booked to appear on *Top of the Pops*. For once, Nigel said no way.

'They've worked for fifty days without a day off, so it's out of the question. Well, unless you buy all of the boys a watch.'

'What kind of watch?'

'A £300 Tag Heuer should do it.'

We performed 'Relight' for the first time on *Top of The Pops* and two weeks later, on 9 October, it entered the charts at No. 1 and was followed two weeks afterwards by our new album, which also went straight to the top of the album charts. All this success gave us the chance of mounting our biggest tour so far. We did twenty-one dates in all, including one in Dublin. We knew we must be getting more successful as we were given days off between some of the gigs – not too many, mind you.

A longer tour meant better staging, better effects and a bigger and more exciting show overall. In contrast to the bigger better theme, Rob introduced another of his little touches, the devil's horns during 'Relight'. He is a consummate showman, a real vaudevillian. At times his humour reminds me of Freddie Starr's.

It wasn't the dancing but the rehearsing I hated – that and the fact that the four people I was stood next to were bloody good at it. We'd practise constantly, in hotel corridors, anywhere, you name it. Howard would take the piss out of my dancing – we'd all take the piss out of each other – and everyone would be laughing, but when Rob did it there was always an edge, something deeper that didn't make you laugh the same way. He's so sharp and quick-witted, but there's always a little message. Rob's not to be underestimated, ever – maybe that was my mistake.

After the tour was over we again swept the boards at the *Smash Hits* Pollwinners Party on 5 December, and we followed that with our third single from the second album. 'Babe', Mark's first lead vocal, went straight to the top of the charts on 18 December. Unfortunately we didn't hang on to be the Christmas No. 1 as we were deposed by Mr Blobby.

We had Christmas off, which was something of a tradition for us. Throughout my time with the band it was the same story – we would be given time off and it would be, 'Off you go, have a nice time everyone,' and I'd go home and start a new record. At this point in my life it wasn't just the only thing I knew how to do, it was the only thing I wanted to do. That's why it was so great for me meeting someone like Elton. I suppose Elton responded to me because I was the songwriter in the band, but he also understood my drive. I remember the second time I met him we sat and listened to music together for hours. It was a Sunday, I was on my way to London and I'd dropped by. Elton wanted to play me his album so he said, 'Come and listen to it in the car.' That's where he always listens to music.

So we sat in the two front seats of his beautiful Rolls Royce, which is like sitting in someone's lounge, with its state-of-the-art speakers all beautifully tuned, parked outside his back door, listening to *Made in England*. Then when that was done he said, 'Oh, have you heard this record?' so we listened to that, and then I had some new stuff in my bag, so we listened to that. In the end we were sat there for about six hours.

Right after Christmas it was back on the road for promotional trips to Europe, starting with Belgium, Germany and France. It was the beginning of a relentless year – the BRITs in February, followed by the San Remo Song Festival, shooting the video of 'Everything Changes' and then rehearsing the *Everything Changes* European Tour in Spain. The tour opened in Hamburg on 24 March and took in Belgium, Germany, Denmark, Sweden and Finland, finishing just over two weeks later in Helsinki.

I think a promo trip to Germany was one of the rare times I stood up to Nigel during that spell. We were being made up by Mark the make-up before a PA. Perhaps because they had once been a couple, Nigel used to try all the same put-downs with Mark as he tried with us. He always liked to remind you of what you were before he transformed your existence. 'You're just a bin man, Mark,' he'd say. 'You were a bin man when I met you, and now look what I've made you.' This would go on night after night and he was on at him all the time.

I think on that particular night Mark had committed the crime of forgetting to get Nigel's bag out of the van.

'My fucking bag was in that van!' he yelled. 'And you, you're working for *me* when you're here. I'm paying you to be here.' I was sitting in the make-up chair between them, with Nigel raging over my head, and I'd had enough. I lost it. It was the endless travelling combined with the relentless narking at us that pushed me over the edge.

'Nigel, do you know what? I'm sick to fucking death of you two bitching. Right, that's it. Nigel, fuck off out of this studio and go back to the hotel right now. Go!'

I'm normally fairly steady, so all the boys looked up, their faces saying, 'Hey, ho, what's going on here?'

Nigel turned a shade of purple and stormed out the door, slamming it in fury.

There was quite a silence after he left, with the five of us all looking at each other. Then someone said, 'Fucking hell, what are we going to do now?'

I think that gave me a second wind, as I said, 'Right, we're going back to the hotel to see him. I'm really going to give it to him.'

We all trooped back to his hotel and up to his room. We knocked on the door. No answer. I hammered at the door again .

'Nigel, we're going to sort this out, right? Nigel, open up!' I was really itching for a fight by this stage.

When Nigel came to the door he was crying. Inconsolable. Because that's the confusing thing about Nigel: he does have a gentle side; he's emotional and the smallest thing can hurt him. He left early the next morning, before any of us were up, and he apologised – he could be generous that way. He also stopped bitching – for about two weeks.

In May I was invited to a lunch at the Savoy in London to receive an Ivor Novello award for Songwriter of the Year and another for 'Pray', I'm not sure I quite took in what it meant. I thought the whole thing was going to be pretty boring, so I said to the others, 'Don't worry, I'll just go by myself,' although I did take my mum. Nigel gave up his seat so she could go with me, and he also bought me a lovely Versace suit. When I got there I realised this was something very different. What makes the Ivor Novello awards so significant is that the British Academy of Composers and Songwriters awards them, so it's recognition from your peers. And there was Elton to present me with my award. I was totally overwhelmed.

In my acceptance speech, I told people that while we hadn't set out to be anything but successful, we didn't have any idea of what was going to happen. In a sense winning the award made me start considering the direction my career would take. In their different ways I think everyone else in the band was beginning to as well.

Everything became a little bit more serious. When you're on the way up it's one thing; when you get there there's a whole lot more to think about.

Later that month we headed east for another trip to Hong Kong, Korea and Japan. By now we had worked out some of our Japanese fans' idiosyncrasies, especially the girls. They would rent a room between them and then slip notes to us when we were in the hotel reception. We used to call it 'CCing' – corridor creeping. We would collect all our notes together with the various room numbers on them – it was like going to Tesco's meat counter – then we'd turn up at a room, knock on the door and inside there would be thirty girls.

Rob and I had a great trick we used to pull.

'OK everyone, quieten down,' I'd say. 'I'm going to hypnotise Robbie. Robbie you are now under my control. You will go to the minibar and take out four beers, then you are going to leave the room.'

Once he'd gone, I'd say, 'I will now disappear.'

I would then shoot out the room and dash up the corridor. I know it sounds stupid, but that's the sort of thing you end up doing when you're on the road – anything to pass the time.

While we were in Japan we got a call from Nigel.

'Lads, I've booked you for a week in Australia, seeing as you're in that neck of the woods.'

We replied, 'Nige, it's an eleven-hour flight.'

'Well never mind, you're over that way.' This from Nigel who needed a lie-down after a flight between London and Manchester.

When we arrived in Australia there were fans waiting for us; not as many as we would get in London, but we still had to run the gauntlet at the airport. Francis from BMG met us and shepherded us into a trusty Toyota Previa and then we were off to the hotel, followed by kids on motorbikes and in cars. After our first trip to Japan, where every minute of every day was filled, Nigel insisted that from then on when we arrived in any country outside of Europe we should have the first day to ourselves to relax and recover. Chrissie Harwood accompanied us on this trip to Australia, and before we left Japan she told us that the label wanted to take us on a boat trip around Sydney Harbour the day after we arrived.

'They're not going anywhere, it's their day off,' said Nigel on the phone to Chrissie.

'He's right, we're not going anywhere, it's our day off,' we chorused.

When we got there Chrissie said, 'Are you sure you don't want to go on the boat trip? It's such a nice thing to do; it'll be a lot of fun.'

Naturally we went.

'God, I hate this life!' I said, probably speaking for all five of us.

I ended up dancing with a girl to Billy Joel's 'Just The Way You Are' as we went under Sydney Harbour Bridge with the lads, led by Rob, chanting our song: 'We're naughty, we're naughty, we're off our fucking heads.'

8

The Grand Tour

Sometime in early 1994 everything started to become unreal. We were so hot that we lost our footings. It got to the stage where I thought, this is it; this is how the rest of my life is going to be. It's never going to change; life will never be any different from this. I felt totally comfortable, as if the rug could never be pulled from underneath me. It was like sitting in your favourite chair, your remote control programmed to your favourite channels. We were all in that seat, we were on the radio and TV all the time, and in all the newspapers – it seemed like a Take That world. Despite the fact that we were working hard, everything was to order, things happened when we expected them to happen, everyone around us was there to fulfil our needs. Writing was easy: I could sit at a piano and just write a hit. Everything was going right on a daily basis. We had stopped climbing the hill, we were there.

I decided it was time to move house. I found a place in Plumley, which seemed to me to be the kind of house that someone with aspirations to become Elton might buy. It was on sale for £300,000 and it was secluded; it even had gates. I took my dad to look at it. Perhaps because I'd been away from home for a while I noticed that he seemed to have aged quite a bit since he'd retired. I was actually quite shocked by how he looked; he was so grey.

'What are you doing with yourself, Dad?'

'Well, I've been playing bowls a lot.'

My dad's an active man and I felt that retirement – he had retired early having been made a good offer – didn't suit him. When we arrived in Plumley we found the house, which was called Moorside, and we were met by the agent who showed us around. I immediately went inside while Dad walked around the acre of grounds. When we met up about an hour or so later he said, 'You know what, Gary? I could do the garden.'

That was it, I decided to buy it and immediately agreed a price with my dad for him to become the gardener. Once I moved in I paid an even bigger price. Every morning, or so it seemed, at seven o'clock it was brrm, brrm. My dad would start up some piece of machinery – a mower, a strimmer, a chainsaw, or hedge-cutters. Mind you, I ended up with a fantastic garden, and of course you can't sack your dad.

Pretty soon Dad started making a pond, maybe it wasn't a lake like Elton's, but it was a start. Best of all, though, I got to spend time with him. I realised that I hadn't spent a lot of time with him when I was growing up because he always seemed to be at work. While I lived in Plumley the two of us would regularly go and have lunch at the pub; it turned out to be a great time in my life.

I was also seeing a lot of Elton. One day I was round at his place for lunch and we got to talking.

'It's really hard living on your own, working so hard and trying to keep your life going smoothly, I said.'

'What you need, Gary, is a butler. Someone who takes care of everything.'

'A butler?' I was incredulous.

'Yeah, they're great. They pack your bag, unpack your bag, wash your clothes, iron them, and even do the cooking if you're lucky enough to find a good one. They can answer the phone, take messages, it's brilliant.'

Next thing I was doing interviews. The third guy I saw was just perfect; Maurice was his name, straight-backed, slightly camp and just the business. He got the job and lived in the bungalow at Knutsford, then when I was away he stayed at Plumley, so there was the added bonus of security. While having Maurice had many upsides, you can imagine how the others took the piss out of me. They all used to rush to my room when we travelled anywhere just to see how much tissue paper he had used to pack my suitcase.

'Hello, Moorside,' was how Maurice, in his soft voice, answered the phone, the inflection gently rising as he said 'side'. People may laugh about it, and none more than me, but he made my life so much easier. He organised everything. He would cook wonderful dinner parties, and nothing was ever too much trouble. My home life became like a scene out of Jeeves and Wooster – it was a gentleman's thing. This was all fine until Dawn and I got together: she took one look at him and said, 'He can go. I'm not having him mincing around.'

It was the first manifestation of Dawn keeping my feet on the ground.

Early in June 1994 a new guy joined the Take That family. His name was Chris Healey and Nigel took him on as our new tour manager. Chris had worked with Go West and the Kids From Fame, among others, having started off with a heavy metal band called Uriah Heep – his *Spinal Tap* years. You'd never know it to look at him, though, he's the straightest guy you'll ever meet, and looks more like a bank manager than a road rat. Chris stayed on and worked for me after I left the band and came back to work with us on the Ultimate tour in 2006, and became a really trusted mate. We first met him in late July at Stanbridge Farm, near Handcross in West Sussex; we were rehearsing at the 500-year-old farmhouse for our summer tour. We spent days working on dance routines and vocal harmonies in a marquee in the grounds. It proved to be a much better place to rehearse than Wales – at least we got the chance to go to Brighton or London on our nights off. We had to break off from rehearsals to film the video for 'Sure', a much more ambitious production than any of our earlier efforts. We acted on that video, another first for us; it's my daughter's favourite because the little girl who appeared in it was also called Emily.

While we rehearsed, production rehearsals were under way at Docklands, where our stage had been set up. It was there that tragedy struck when Tim Warhurst, the front-of-house sound engineer, fell off the PA stack and was killed. Neither I nor any of the others were there, but it shook and upset us all and we've never forgotten it. On every tour since we've been aware of the potential dangers on stage.

Shortly before we started rehearsals 'Love Ain't Here Anymore' came out. It was the sixth single to be taken off the *Everything Changes* album and perhaps none too surprisingly it only made No. 3 on the charts, having followed on from four straight number ones. The Pops tour, as it was called, opened in Glasgow at the SECC on Thursday, 24 August.

It was on this tour that we introduced the Beatles Medley into the show, and what we call the B stage, where a bridge is lowered and we walk over from the main stage to the centre of the arena and perform on a small circular stage. From the very first night this was an amazing success. We got to do something completely different, the fans near the B stage had a terrific view of us and it was another wow in a wow-filled show. However, not every venue saw it the way we did and quite a number, including Glasgow, banned us from using it for what they regarded as safety issues. We have used the B stage ever since, and even reprised it for the 2006 tour – it gives us all a great feeling being so close to the fans.

Every time we'd go out to the B stage I'd look down and see Chris Healey's face looking up at me.

'Heals, don't ever miss a single night, it's good luck for us,' I'd tell him.

He never has. Chris has another skill that's valued by everyone in Take That; he makes the best cheese toasties on the tour bus!

Another difference on this tour was the support act. We had the idea of having a mini Take That band: they were about nine or ten and came from the Sylvia Young Stage School; they were brilliant. Every time we changed our hairstyles they did, too.

Compared to what had gone before, this tour was enormous – this was work. While we weren't doing back-to-back shows, we were doing five or six nights on the trot, which even for fit young lads like us was still shattering; it felt like we were on a treadmill at the time. If you doubt me, you try dancing full-on for ninety minutes *and* singing. Days off were usually a travel day and we would frequently argue the toss about what time we had to leave the hotel.

'Six forty-five wake-up, seven thirty departure? You have to be fucking joking.' We knew they weren't and we knew we had no choice, but we always protested.

We were comfortable enough in our roles in the band now that we could be a bit more separate. Our rooms showed our differences. If you walked along the hotel corridor and went into my or Howard's room, they'd be not tidy, but not untidy either. But if you went into Rob's room there'd be clothes everywhere, shirts hanging off the lights, massive bags spilling over with stuff, a plate of chips with tomato sauce lurking under a sock . . . it would give you a headache. Go into Jason's room and you could spot the lad who's looked after himself from an early age – Jason keeps everything orderly, his clothes and socks are all beautifully folded. Knock on the door of Mark's room and it would be shrouded in darkness, joss sticks burning and Indian music playing . . .

Leaving our hotel to go to the gigs was much more chaotic

than on any of the earlier tours. There were hundreds of girls waiting for us outside and we had to almost fight our way on to the tour bus. As we pulled away they ran alongside, banging on the bus. They screamed, they cried – it was pandemonium. We worried that someone might be run over, hurt or worse. When we arrived at every gig it was the same routine in reverse, and sometimes we needed a police escort to get out after a show.

Mark was unbelievable with the fans: he'd spend whole afternoons signing autographs. He was so good I'd feel guilty about not giving them enough time. Jason was like me; he did his duty. Howard found it quite hard, because he's shy, so he didn't go overboard with them. Robbie was often odd with the fans; he could be quite dismissive and a few times he embarrassed us by turning his back on them.

Every minute of every day seemed to be taken up with something. There were interviews at the gig with radio stations, magazines, newspapers and local TV; everyone drains a little bit from you. Every interview was the same, every question we'd heard a thousand times before, and believe me they were even more inane then. It felt like we really were turning into performing monkeys.

The tour bus had become more than a bus – it had ten bunk-beds upstairs, a lounge at the back, the cheese toastie maker, a coffee machine, Grahams in the cupboard . . . We used to have our band meetings in the back – nothing wound up Nigel more than calling one of us and being told we were in a band meeting because he'd think we were talking about things that should have involved him. Basically we'd be moaning: 'We shouldn't be doing *Smash Hits* – we're past all that now', 'When are we going to get a day off?' 'I can't believe he booked us in for another road show', or we'd be planning how make the shows bigger and better. And I'd be taking notes because it was always me who had to call Nigel and relay the latest.

By now we'd all started smoking – partly through boredom on

the never-ending journeys. Rob had always smoked, ever since I first met him, then a few years later Mark started, I was not much after and then Howard joined us. Jason, being Mr Health, decided he was going to be different and started smoking cigars. When we pulled up somewhere and the tour bus door opened there'd be plumes of smoke billowing out. God knows how we had the puff to get through our live shows.

There was a great infrastructure that went with touring and it felt like a big travelling party. I loved saying, 'After the show tonight, shall we take everyone for dinner?' and the bus would pick everyone up and take us to a restaurant where there'd be a table for twenty-five. You'd mix around, moving from person to person – you'd know all the faces – having a chat with everyone. I've always loved that family feeling.

But it was getting to the point where being on the road was the only comfortable place to be. We had five security guys, one for each of us. James Gentles and Paul Medley were with us – in fact, they still are now. They have been rocks for us and we trust them absolutely. Life without them, both on the road and when we're working, would be a nightmare. But when the tour ended, we were suddenly on our own.

It wasn't just that Nigel wasn't much help, no one was. We were prisoners in our own homes and everything we did was difficult. I would go to the supermarket and be followed by six cars or pounced upon by a photographer.

'Hold that Asda bag up.'

When I made it back to my car there would be notes under the windscreen wipers, and messages in lipstick on my door or window. Or I'd come back from four and a half months on tour and be trying to get to sleep on a hot summer's night when through my open windows I'd hear 200 Italian girls singing 'Could It Be Magic' at the tops of their voices. It sounds funny now, but at the time I just remember thinking, this is my house, I wanna get to sleep and I can't. Where can I go?

Whenever we got together after a few weeks off we'd always compare stories.

'You'll never guess what happened to me.'

'That's nothing, mate!'

A three-hour therapy session would ensue. Managers, security and other people around you can sympathise, but they can only imagine what it's like to be the centre of such obsessive attention. I know that it's our egos, that we invited it all to happen, but it's still difficult to come to terms with.

The fans had become an unbeatable force. They were renowned for their persistence. The ones that used to get me the most were the ones at the airport – 'the elite 8' we called them – and there was no escaping them. No matter how late you planned your trip, they would be there. They had cars and some of them had mobile phones and would operate like a tag team. There'd be one pitched outside the house, and then as you left, there'd be another at the end of the road to catch you, and so on until you reached your destination. And once they knew where you were going, the rest would appear. Most of the fans were sweet, but I have to say there were a few that wound me up because they were so sly. It wasn't just the waiting outside your house, they would think nothing of knocking on your mum's door, finding your old friends, stealing your mail – and they knew their rights. If you objected they'd say, 'You've got to talk to us because we're your fans, and if you don't we'll be off to the newspapers.' Life became a game of cat-and-mouse. I now realise that for those fans it was an obsession; for them it was real life. They didn't understand what an invasion it was for us – time off was hell.

On this tour Paula Yates seemed to be an ever-present feature. Having met Nigel at Elton's house she would even sometimes go to his place for the weekend. She didn't spend time with any one of us in particular – she certainly never slept with any of us – I think she just liked hanging out with bands and performers. She used to go to Sotheby's and bring me presents; once she turned up with a beautiful silver sugar bowl and spoon that I still treasure.

One night we were in the hotel in Sheffield after a show, standing at the bar, when I noticed my dad talking to Paula. What the bloody hell is he saying to her? I wondered. Anyway, I had my cheese toastie and a couple more drinks and looked back over to where they were standing, and he was still there chewing her ear off. I tried to break away from my conversation to go and rescue Paula. Finally, twenty minutes or more later, I went over to them and heard my dad say, 'You know what I love? I love prisons and the *Titanic*, that's what I love.'

That's it. 'Come on, Paula,' I said.

'Anyway, love, who are you with?' said my dad as I dragged her away. 'Are you the wife of someone working on the show?'

We would sometimes arrive in a place and Paula would be there. Once we got off an aircraft in Amsterdam and there she was waiting for us; not even Nigel knew she was going to turn up. I found it difficult to reconcile Paula hanging out with us when she was married to Bob and had kids. She'd written books about how much she loved being a mum, so why wasn't she at home with them? I even thought, that's not being a proper mother. Then one day at a gig she was backstage with her children, and I got to see just how wonderful she was with them; she was such a lovely mum. I talked to her about Bob and when she spoke about him and his Live Aid work it was clear that she respected and loved him. I can honestly say I could never quite work her out, but she was a very intelligent woman and she wrote some great pieces about us for the *Daily Mirror*. Other people would say to me, 'I'm not keen on Paula Yates,' but I liked her a lot, enjoyed her company and, though we lost touch with her when she was with Michael Hutchence, we were all incredibly saddened by her death.

It was on this tour that Rob got in with his own a group of people, or more correctly they got in with Rob. There were five of them, four guys and a girl, and Rob called them the Diamond Dogs. They were just a bunch of liggers and freeloaders, and they were always around, ordering drinks and putting them on Rob's bill. They were exactly what I imagined liggers would be like, real fashion poseurs, and none of us could stand them. It particularly annoyed Mark, who had always been close to Rob, because he found himself pushed to one side. Maybe it was just that Rob was the top of the pile with these people. Everyone in our world worked for us and here was a group who upset that delicate balance.

Just before starting rehearsals for the tour, we were in the dressing room before appearing on *Going Live* when Nigel produced not so much a rabbit out of a hat as some dolls' heads from a bag.

'What the fuck are they?' said someone.

'They, lads, are the heads to the new Take That dolls,' said Nigel proudly. He went on to explain that he had done a deal and we would get money from every doll that was sold through a licensing arrangement. We were given the complete dolls while we were in Dublin.

I think Rob spoke for the rest of us when he said, 'It looks fuck all like me.' We were all sat around having our dinner before the show, not quite believing what we were seeing.

'It's all downhill from here,' said Jay dolefully.

Everyone in the catering room, crew, band and us collapsed with laughter. Rob's doll had a bit of a mishap as he plunged it head first into a huge bowl of trifle.

When I got home after the tour I decided to take a trip to Toys 'Я' Us in Chester to see if they had any of the Take That dolls. Dressed in my regulation pop-star sunglasses and a baseball hat, I slipped into the store and started looking around. No dolls in sight. I decided to ask someone.

'Excuse me, where are the, er, Take That dolls?'

'Oh them, they're down the back. Follow me, I'll show you.'

We finally got to the Take That dolls, piled high in another part of the store, but there wasn't one of me as far as I could see. Blimey, I thought, they must have sold out. Local boy makes good!

'Have you got any Gary Barlows left?' I asked.

'Well, no we haven't,' she said. 'You see, you have to buy a Mark, a Howard, a Jason and a Robbie doll, then you collect the coupons and get a Gary Barlow doll for free.'

What? I was on the phone to Nigel the instant I got home.

'Nigel, what's this about the Gary dolls being free?'

On the Sunday after the Pops tour ended in Belfast, 'Sure' made the charts and went to No. 1; it was the first song I had written with any of the other boys – Mark and Rob wrote the rhyming rap in the middle. We soon headed off again to do some European promo work with a difference. The first stop, Holland, was run-of-the-mill stuff, but from there we flew to Milan, and from the airport we were driven to the Hotel Castello di Pomerio, high in the hills above Lake Como. Originally a twelfth-century castle, we were there with Italian *Vogue* and Versace for a photo shoot; Donatella Versace was overseeing things. This really was the big time – goodbye *Smash Hits*, *ciao L'Uomo Vogue*! Afterwards we went to the Villa Le Fontanelle, Gianni Versace's house on Lake Como, for a dinner party. By this time we were getting used to this kind of thing; and to make as feel more at home, Elton was there, too; he and Gianni were great friends. I revelled in Gianni's home as it mirrored my newly acquired tastes – if a little more ornate than even I aspired to! Afterwards we went for a walk by the lake and later Elton tinkled the ivories – 'Candle In The Wind' had never sounded better.

Next day we were off to Bologna and then Berlin to do more promo, more telly and more interviews. It was routine: airport, aircraft, airport, hotel, TV studio, press conference, hotel, airport. Our lives had become one long schedule, even though we were doing less of the frenetic stuff and had definitely entered a less-is-more phase. Make no mistake, however, we were in control of none of this, we just acted under orders, most of which came from Nigel or the label. What these European trips did for us, besides promoting our career, was to get us out of Britain, helping at times to create a vacuum in the media, something Nigel was very keen on in the run-up to the release of a new single or album.

Gianni's house might have verged on overkill, but it didn't slow down my relentless spending. Wherever we were, I'd go shopping. On a free morning in Paris, say – Paris was always dangerous – Mark and Rob might go shopping for clothes, but I'd head off in search of antiques. Howard sometimes came with me as he liked to browse, or else I'd go alone with a security guy, and I'd spend. I used to call it the Grand Tour. If I saw a painting or a piece of furniture I liked, within minutes I'd have said, 'How much is that? I'll take it.' £75,000 for a pair of paintings was a snip to me, and it wasn't just one pair: I bought countless Italian oils: Giordano, Panini, battle scenes, cupids. I also loved anything marble – I remember an inkwell with bronze figures that I just had to have – or anything edged with ormolu or gilt. I was so obsessed that I arrived home to find crates of things I couldn't even recall buying.

In a way, the fascinating thing for me has been to see what happens when you take six people and give them all a load of money and life experience. Once you live in a certain world you step up to the bar. To a degree we all did that. Howard bought an enormous place in Cheshire – he has beautiful taste in houses. Mark bought a nice run-down house and did it all up himself. Jason bought lots of small properties. Only Nigel lives a life very like the one he had before Take That. He's bought a larger house, but he still goes on holiday to Gran Canaria every year, to the same hotel he visited when I first met him. Of all of us I went the farthest.

We got back from Europe on Friday 25 November and headed straight for the Conrad Hotel in London. We were sort of there by royal command. Princess Diana had called Nigel and asked if we would play at her Concert For Hope at Wembley.

'Absolutely no problem,' said Nige.

She asked us, through her equerry and Nigel, if we would all like to go round for tea. Before we left the Conrad we were visited by a guy who talked to us about how we should behave.

'There'll be some ladies-in-waiting there and you should address Her Royal Highness as Ma'am.'

He filled us in on background information on the Princess. We all thought, let's just get on with it. After he finished we shot round to Kensington Palace – there was no security, we all just drove in. We could have had anything in the boot.

At the palace Diana was all over Nigel – she loved him, you practically had to peel her off him – while we ended up with the ladies-in-waiting. Jason had made a big effort and got dressed up in a nice new denim shirt and jeans; he spent most of the time trying to get a word in edgeways, but couldn't because of Nigel. The following night, before the Concert of Hope, Princess Di came along the line to meet all the artists that were appearing. Besides us there was Eddi Reader, China Black and Lulu. When she reached Jason, he said, 'You're looking lovely tonight, ma'am.'

'And you haven't changed,' said Diana.

He was wearing the same shirt as the day before. He was destroyed, completely destroyed.

As soon as Christmas was out of the way it was back to work on the new album. We were working with a new producer, Chris Porter. Chris turned down working with the band early on in our career, but now he got in with both feet. He's such a top man, down to earth, serious about music, picky with vocals, but great fun to work with – he has the longest Mutley laugh you ever heard. I had bought a Euphonix desk, which set me back about £80,000, but it meant my studio was good enough to produce more than just demos. Chris said to me, 'Look, you've got all the gear that I've got, so it'll be a lot easier if I come to you. We can get all the boys in to do their vocals and save everyone having to come to London.' We started recording in my home studio with Chris producing tracks like 'Back For Good' and a few others.

Chris Porter arrived with Chris Cameron, who played most of the keyboard parts on the tracks we recorded together. He had worked with George Michael and was a multi-talented guy. Besides 'Back For Good' we did 'Nobody Else', 'Hate It' and 'The Day After Tomorrow'. Of course recording was made far easier with Maurice on hand to feed us. In fact, the harder we worked the more he cooked – I put on pounds.

Soon it was February, and February meant the BRITs. What had started as a slightly shambolic way to rustle up music industry sales in a dead month was now the highlight of the musical calendar. If you were invited to appear it was an honour, and whatever the organisers asked you to do, you did – unless you had Nigel as a manager. It was a time when his bull-at-the-gate style came into its own. The year before, the organisers had wanted us to sing a duet with someone else, but Nigel, ignoring the fact that we weren't the only band on the block, took a chance and said there was no way we'd appear unless we could do it solo. Amazingly they agreed, which is how we came to perform the Beatles Medley. Kim Gavin devised an incredible set with seventy dancers, including Dawn – we caught each other's eye again – and had the whole thing filmed in black and white.

This year Nigel pulled another brilliant flanker. Only a week before the show he announced, 'Lads, I've just been to a meeting and the BRITs want you to appear.'

'That's great,' we said.

'I told them you'd play your new single. They said that their policy was not to have artists performing their latest record, so I said stuff it, we wouldn't perform and upped and left the meeting.'

'Oh, OK,' we replied.

The next day Nigel got a call from the organisers agreeing to let us play 'Back For Good'. While pulling stunts like that won Nigel no friends, it helped our careers no end. It was probably one of the few occasions that nerves played any part in our performance. Playing a song we had never performed live before in front of the cream of the music biz gave our performance an added edge, and for me it was a moment when everything combined to produce four minutes of perfection. It reflected our togetherness as a band, but it also paid tribute to Nigel's skill in getting us there. Kim Gavin surpassed himself. This year everyone had followed our lead from the year before and decided big was beautiful – the Pet Shop Boys appeared with fifty or sixty coal miners – so Kim went the opposite way: a stroke of brilliance. He told the director to go in tight on our faces and when we rehearsed he said, 'No, I mean really tight, no fringes, nothing.'

With help from Kim and the team we stole the show.

The day after the BRITs we flew to San Remo for the song festival. Backstage before the show, as the five of us sat eating dinner together, we got into a lengthy discussion about our musicians and how we could better our sound by perhaps using some different people. Everyone had a point of view and some agreed with me; Jay, for the most part, was the voice of reason. The only one who didn't have much to say was Rob – actually he had nothing to say. It was a typical example of him standing on the outside, not having an opinion. I always thought it was because he was young, but maybe it was for other reasons.

With all the highs, the adulation and the constant full-on schedule, life in Take That was slowly but surely becoming unbearable. I was even beginning to tire of the unending menu of girls. It was beginning to feel like it had less and less to do with me, as if it was taking me away from who I was. You name it, I'd tried it, all varieties, every scenario, things I can't write about here

– I've got kids now! – but what had started out as an amazing adventure had become, and it feels sordid to say this, a chore; just another part of the routine. There was no effort in it, no chatting them up, not even for five minutes, but there was always some girl who'd come up and say, 'Take me back with you.' I wouldn't even spend the night with them – I wanted a good night's sleep. You'd get them back to your room, do the business and then say, 'Right, out.' I'd started off polite but now I couldn't be bothered. Sometimes they'd be shocked, sometimes they'd be tearful and sometimes I'd feel like a shit, but it's amazing how desensitised you become if it's continuous.

I felt like I'd had enough. There wasn't a specific moment when I realised, I can't do this any more, it was more like internally I tipped on to a different counter. I think I recognised that I was missing love.

Nick Raymonde was always looking for people for us to work with, people who might keep our sound one step ahead. With his background in dance music, he came up with the idea of working with David Morales, a guy I'd never even heard of but who was a big DJ/producer in the dance world. Nick and I headed to New York, having been given an address in Brooklyn. When we arrived we found no one at home, so we hung around for about an hour, growing more and more conspicuous; the longer we stood there the whiter we became. Cars full of black guys kept driving by until eventually a car approached us; it was almost true to say we heard him before we saw him arrive in what could best be described as a mobile disco – the car was built around a pair of the most enormous sub-woofers. Out climbed Morales, who had the best body I've ever seen on a guy – he looked the business.

'Yo yo yo, howz ya doin.'

We walked down the stairs to his basement studio. He bent over to turn on the power and in his back pocket was a seven-inch blade. I thought, bugger me, if he says the second verse goes there

I'm not going to argue. Soon afterwards another guy showed up; he was a keyboard player and programmer. Between us we got 'Hanging Onto Your Love' together, with me writing a melody and some lyrics over the top of what they'd laid down. Halfway through the session the phone went and I worked out that the caller had not returned something that Morales thought he should have.

'Yo yo, motherfucker,' yelled Morales, 'I'm gonna cut youz up, starting at your toes and slicing each one off.'

Well, that was it, I went into hyperdrive. I finished the second verse so fast; I wanted out of there.

'David,' I said, 'I'm quite jet-lagged. I think I need to get back to the hotel.'

'Yo yo man, no worries. I've got me some business to take care of.'

I bet you have, I thought.

The next day, with the vocals still to do, Nick booked a studio up town, David came along and we finished the song and on the third day he called us up and took us out for some sushi – he turned out to be a real sweetheart.

From New York Nick and I flew straight to San Francisco to meet with Narada Michael Walden, a songwriter I have always admired. At his studio we sat and talked and I noticed that he wrote down things I was saying.

'Are you getting lyrics from what I say?' I asked.

'Sure. I learned very early on that it's a great trick. I was once working with Aretha Franklin and we were talking about the music business and she said, "Who's zoomin who." You know, who's doing what to who in the biz. That's how we came up with that song.'

We had a whole jumble of lyrics and just got on with writing a song. Also at the studio was a guy called Walter Afanasieff, who was a programmer who had worked for Narada for about six years. We spent an hour in the studio with a drum machine, and

Narada played chords. He would shout out lines like 'Old school friend' and say, 'Now sing something with that in it.'

'Old school friend, let's see each other again,' I sang.

After about an hour of this process I said, 'I don't get it.'

'Don't worry, Gary, with what you have sung, by the time you come back tomorrow my assistant will have made these into songs.'

'Oh, right,' I said, rather doubtfully.

Nick and I went to his studio the following day to find that Narada's assistant had cut up all the bits and pieces and turned them into a verse and a bridge. We then did the same thing all over again. And before you ask, nothing came of those lines, but I've still got the tapes somewhere.

It shows how differently songwriters work. Narada and David were two sides of the American writing style. Narada had no idea who Take That were; David, on the other hand, used to come to England and understood the scene. Having said all that, I've used Narada's technique of writing down what people say many times as conversational lyrics often work so much better: there's a poetry to things that trip off the tongue. And if you listen to the lyrics to 'Hanging Onto Your Love', they're neither conversational nor very much else for that matter, but then again, they're not bad for a man scared out of his wits.

Work continued on the rest of the album, much of it at Moorside. Dave Seaman and Steve Anderson, who worked professionally as the Brothers in Rhythm, came and enjoyed Maurice's meals. One day, while I was at home working, the police turned up. Outside were a couple of coachloads of young Italian girls; most of them sitting having a picnic. I assumed it was something to do with the fans, either that or the policemen wanted an autograph, which wasn't unheard of. What they wanted, however, was a serious chat.

'Could we come in?' they said.

'Of course,' I replied, ushering them inside.

'There's something rather unpleasant happening on your doorstep and we need to talk to you because we might have to monitor the situation.'

They went on to explain that the other boys and I had had our addresses posted on a paedophile's website.

'Your homes are being watched by paedophiles and we would like a room where we could watch what's happening.'

Moorside was right next to a pub with a large car park, and when we went upstairs to one of the bedrooms overlooking it, we could see three cars with guys sitting in them, watching the kids. It was all so seedy. From then on the police regularly turned up and moved on the guys who were watching the girls who were on my driveway watching me.

In March 1995, during rehearsals for our upcoming European tour, Rob and I were talking when out of the blue he said, 'I've had enough. I want to go, I want to leave.'

'Why's that, Bob? Why would you want to do that?'

I was shocked, it made no sense.

'I want to leave, I'm bored.'

'That's as maybe, but what would you do? It's been a great opportunity being in the band.'

We talked it over for a while and then Rob finished up by saying something that stunned me at the time.

'Well, I would have been a success anyway, I'd have made it with some other group or even on my own.'

There seemed to be no logic to what he was saying, but I could see he absolutely meant it. I told him he was daft to want to leave and we never spoke about it again. I'm not sure whether any of the others had a similar conversation with him. The previous summer's big tour was the worst we'd had in terms of pressure and thought that probably had a bearing on Rob's mind-set.

Just before we left for the tour Nigel popped into Moorside one day on the way to his place in Wales – he often went there to fish,

GARY
HOWARD
MARK

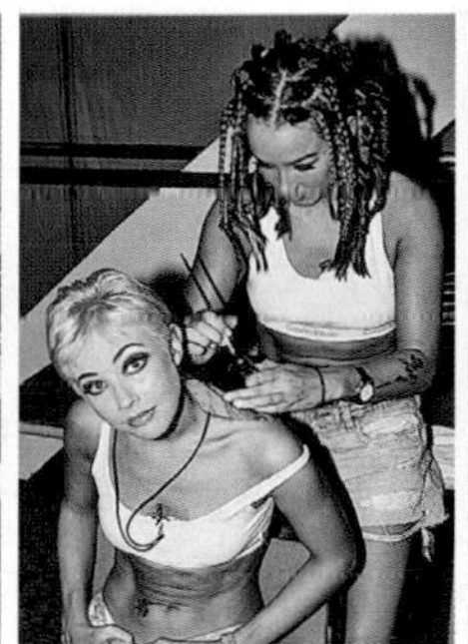

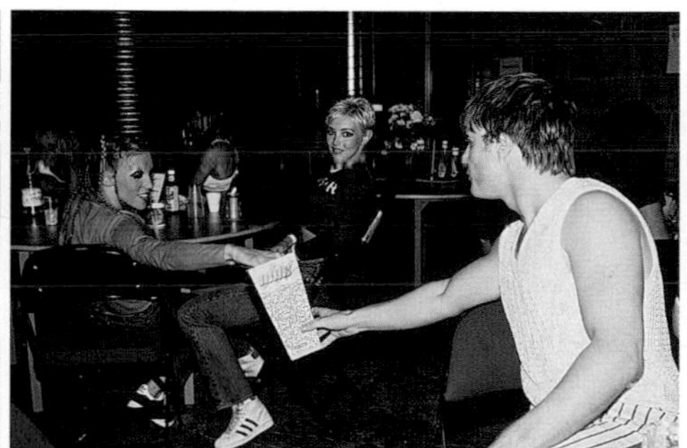

Previous page: Four lads at large in Australia, the Far East and America, 1995

This page: Dawn and I got it together on the Nobody Else tour

The Nobody Else tour

PREMIER
PREMIER
YAMAHA Clavinova PF
Thunderbird

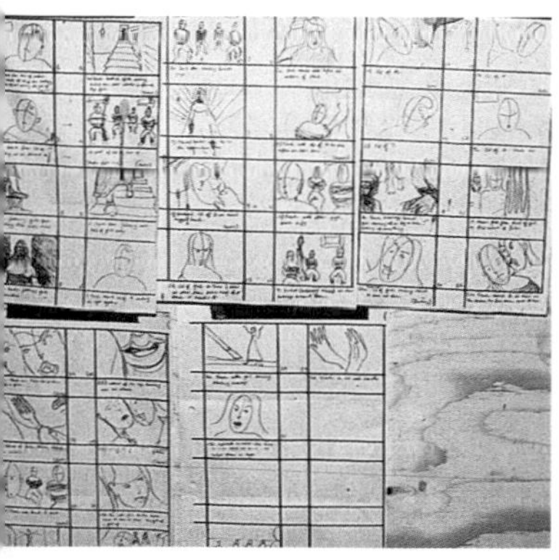

Above: Shooting the video for 'How Deep is Your Love'

The break-up press conference, 13 February 1996

angling is his passion, though you'd never guess it if you met him. He planted a seed in my mind about buying a bigger house by showing me some places in *Cheshire Life*.

Later, on tour in Germany, I called my mum from Berlin around lunchtime just to check in and asked them what they were up to.

'We're trying to think of something to do, Gary.'

'Well, why don't you go to a few estate agents and see if there are any houses you could look at for me to buy, say seven or eight bedrooms.'

I wasn't that serious about moving, I was just trying to give them a project, but by 7 p.m. that night they were back on the phone.

'We've found this place. It's in a road we've never ever driven down and it's only four miles from Frodsham. Here, your Dad wants to talk to you.'

Blimey, I thought, they must be serious.

'Gary, the man took us round on a golf buggy it were that big. And there's a little house where me and your mum could live.'

I knew how difficult it was for them, as well as our Ian, living in Frodsham. They were forever being doorstepped by the papers and collared in the street, so I thought this might be the solution.

'Well, there's nothing I can do for six weeks until I get back,' I said.

When I got home we went to Delamere Manor to have a look at it. Halfway up the drive I said, 'I'll have it.' Elton would have been proud of me.

There was a third house on the property that was perfect for our Ian, but people were living in it. I was sure they didn't want to be faced with me as a neighbour, so I suggested they go and have a look at Moorside – not to buy it but to see what awaited them if they stayed put. On the day they drove over there were about 400 fans camped on the drive. They soon agreed to sell their house to me. Our Ian moved in first and started work on the main house in

August – soon Delamere Manor was to become our very own Ramsay Street.

I suppose when you're successful you need to mark it with a purchase – you just get to a level where you think, I need that now, whether it's a sports car or a house. I'd already been rattling round Plumley like a pensioner, but Delamere was five times the size. It had nineteen rooms, 117 acres of grounds and an enormous lake. It was a statement all right.

I set about furnishing it with a vengeance. Marble sinks in the bathrooms, trompe l'oeil murals in the corridors, antiques everywhere. This was no hobby, I was serious, and in the end I spent £1.5 million on antiques, almost all of which filled rooms at Delamere that we only used every other Christmas. This time my dad's input went beyond mere gardening; I got him to build an obelisk at the end of the lime walk.

While we were in Germany we got the midweek chart placings and 'Back For Good' was at No. 1. We had sold 150,000 copies in three days. It was phenomenal. By the end of the week it was of course, still at the top, and it stayed there for four weeks; I think it remains the fastest-selling non-charity record of all time. Such was the demand for the song after the BRITs that we pulled the release date forward by two weeks. It was No. 1 in thirty-one countries and it marked the pinnacle of our achievement as a singles band; since then it's been covered eighty-nine times in every style imaginable, including reggae. A month later our third album, *Nobody Else*, entered the album chart; it too made No. 1 and stayed in the charts for the rest of the year.

Fan mania reached new heights on this tour when one group of girls followed us all around Europe in a hire car. They went to our first gig and then just tagged along behind our bus for the rest of the tour. I have no idea where they stayed when they got to each city because the hotels that we booked into were good about not accepting bookings from people that sounded like fans. But everywhere we went, they went too. James and Paul, our security, were constantly on their guard. Interestingly, the group have turned up again on the 2006 tour; times have changed a lot because James and Paul chat to them now.

We were red hot, but it's impossible for things to keep getting better – nothing improves, or lasts, for ever. At some point you either plateau or start going downhill and in pop music usually it's the latter. Your audience starts growing up and your fans don't so much move on to other performers as just move on in their lives. Pop is fundamentally a fashion item.

We, too, were moving on and Rob was the keenest of all of us for a change.

9

The End Beginning

It was in Berlin that Take That as a five-piece started to unravel, or finally unravelled, depending on your point of view. We were there for the first MTV Europe Music Awards; we'd won Best Group award in the video category for 'Sure'. This was an important show for us because it was being aired in the USA as well as in Europe and, it was to be our first coast-to-coast TV appearance in America. We flew to Berlin on 1 June 1995 and went straight to the Hilton, where all the artists were staying.

After checking in to the hotel we went off to rehearse in a large temporary structure which had been set up in front of the Brandenburg Gate. The rehearsals went on for most of the afternoon and evening and we learned a whole new routine for the opening of 'Sure', which involved working with a large group of dancers. As you can imagine, I loved it.

Wandering around the hotel was crazy as everyone in the music business seemed to be there. George Michael was hanging out in the bar chatting, and there was Tom Jones, who hosted the awards, and Prince. Literally everywhere you looked there was someone you recognised. It was as though every one of its 600 bedrooms had a star inside. I went back to the Hilton after the show ended and walked into reception to see this black girl looking all knock-kneed; she had dropped the contents of her handbag and was scrabbling around picking everything up. It was Naomi Campbell. The night before the show we had taken over the basement bar and it was wild, like a rock 'n' roll dream sequence with girls hanging off everyone. The party went on until 5 a.m. and we were all there, with Rob going up and down to Kate Moss and Naomi's rooms all night.

By all accounts Rob had had no sleep for over twenty-four hours when it was time to head off for rehearsals. The first I heard about it was shortly before we were due to leave the hotel in the late afternoon. Chris Healey told me in sketchy detail what had happened. Nigel had gone to Rob's room first and gave him a glass of fresh orange juice, which made him sick everywhere, so the room was covered in vomit. Then Chris was called up to Rob's room to try to get some dry toast down him to bring him back to normal. The problem was that no one working in the hotel seemed to see the urgency of the situation and Chris ended up screaming at the hotel management, 'GET DRY TOAST!'

Nicki C. found out that there was a local doctor accompanying Prince 24/7, so she went and tracked him down. Apparently he was dressed completely in white, including white wellies! After much gesticulating and struggling with his broken English and her non-existent German, she made him aware of what she needed and waved a lot of money under his nose. He gave Rob a shot of penicillin, which brought him back from wherever he'd been.

Sitting on the bus to the gig Rob looked bloody awful. Backstage before we went on he was the master of understatement.

'I had a bit of a heavy night last night,' he said.

I don't recall being worried, and nor were any of the other lads. We were so used to just stepping on stage and it all working that we'd almost stopped thinking about it. It was as though we were on autopilot.

Everyone else, Nigel included, was much more concerned, not

least because the headlines the next day were Nigel's worst nightmare.

Looking back at this period in our career we were in a strange place. Having worked bloody hard to make it we had retreated further into planet celebrity and the Take That bubble; it was as though everything happened around us rather than to us. It probably explains why the bender in Berlin made so little impact. In many ways we failed to see what had been happening to us, or to Rob. I hadn't taken Rob seriously when he spoke to me about leaving; would he still have gone if I had? Who knows. One thing I am sure of is that what happened to Rob that night scared him; I know it would have done me. But I was so wrapped up in myself that I was unconscious, even uncaring, of what he was going through. I never stopped to say, 'Are you OK, mate?'

We were becoming more and more cocooned from the outside world, while our bubble got bigger and bigger to protect us, or so I thought. I was in my own individual pressure chamber, thinking constantly about the next record, and it felt like a kind of heaven and hell all rolled into one. I'm not sure how else you can handle a situation like that, and it's probably why bands that enjoy such extreme popularity almost inevitably break up. With all that's happened to me since Take That split, I have come to understand that you have to work at your career to keep it on track, and when you're in a band you certainly have to work at the relationships between you all. You need to look out for one another, be there for each other but at the same time try to keep a sense of proportion. Our youth, our fame and our relationship with Nigel all helped to make that an almost impossible task. That isn't to say that we didn't try, but as young guys we didn't have the emotional equipment.

It felt as if my age stood still when Take That started. Although I was, in some respects, the most mature member of the band, and certainly the most business savvy, mentally I felt no older when we broke up. Rob had only just turned twenty-one when Berlin happened, but I think that, like me, he stopped growing when he joined Take That, which would have made him only sixteen and a half.

We had another tour coming up, and as usual Nigel wanted us to keep a low profile. It was a policy that usually worked, so after the MTV Awards we were keeping our heads down and not doing any interviews, appearances or telly in order to create a media vacuum. Everyone apart from Rob, that is. One day I turned on the TV and there was Rob with his mum at Ascot giving an interview, and a few days later there were pictures in the papers of him coming out of a club with Liam Gallagher. It was irritating because of what we'd agreed – you can't say you're not giving interviews when they've just seen Rob on daytime TV. But I just thought, you silly bugger, we're supposed to be lying low, and I said nothing. In retrospect I don't think he was trying to do anything to harm the band, he was just starting to play his own game.

The next thing that happened, of course, was Rob's appearance at Glastonbury on stage with Oasis, off his face, sounding like shit and making a complete arse of himself. We were recording at my house in the last week of June, not long after, and he couldn't sing because his voice was shot. We all gave him a hard time about it, and at one point we sat him down in the back garden and said, 'What are you doing? What's going on here? We'd have loved to be at Glastonbury but we agreed to keep out of the press.'

We were worried about the image of the band, worried for each other and worried for Rob, who seemed to have lost the plot. And yeah, maybe we were a bit jealous too – we'd all have liked to have been there, but being in a band means pulling together, and that certainly stopped being a priority for Rob. We were apprehensive, but Rob seemed oblivious.

As soon as we finished recording, rehearsals began in Stockport. When Rob appeared in the morning, we never knew if he'd been drinking all night or what he'd been up to and it started to undermine everyone's confidence in him, not least Jay's. There was a move in the show where Rob would take Jay's foot and flip him backwards in a somersault so he'd land on his feet. One day Jay said to Rob, 'You'd never take anything before a show would you, Rob? Because this is dangerous, I could break my neck doing this if you don't do your bit right.'

We were all losing faith in him.

One day Rob showed up at rehearsals and out of the blue announced, 'I'm gonna leave the band at the end of the tour.'

Our reaction was, 'Fine. If you don't want to be in the band then that's the best thing.' He told us this just before we were due to have a curry night with a couple of competition winners and straight after we finished our curry I rang Nigel to tell him what had happened. He said he wanted to see us right away. Howard and Mark didn't go; it was just Jay and I.

'Don't let him do this, Rob just wants to sing a swan song,' was Nigel's take on it. He thought it would turn into the farewell Robbie tour and that he would try to upstage the band. Nigel was adamant he had to go right away, or agree to stay in the band and not go after the tour. The legal position, according to Nigel, was that he had to be given the option, but the band's position had nothing to do with legalities: we had all just lost patience with him. I can't speak for the others, but I was concerned for our futures. I wasn't that bothered about what Rob wanted because he wasn't showing any loyalty to me and the other three lads.

The next day Rob appeared looking like he didn't want to be helped, or couldn't be helped. I'd never seen Rob look that bad, or anything close to it, in all the time we'd known each other. Actually, it didn't even look like Rob, it felt like he hadn't brought himself along. The five of us sat down to talk; Jay, Howard, Mark and I like wolves surrounding our prey. True to our training, though, we four wolves became the puppets Nigel had taught us to be and repeated Nigel's line about either staying or going. I say 'we', but it was actually Jay who spoke, with us three nodding our heads in agreement.

Rob hardly said a word, and when Jay had finished he pushed his chair back, got up and walked towards the door. As he passed the fruit bowl he said, 'Can I take a piece with me?'

'Sure,' one of us said.

He opened the door, turned and said, 'I'm off then, I'm going, see ya.'

'See ya, mate.'

'See you, Rob.'

'Bye, mate.'

'Bye.'

With that he closed the door. We exchanged glances and then the door opened again.

'I'm off then, I'll see ya.'

Then he closed the door and was gone.

I would have put every penny I had ever made on Rob coming back. It was only when I saw the pictures of him a couple of days later on a boat in St Tropez with George Michael and Paula Yates that I knew he'd really gone for good.

Straight after Rob had left we carried on rehearsing with Kim Gavin. There were five dancers who were there to partner each of us. 'Kim, I don't think we'll be needing the middle girl,' I said. 'Rob's left the band.' She went back to the hotel and we began reworking everything for four not five. For the well-oiled machine that we had become, it was just another day in the life of a boy band and not the devastating blow it seemed to everyone else.

Out of all of us, Mark was closest to Rob, although they had drifted apart and stopped going out together over the previous year. Even so, Mark thought about chucking it in for a couple of days, before he realised how much the band meant to him. Like the rest of us, he was convinced that we were unfinished business. I think Jay felt the loss most – he's such a team player and has taught us all a lot about responsibility – it was a huge disappointment for him. I had no idea what I had lost. I'd been so busy thinking of my own career, and the band's career, that I hadn't stopped to think about Rob and whether he was unhappy or unfulfilled, or about the role he played in our set-up.

In a way there weren't many signs to spot. Rob was never horrible, or anything close to it, to me or any of the others while he was in the band. Strangely, when it came to the music, Rob used to be one of my biggest supporters – he was always saying how good my songs were. There are many things I remember about him with affection. One thing I loved about him was that it never mattered what time you woke him or got in touch, he was always up for it, whatever it might be. Rob would often show up at my house in Plumley at all sorts of odd times. It was fairly close to Manchester Airport and he would go to Dublin for a few days, then when he got back he'd come straight to Moorside. He would disappear off to bed and that would be that last I'd see of him for twenty-four hours. When he'd get up, Maurice the butler would be on hand to make him toast and then he'd just hang out. I liked him popping in and the others would do the same because we all lived around Manchester. Thanks to Maurice there was always food on the go at my place and I think that was an added attraction. Rob was friendly with Samantha Beckinsale at the time and the two of them would often drop in for something to eat. The point is that there was no feud between us when he was in the band, no rift or any bad feeling. Years later I was to find out that he and others had a very different version of what went on, but I'm sure in Rob's case that some of that has come with hindsight.

I was certainly blind to the antagonism between Rob and Nigel. I knew they were uncomfortable around each other – Rob has the ability to home in on people and say the things that other people only think, and Nigel is exactly the same. Nigel never seemed to have any time for Rob. He was the youngest, and he couldn't seem to take him seriously; to him, he was an afterthought. But to be fair to Nigel, while Rob was in the band he never gave Nigel much reason to think otherwise. Whenever we had a meeting to talk about something to do with the tour, or our music, if Rob was asked for his views, he would say, 'Whatever.'

'We've got this new song, Rob, what do you think?'

'I'll go along with anything,' said Rob.

To me it seemed like there was never any desire, no real hunger in him, he seemed quite lazy. Maybe he didn't want to take responsibility or maybe he was frustrated by being in Take That. I remember once, in an interview in Australia, we were joking about, saying, 'Why not go out and buy one of our records.' 'Buy two, or three or four,' said Jay, 'and a poster.' But Rob said 'Don't buy us, buy U-2, they're better.'

We had been so close, such a tight unit, that when Rob did go it was a bit like a marriage breaking up. Destructive things were said on both sides in the heat of the aftermath. The fact that we all lived out of London meant that, for the most part, we weren't part of the media feeding frenzy, but once he was on his own Rob became part of that world. Almost overnight he seemed to acquire loads of new best friends, people he hadn't even known before.

Looking back, I think things first started to unravel around about the time the Diamond Dogs appeared on the scene, during the UK tour in the summer of the previous year. Nigel would say things like, 'Did you see Rob when he came on stage? His eyes were bulging and he held up two fingers to those bloody friends of his, as if to say, "I've had two Es."'

'He's probably on nowt, he just wants you to think he is,' was my reaction, but I must admit I'm still unsure. One thing's for certain: Rob wanted people to think he was taking drugs. People would say he was high all the time, but I don't believe it – Rob's far too clever for that – and I'm still confused as to whether or not it was true. Part of me thinks it was just for the sake of a good story as the Take That show was too intricate and difficult to do if you were out of it. There's certainly no way he could have managed to do what he did on stage if he was that far gone. Rob was always fully functioning, and to perform as Take That you had to be at the top of your game.

It was also around this time that things started to feel repetitious for me. All the goals I had written in my Filofax had a tick against them. Now I no longer had to save for months and wait six long weeks for a new piece of kit to be delivered, I could phone up and be playing it by the next day. It had all become too easy. That's one of the reasons why our live shows became bigger and better – it was the only challenge left for us. It was also the only time we had to think as a band, with no input from Nigel. In a way, Rob's leaving gave us another challenge, something new to focus on. It just meant we needed to step up a gear. It didn't seem any more worrying than that.

What we hadn't reckoned on was the speed with which Rob started to attack the band. His eagerness to say things against me and the band was probably a result of being egged on by those around him. Perhaps they thought it was good for his career, or perhaps it was his retaliation for the good reviews our final tour had got without him. Either way, the newspaper battle that ensued helped contribute to knocking down the house of Take That. We had been careful about building our house and watching it be destroyed was dreadful.

Take That had been micro-managed for years, and Rob suffered from being the youngest. Robbie wasn't a team player, and I can say that because I wasn't either – I wanted to be team leader, and so did he. I think he found it annoying playing second fiddle to anyone; it's not in his nature. He'd been the only man in his house since his dad left when he was three and he was used to being number one. What Rob went on to do was a massive achievement – to make that kind of transition takes guts. But the truth was that when Rob left the band he wasn't Robbie Williams, he was just Robbie from Take That. All of us were just a Christian name with the same double-barrelled surname. If Rob hadn't have gone on to become the megastar he did, he would have been just another few pages in the Take That story. As it was, he excelled at being free.

10

The Twist of Separation

With Rob gone we were faced with some tough rehearsals, having to rework everything for four, not five. We used the Territorial Army HQ in Hammersmith to work on new dance routines before production rehearsals began on 1 August. The Nobody Else tour began at Manchester's newest venue, the Nynex Arena, which had only been open for three weeks. We were there for an unprecedented ten nights, followed by another ten at London's Earls Court. If we thought there was going to be a backlash following Rob's departure it didn't seem to be happening. It felt like the biggest and best show of our career so far. Such was the demand for tickets, we could easily have done another ten nights.

One night during the Earls Court run we had a VIP visitor. Clive Davis, the head of Arista Records in America, a company owned by BMG, was in London especially to meet us, having recently signed us to his label. He loved 'Back For Good'. He came to see the show and afterwards we were all invited to go for dinner in his suite at the Dorchester. Even though Clive has a definite air of importance about him – he's like an old, stuffed film star and very charming and urbane – we didn't instantly register him as someone we needed to impress. As we sat around the big dining-room table being served pizza and ice cream, Clive gave us the benefit of his years of experience.

'Hey, boys, I hated the show.'

We all thought he was joking and laughed. He wasn't.

'The costumes were awful. I mean, you know it would never work in America.'

It became apparent that he wanted to release 'Back For Good', but he didn't want us to tour America to support it, he would just use the video. He felt the image of the band was totally wrong for the single – we were too camp and too cabaret. We came away that night thinking, well, we've been signed in America but the head of the label doesn't like us. And instead of jumping to our defence, Nigel had just lain on his back, rolled over and played dead. It was the first time he hadn't retaliated against someone insulting us.

The day before the tour opened, our new single, 'Never Forget' came out. It went to No. 1 on the following Sunday's chart and money from the sale of the record went to support Nordoff-Robbins, the music industry's charity. A few days into the Manchester run 'Back For Good' entered the American Hot 100, where it eventually climbed to No. 7 and stayed in the charts for the rest of the year and on into 1996. A couple of days after Clive visited us the American version of *Nobody Else* made the US album chart. Because of everything that followed I can't even recall if we were even excited about finally getting an American chart placing. We were so big in Britain and Europe that America did not seem that big a priority. Nor, at this point, did I have any inkling of the massive effect that Clive Davis would have on my life.

Robbie, meanwhile, seemed to be in a bit of a mess. I've lost count of the number of people who called me up during that time and told me they'd met Robbie in the street and what a state he was in. It got to the point where I would say, 'Tell me, did he burst into tears, fling his arms around you and sob that he was so unhappy, that Take That was a prison he had to escape and he doesn't know what to do?' Rob was constantly in the papers, every other day there'd be a shot of him coming out of a club wrapped around a model or a member of Oasis.

I remember us all feeling fine about everything then, but I was probably feeling better than anyone, and it had nothing to do with Robbie leaving. I'd met Dawn. She was working on our final tour – I remember going into one of the rehearsals in the Docklands and there she was: tall, blonde, beautiful and as shy as ever. She came into the canteen and we got talking. It's weird to think of now that my life's so different, but I'd been on a girl bender for years and was ready for something different. I wanted someone to wake up to in the morning, someone to hang around with all day – a relationship. As I was talking to Dawn I remember thinking, this could be good, this.

On tour everyone splits off into little groups and I made sure I got in with Dawn's circle. But God, was it slow going! Dawn is quiet and much more reserved than me, she had only ever had one boyfriend.

I was dropping hints like bricks. 'So, you know, should we, er . . . should we do something, er, together . . . sometime . . .?' and getting nowhere. We were about halfway through the tour when Mark said to me, 'How's it going, then?'

'I'll be honest,' I said, 'if I don't get a kiss or something tonight, I'm moving on. I don't mind a bit of hard work, but this is ridiculous!'

We headed out to a club that night, but as we were surrounded by crew, bodyguards and the whole entourage, it wasn't exactly private. But Dawn and I danced face to face all night. At one point Mark came over and said, 'This is it, mate!' When we left the club and got in the van, we were all squeezed in – there must have been sixteen of us going back to the hotel and it was quite a small van – and I said to Dawn, 'Sit on my knee.' As she sat down she turned round. That was our first kiss and it lasted all the way back to the hotel. I was staying at home, so I left her there that night, but pretty soon after that we became inseparable.

Dawn was a breath of fresh air in my life. On the one hand she understood the business – she'd left home in Worcester at fifteen to take up a dance scholarship at the Laine Theatre Arts College and had been dancing and modelling ever since – but on the other, she was more in touch with everyday life than I was. She loved to go shopping, eat out and spend time together. I remember her coming to my house one night and switching the TV on. It had hardly been turned on since I'd bought it and I was about to slope off to the studio when she said, 'Where're you going?'

'I'm going to do some –'

'You're going to work now? It's eight o'clock at night! Let's just watch TV.'

I sat in the chair, tensed up and stiff as a board. I didn't know how to relax. It was so long since I'd sat back for an evening and done something other than music.

Dawn wanted a real life, not a showbiz life. When we first started going out I'd say, 'I'm going for dinner with BMG tonight, do you want to come?' and she'd come along. After about five dinners I said, 'Come on, we're going out with so-and-so tonight,' and Dawn said, 'Do you know what? I don't think I'll bother.'

'Why?'

'Well, everybody wants to talk to you and I'm just sat there. If someone gets stuck talking to me I know they don't want to, so I'd rather not go.'

'Nobody feels like that,' I said. 'They couldn't.'

'No, Gary,' Dawn said gently, 'they do. You're just blind to it, that's all.'

From that moment on Dawn detached herself from that side of my life, and I suppose because of her I became less involved in it, too.

We were about to go on a tour of the Far East and Australia and I said to Dawn, 'Why don't you come with me?'

'How can I?' she said.

I assumed she was talking about the cost or something and said, 'Don't be daft, I'll pay.'

'I can't come with you. I have a job to do. I'm dancing on *Top of the Pops* next week with Cher.'

'Stuff that, just tell 'em you're coming with me.'

'Gary, you don't understand. I have a job and I need to do it. They're expecting me to work and that's what I'm going to do.'

I was stunned. Clearly Dawn was going to be the adult in our relationship, at least for a good while.

We flew to Australia and checked into our hotel; it was a case of, now then, where are we today? Not that it mattered to us, we were just rolling along, floating on our entourage cushion. Where once we'd travelled with one or two people from BMG, now we moved in a crowd of forty-six. By the time we got to the gig at the Adelaide Entertainment Centre on 25 September we'd at least worked out that we were in Oz. Fifteen minutes before we were due on stage the promoter came to see us, which was unusual as promoters almost never came to see us.

'I've got a little bit of bad news. I'm afraid we've not quite sold out, but don't worry, we've screened off the areas that haven't sold.'

We went on stage and as the curtain went up, with no word of a lie, there were maybe 200 kids in the audience. It felt like there were more of us on stage than there were in the audience. As we looked out we could see a huge bare area of floor behind the crowd where the mixing desk was located. The promoter had had to cover up vast areas of the 9,000 seat arena. He must have used every single curtain in Adelaide.

We finished the first song and the audience clapped, but while we were used to a wall of sound for applause, this time we could hear each individual handclap. And to make things worse, someone had brought a dog with them, and it howled along with the claps. We could see the funny side and managed to laugh about the whole thing. If it had happened earlier in our careers we would have been thrown by it, but as it was we just carried on with barely a second thought. Things didn't get much better at the second gig in Melbourne, where I think we doubled the audience. By the time we got to our fifth and final Australian gig there were maybe 5,000 people in the audience, but that might be wishful thinking on my part. Then we found out the reason: the tickets went on sale the day the announcement was made about Rob leaving, so it looked like everyone had doubted that we would show up. We had sold a lot of records in Australia, but this was our first live show down under, although we had done promotional tours which had gone well. There seemed to be more fans at the airports than there were at the gigs and there were very definitely more guys outside the hotel than girls, which had never happened before. But the truth is I spent my time in Australia in a daze; all I could think about was Dawn. From the moment I arrived and throughout the tour, I wrote her a handwritten letter and sent it home every day.

Not long after Dawn and I started going out I'd felt there was something I needed to tell her. I sat her down and started, 'Dawn, listen, I feel I should tell you . . . I've . . . we've had very different paths, you and I. I've done a lot of things, I, er . . .'

'Well, of course you have,' said Dawn. 'You've been in Take That for five years.'

That was it. She didn't want to know details. She didn't say, 'That's fine but the playing around stops here.' I think she knew she didn't need to.

After Australia we went to Bangkok and Singapore, where thankfully it was business as usual, with a bonus: Dawn had managed to get six days off and she flew out to Thailand to join me, which made our time there absolutely brilliant for me. After Dawn flew home we did two great shows in Tokyo and then a final show in Indonesia. From there we flew to Los Angeles, because 'Back For Good' was moving steadily up the American Hot 100. Clive Davis had relented slightly and was allowing us to show our faces in America.

When we arrived in Los Angeles Clive, who was based in New York, came to California to see us. He stayed in his bungalow at the Beverly Hills Hotel, which is his Californian home away from home. He seemed eager to make an impression on us and played us Whitney Houston's new record. We felt flattered by the attention, even if he didn't like our stage shows. Unusually for him, Nigel also flew out to LA; he'd spent so little time with us on tour that it now felt odd when he was around. Nigel, worried that everyone in America didn't respect him enough, was on vintage form, bollocking the record company and everyone else around him. About the only people he didn't bollock were the four of us – maybe he'd given up on the band already?

For the first time in my professional life I felt like I couldn't be bothered. In the past when we worked a country, and especially one with such a huge upside, we put in a lot of effort to ratchet things up a gear, but not this time. While I had Dawn as my distraction, the others were feeling a similar lethargy, though for different reasons. Mark had lost his closest mate in the band when Robbie left, and I think he felt let down. And for Jay, because he was so big on the band being one, on it being us against the world, Rob's departure left a real hole. None of us thought this was our big chance to break America. We had reached that point where we were looking forward to the time off more than the work. Not that we had talked about knocking things on the head – just the opposite, we discussed making a new record while we were in Los Angeles – we were just all on go slow and had stopped feeling as if the Take That life was ours for ever.

While we were in New York I had another meeting with Clive Davis. I had a load of new songs I'd written and I went to see him with all my new material. He didn't like any of it. I thought, never mind I'll go back home and write some more stuff. I was a bit pissed off, but Clive intrigued me: no one had told me they didn't like my stuff for years.

Despite talk of making a Take That album, I was also thinking about my own career. It was as if Rob leaving had reactivated the part of me that had viewed Take That as a stepping stone, and with the rumours that Rob was planning on making a solo record, I felt forced into thinking of going solo, too, though when I say forced, there was no one pushing me at this point other than myself.

When we got back to London at the end of October, Nigel did the worst thing possible for the future of the band: he gave us a long holiday – time apart and time to think. All we had in the diary was the inevitable appearance at the *Smash Hits* Pollwinners Party, the MTV Awards in Paris and a recording session for a new single. We went to Paris to receive our award as Best Live Band and Rob was there; he hugged all of us. He seemed just the same, maybe a little heavier.

Our new single was 'How Deep Is Your Love', which we recorded in my studio at Moorside with Chris Porter. The idea to record the song was not something sudden; I used to play it on the organ back in my club days, we had talked about covering it shortly after the first album came out and we would sometimes sing it a cappella backstage, especially during the Pops tour in the summer of 1994. There had also been talk of us releasing a greatest hits album, and shortly before Christmas we agreed with BMG that it should come out in the spring.

After Christmas Nigel decided to call a meeting, but I couldn't go because I was ill with flu. I'm not completely sure why it was being held but I think he was anxious to bring some band business to a head. Very early on in our careers, when Jay, Mark, and Howard started to have a bit of money coming in, they had sought advice on what to do with it. Jay's brother, Simon, was a financial adviser, and he helped them make the most of their earnings. I had made considerably more than the others because of my songwriting royalties, so I had a lot of money sitting in the bank doing nothing and when Mark told me about Jay's brother, I decided to have a meeting with him. It wasn't just investments I needed help with, my financial affairs were chaotic. As a band we were well advised, but personally things were a mess.

I outlined my predicament to Simon, who advised me that the company he worked for only dealt in investments. I wanted someone to look after everything, from negotiating and buying my houses to ensuring my electricity wasn't cut off if I was away from home for six weeks. He said that he would have to ask his business partners if they could provide such a service. When we met again Simon told me that under the Financial Services Act they couldn't act for me that fully unless they had my written permission to do so. I was more than happy to do this and put all my financial affairs in Simon's hands, giving him power of attorney. He was still reluctant to take the responsibility and advised me that I shouldn't give him or anyone that much power, but I explained that it was exactly what I needed and that I was a good judge of character. I joked that he wasn't going to rip me off, so there was no risk, and Simon finally agreed. I had been spending money like it was going out of fashion – on the house, antiques, you name it – and Simon was brilliant at dealing with these things, making sure I was treated fairly.

I remember Simon insisting on going through all the investments he thought I should make, but I wasn't interested in the detail. So he eventually gave up explaining them to me and I just signed wherever he told me to. The situation was ideal for me –

knowing Simon was taking care of things meant I didn't have to worry.

Nigel had not been very keen on any of the band's family members being involved with Take That, so he didn't like the fact that Simon was doing investments for us, and never missed an opportunity to have a go at him. Nigel called the meeting with the band, Simon and the accountant and started having another go at Simon, but everyone put Nigel firmly in his place. He left the meeting fuming, and Jay, Simon and the accountants were also very annoyed.

The next afternoon Nigel turned up at my house with Nick Raymonde and dropped a bombshell.

'Gary, you need to go solo as quickly as possible because I can't manage this band any more.'

Nigel explained that he had irreconcilably fallen out with Jay over Simon's involvement – Nigel, with his desire to control everything couldn't deal with a situation where he wasn't in the driving seat. In a TV show interview quite early on, Jay had said something that Nigel quoted back to me that day and on more occasions since than I can count: 'I'm so in control of being in Take That that I've let someone else take control.' I was confused, because I totally trusted Simon, in part because he was Jay's brother.

Nigel and Nick left without us reaching a firm conclusion because I felt too lousy to think about the rest of my life.

We'd all had enough. In January we were in London for something or other and we met at the Athenaeum Hotel on Piccadilly. It was just Nigel and the four of us and we talked about what we should do next.

'Should we be thinking about splitting up?' I asked. 'We've achieved everything and more than we ever expected.' It wasn't something we'd discussed, it was just an instinct.

Without missing a beat the other three agreed with me and started talking about what they wanted to do. Mark wanted to develop his singing and had solo ideas; Jason was ready for it all just to stop – he wanted time out, to travel at his own pace to all the places we'd missed out on seeing during the Take That merry-go-round. Howard was the only one who said nothing. I was excited about the idea of a solo career and about being with Dawn – for me, every minute we spent apart was a minute lost. The conversation seemed to come to its own conclusion. We decided to announce the split at the BRITs in February.

A few weeks later we appeared on Des O'Connor's TV show for the first play of 'How Deep Is Your Love'. Two days after that we went out to Hayes and to a quarry near Aylesbury to make what was the worst video of our entire career, and that's saying something. We were always a pushover when it came to dumb video ideas, and you can see the boredom on our faces as Paula Hamilton – the girl from the VW advert – acts out a bizarre cameo. I think we all said 'It's crap' at the time, but no one could be bothered to object. Mentally we had already left the band.

Keeping a secret that big was impossible. Three days after the video shoot, the *Sun* ran a story about us splitting up, and the day after, on 13 February, we held a press conference at the Manchester Airport Hilton. We trooped in, sat down and Mark assumed the position of spokesman.

'Well, first . . . we do care very much about our fans . . . We've done all that we can do as Take That, we took it to a level well beyond any of our expectations and, I suppose, beyond many of your expectations . . . For now, it's the end of Take That, but we'll still be around, our mugs will turn up on the TV and doing things for numbers of years to come. We've taken it as far as we can go at the moment, but there may be more to come . . .'

There were some funny questions, and some funny answers from us, though strangely I didn't say that much. One thing I did say was, 'Like Mark said, it's something that's been growing over the last six months, but, you know, it's a career move for all of us.

Our dream is that after five or ten years we'll come back and do it all again.'

As we were closing up we were asked what record we'd like played the following morning. Howard was spot on when he suggested 'Keeping The Dream Alive' by Freiheit. What had passed us all by, but the press picked up on, was the fact that 13 February was Rob's birthday. I was asked in the interview about it and I had to admit I'd forgotten.

We were totally unprepared for the scale of the reaction. The split made *News at Ten*, and a special Samaritans' helpline for distraught fans was launched. It was staggering to think that it was the end of an era for all our supporters as well as for us.

After the press conference the papers were full of stories, conjecture and the usual tittle-tattle – Ladbrokes had odds on our solo careers: Gary 6/4, Robbie 2/1 – but I think it was Mike Stock of Stock, Aitken and Waterman who summed it up best when he said of the band: 'They were like a jigsaw where all the pieces fitted together perfectly. Other groups always had a piece or two missing.'

With the *Greatest Hits* CD coming out in April we agreed with the label that we would promote it throughout Europe. Before we left we played the BRITs and the day after we went to the Song Festival in San Remo – it was the start of six busy but thoroughly enjoyable weeks, possibly the most enjoyable we ever spent as a band. That said, it didn't get off to a very good start. On our way back from Italy to Monte Carlo we were arrested. One of our vehicles had apparently driven over a fan's foot when we were en route to Italy and the Gendarmerie had been mobilised to intercept us when we crossed back over the border. It turned into something of a farce. Despite keeping us in jail for a few hours, we all knew nothing would come of it, we were just irritated as we'd been looking forward to a drink at the bar.

We got home and headed to Manchester for the launch of the

Greatest Hits album, then two weeks later 'How Deep Is Your Love' was released and went straight to No. 1. Between these two dates we went to Geneva for a TV show and I flew home alone. As usual, to avoid the gaze of my fellow passengers and travel incognito, I was wearing the obligatory sunglasses and baseball hat. When I got off the plane I was standing waiting for my luggage when I noticed Eric Clapton was standing three feet away. He was dressed in perfectly normal clothes, no sunglasses, no funny hat and no one took a blind bit of notice. That was a lesson learned.

Our promotional swan song continued with visits to Norway, Denmark, Sweden, Spain, Switzerland, Austria, Germany, Belgium, and then it was back to London to pick up an Ivor Novello award for 'Back For Good'. Howard and Dawn accompanied me, though none of us had any idea of how Howard, who is always so self-contained, was feeling at the time. It wasn't until we were making the documentary in 2005 that he revealed he had felt almost suicidal about the break-up of the band. For Howard, who like Jay is from a big family of six kids, the loss of the band was incredibly unsettling. I thought we shared a sense of relief that it was over and felt glad that it was us that called a halt to the band rather than waiting till our popularity waned.

It was just after the Novellos that the story of my relationship with Dawn appeared in the press. 'Heart-throb singer fell for stunning blonde Dawn Andrews, 23, when she appeared on the group's last-ever tour,' wrote the *Daily Mirror*'s Matthew Wright. We were spotted walking along the King's Road and there was a picture to prove it. It was all Dawn's fault – I wouldn't have gone out but she was always saying, 'What do you mean you can't go out? Don't be daft. That's no way to live your life.'

It was Dawn that put life back into my being. Over the next few years, and still today, it's Dawn who has saved me. I don't think I had ever communicated properly with any of my other girlfriends. I don't remember having a decent conversation with any of them. Dawn dealt with my enormous ego and centred me, and without her I know things would have gone seriously wrong. With my solo career looming, my personal life was better than I could ever have imagined – I knew Dawn was my partner for life.

Take That's final fling was not at Wembley Stadium but on the Ivo Niehe TV show in Holland. We all had a good time staying at the Amstel Hotel, ordering in food from our favourite Indian restaurant, but thanks to Nigel it was a bit like the second sitting of the Last Supper. On that night of all nights, when there was absolutely no need to upset anyone, he couldn't resist upsetting some of the label people. We flew from Amsterdam to Manchester to be greeted with one last flourish: the *Greatest Hits* album went straight into the charts at No. 1.

Years later I saw Chris Healey's diary the entry for that day: 'End of Promo. End of Take That.'

Little did he know . . .

11

Walking the Line as One

26 February 1997

Sitting just across the aisle from me are Eric Clapton and Sheryl Crow. I think they must be dating because she's fallen asleep with her head on his lap. Sean 'Puffy' Coombs is behind me with Big E, and Sting is just in front. I'm on Concorde, it's the morning after the night before and I'm on cloud nine – no, make that ten.

Forget the BRITs. Clive Davis had asked me to sing at his world-famous pre-Grammy party. Every year Arista stage this event on the night before the Grammys in a bid to break new artists – and to be fair it usually does. It's an intimate gathering for 400 of the most-loved media people as well as a host of famous artists and producers. Fuck, I'm showcasing for America tonight!

They're all talking about the Grammys and I'm buzzing. To have had a personal call from Clive really got me going, but playing at this event tonight is truly amazing. I don't even know what I'm going to sing yet. With the new album finished I'll probably do something from that, along with 'Back For Good', because it was a big hit in the US.

'I'm going to see Whitney Houston perform at Clive's pre-Grammy party tonight,' I hear Eric say. Jeepers, this is it, folks, she's probably my warm-up!

There's one thing bothering me. If Nigel had still been my manager he would have been here with me, no matter what. Simon Fuller's been my manager for about three months now and I'm a bit surprised that he's decided not to come. This is after all the most important gig I'll ever do. Instead he's sent some new guy from his office called Ian Pirrie. I wanted Chris Healey to be with me, but Simon insisted that it should be his man. He's not really my kind of guy, but hey, I need to be open to these things with a new manager.

In a couple of hours it will be 9 a.m. in New York and we'll be at JFK. I'll have all day to relax before the big show tonight.

I was told I was the new George Michael, the next Elton – you're the talented one, the best British songwriter for years. I was told, forget Robbie, the big money is on you. But almost from the moment I left Take That my self-belief began to fade away.

Any doubts were small at that point though, BMG were hot to trot and so was I. We hadn't released any of the songs I'd written for Take That since the previous August, so I had plenty of material in the bag. I said to Chris Porter, 'Let's go. I want to make an album and let's do it together.'

In fact, Chris and I already had two songs well under way. One was 'Open Road' and the other was 'Forever Love'. Both songs would have ended up on the unmade Take That album.

At that stage I thought that making a solo album would be just like making a Take That album, except without Howard, Mark, Jay or Rob's involvement. Chris and I recorded twelve tracks and I was pretty happy with the result. I had what I reckoned was a strong single – Nigel chose it; he was good at that, he's got a great ear – and the plan was simple: to get 'Forever Love' out, then maybe release another single, probably 'Open Road', and then off the back of that, the album. At least I think that was the plan. To be honest, that period of my life has become something of a blur, though some of what occurred affected me so deeply it's for ever etched on my soul.

One side of me loved the idea of going solo while the other side kept thinking, bloody hell, I'm not sure about this. My ego was rampant, telling myself I had the talent and this was my time. But the real me, the me that's true to myself, was saying, shit! I need to get going here.

The rumours were true: at a midnight press conference on 27 June 1996 Rob announced he was planning a solo career and was splitting from BMG to take up with EMI. I have to be honest, at that stage I didn't think he was much competition. It has nothing to do with whether or not Rob has talent – simply because lately he'd put next to no effort into the band.

One of the conditions of Rob's release from his BMG contract was that he wasn't allowed to release a single before me – 'Forever Love' was scheduled for release in the middle of July and his was due out two weeks after. From the start Robbie and I were pitched against one another. The press wanted to see a battle, the pop equivalent of Oasis versus Blur, so it was bound to get messy.

I wanted my solo career to be a new departure. Take That's fans were growing up and I wanted to grow with them and appeal to a broader market. Nor did I just want to appear in *Smash Hits* and the tabloids, I wanted to be cooler and classier than that. The press girl at BMG had got me a cover slot in *Arena*. I trained like a maniac and went on a diet to present myself in the best possible light. The shots were taken by Norman Watson at the Great Western Hotel in Paddington, Hammersmith Bridge and in Soho and they are fabulous pictures, even if I say so myself.

It was the total opposite of where Robbie was at; he was drinking, eating and partying obsessively. While I'd lost a stone and a half, he'd put it on. What I didn't see coming was the interview Rob gave the gay magazine *Attitude* in the run-up to his single release. He called me 'a clueless wanker' 'really fucking dated' 'selfish, stupid and greedy'. He said he'd been a 'prisoner for six years in Take That' – it was a declaration of war.

At that stage things were going well, so I didn't feel the impact immediately. Things were looking good for the release of the first single, the *Sun* had done a massive splash and I was sure that the album Chris Porter and I had put together had real potential. Nigel loved it, I loved it and it felt like a hit, but BMG were curiously lukewarm. It seemed to take ages to get any kind of reaction and when I did it was non-committal.

It took me a while to fathom that the source of the apathy was America. After the break-up, Nigel had assumed there would be no deal for me with Arista, but it seemed Clive Davis was still interested. Apparently he had called and said, 'You know my feelings on the band, but my interest is in the songwriter. I wanna know what he's doing as a singer.' When I delivered the album, Clive was the first person it had been sent to. 'Great news,' said Nick Raymonde when he called Nigel, 'Clive Davis wants to sign Gary for America. The bad news is he doesn't like some of the record.'

Hanging on America's response, BMG had got cold feet. Yet to me their reasons weren't at all clear: I was a UK-based artist and BMG in the UK was my main label – surely they should call the shots? Nor was Nigel fighting my corner; he was being uncharacteristically meek.

'But Nigel,' I said, 'before BMG started showing signs of not liking the album you were completely sold on it. What's the problem?'

'Well, you know how it is, Gary, they know best about these things.'

When I look back now, my main regret is not making more of a fuss. As the lead singer of Take That I had written six number ones – I was in a much stronger position than I realised. But no one else rated the new songs except for Chris Porter and me. I had dates on hold at the Royal Albert Hall, but there wasn't much point in playing them without a record to promote; so progress was impossible.

With the seeds of doubt sown in my mind I began to question

my material. Maybe it wasn't good enough? I was in a total quandary, and so was Chris, so we retreated back to the studio and started work on some more tracks. Unsurprisingly, nothing came of it, my mind-set was totally wrong. Chris was scratching his head, trying to come up with something better, and I was doing the worst thing imaginable: listening to the radio and trying to write things that reflected other artists' sounds. It was like turning the clock back to 'It Only Takes A Minute' when everyone thought I couldn't write a hit.

Then it came to me – I was a solo artist now and I had to take matters into my own hands. Clive Davis was the answer. He was considered a genius by everyone in the record industry; BMG had sold him to me as a legend who must be obeyed. I decided that if I could just talk to him, play him some of my songs and explain myself, everything would be sorted. Clive would speak and the whole world would listen. I imagined the scene: 'Gary, you've got a hit here.'

'You're absolutely right, Clive.' Chorus the team at BMG in London. Or at least that's how I sold it to myself. In preparation I read his book. When I'd met him with the band during our final tour I hadn't realised quite who or what he is. I now found out that during his long career – he was sixty-two at the time – he has signed just about everyone from Janis Joplin, Bruce Springsteen and Chicago to Barry Manilow, Dionne Warwick, Billy Joel, Aretha Franklin and Whitney Houston. People would kill for ten minutes with this guy, and he'd signed me. You may never have heard of him, but I absolutely guarantee that you'll have heard hundreds of the hits for which he's been responsible. He's been behind records that have sold billions.

Of course there was no question of Clive coming to see me, I had to go to him. He was staying, as usual, at the Beverly Hills Hotel, so I flew to Los Angeles for an audience. It was a bit like going to see the Pope, except that this one's Jewish. Clive's right-hand man was Roy Lott, who Take That had christened 'the chief upper turner downer'. When we had met Clive on our way back from touring Australia and the Far East, Roy's pivotal role in the Arista machine had been to turn the stereo up and down. He was also the chief phoner-upper and he called me at 6 p.m. on the day I arrived in Los Angeles

'Hi, Gary. Roy Lott here,' said Roy in his ultra-slow delivery. No sense in rushing your major task of the day. 'Clive's in bungalow 1C. He wants to meet you at 10 a.m. Please, please, please, PLEASE, do not be late.'

'Listen, Roy, believe me, I know how important this is. It's 2 a.m. in the morning for me right now. I'm going to the Ivy for something to eat, but I'll be in bed by half nine. It'll practically be dinner time for me by the time I meet Clive.'

'Well, Gary, he's expecting you for breakfast, so good luck.'

Good luck? It reminded me of what an enormous move this was for me. But I felt good. I felt *really* good.

I had a routine when I went to Los Angeles. I would check into the Four Seasons, shoot straight round to the Ivy on Robertson Boulevard for some seafood pasta, cookies and hot chocolate, then get back to my room to be in bed by 9 p.m. I would then sleep until 5 a.m., ready to face a full day. While I sat in the Ivy having my dinner I thought to myself, you know, everything's cool, all this business going on at home, with them not believing in my record, I'll make them think again.

Before I'd left England I'd had a couple of late nights, added to which I was stressed from constantly trying to figure out what was going wrong. It was so long since I'd had to worry about the future, Nigel and Take That had taken care of it, but this time even Nigel wasn't behind me. I was feeling very much on my own, and now here in LA I really was alone. Later, as I lay in bed with thoughts racing around my jet-lagged brain, I kept coming back to one certainty: everything was going to be OK because I was going to meet the man who makes megastars. Soon enough I went off to sleep, helped by one of the Four Seasons' great beds –

it's like sleeping in feathers. The one thing I didn't do was to organise a wake-up call. There was no need: I always woke early in Los Angeles because of the eight-hour time difference.

Nine forty-seven a.m., that's what the clock said. That's impossible! I sprang out of bed muttering, 'Right, right.' I was stunned: it was nine forty-seven and the meeting was at ten – I had thought about virtually nothing else all week. I'd brought clothes with me – a hanger full of my best gear so I'd look the business – and I had thirteen minutes to get myself together and over to Clive's hotel. I got dressed faster than I've ever done before because I knew it would take ten minutes to get up to the Beverly Hills Hotel. While I was dressing I thought, bugger I'm starving. I always feel that way after a long sleep, but there was no time to eat.

I went down in the elevator and called out as I ran across the lobby, 'Can you get me a cab? I need a cab, really, really quickly.'

Having stayed there a few times already the guy recognised me and I hit him with $50 to make him move a little faster. Next thing I'm in the back of a cab imploring the driver, 'I want the Beverly Hills Hotel and I need to be there like half an hour ago. Please, just get me there as fast as you can.'

I tried to look in the taxi's rear-view mirror to see how bad I looked. I knew for sure that I didn't look good. I barely waited for the cab to stop before tossing the guy another $50, jumping out and running into reception.

'I'm looking for bungalow 1C,' I said to the first guy I came across.

'Good morning, sir. Yes, sir, you go through here and follow the path to the rear of the property and that's where you'll find bungalow 1C.'

I half walked, half ran, and as I reached the bungalow I looked at my watch: Nine fifty-nine. It was a fucking miracle!

Knock, knock, knock, knock, knock, knock.

No answer.

Knock, knock, knock – still nothing. Knock, knock, and as I hammered slightly harder the door just came ajar. Inside I could hear a voice so I went in, although no one had invited me. Was it even the right bungalow?

'Hello, hello, is anyone here?' I asked.

He was obviously talking on the phone. Next thing a door opened and in walked Clive. Somehow that morning he hardly looked real. True, the glasses he wears are like none I've ever seen, and the make-up threw me a little, but he seemed so tall. This was no mere mortal, this was someone who made music history.

'Hi, Gary, how are you?'

Clive returned to his normal size and demeanour. It's funny how you can be fooled by the way people look when they have power over you.

'Oh, Mr Davis, hi, how're you doing?'

He gave me a hug.

'It's so great to see you, I'm just on the phone, but if you go through you can get yourself some tea.'

The bungalow was massive and Clive was parked at one end, on a sofa by the phone. He ushered me into what would pass as a dining room in a small mansion. On the table there was every drink imaginable: Fanta, Pepsi, root beer, Diet Coke, 7up, big flasks of coffee, every American beer I had ever heard of, and some I hadn't. It was like a buffet, but there was no sign of any tea, or anything that even vaguely resembled it. I didn't want to make a fuss, despite the fact that I was desperate for a cuppa, so I just stood in the room feeling spare, but glad of the time to compose myself. Ten minutes went by, fifteen minutes, and he was still on the phone.

I was starving. On a sideboard there was something I'd seen before but never eaten: a bagel. Next to it was a little pot of cream cheese. I thought it couldn't be that bad – everyone in America seems to eat them – so with Clive still talking away I decided it would be my first ever bagel. I layered on a bit of cream cheese and took a bite. It was lovely. Of course it was, bagels probably cost $10 at the Beverly Hills Hotel. It was gone in an instant. Almost immediately I needed the toilet – though it may also have been nerves.

Clive was still on the phone, so I stood in the doorway jiggling around a bit to get his attention.

'Sorry, Mr Davis, sorry to bother you, sorry to disturb you, I need the toilet.'

'The what? Oh you mean the bathroom. Just go through there, Gary.' He pointed to a door. Feeling a whole lot better I came out, and as he seemed to be finishing his conversation I decided to hover.

'Gary, go back through and finish your tea, I'll just be five minutes.'

Back in the dining room I noticed a plate with a silver lid on it at one end of the table – maybe that's what they call tea I thought. Up North tea is dinner, so in America maybe breakfast is tea! I lifted the lid and there were the best-looking scrambled eggs on toast I've ever seen in my life – $27-worth of scrambled perfection. Toast with the crusts cut off, eggs delicately sprinkled with chives. Nothing was going to hold me back. I tucked in.

As I finished I heard Clive saying goodbye on the phone. I stood up, put the silver dome back on the empty plate and was just brushing the crumbs off myself when he walked into the room.

'Gary, so great to see you. We really need to talk through this record. You just sit over there while I eat my eggs,' he said as he lifted the silver domed lid. Almost simultaneously I fell to my knees.

'Oh no, Mr Davis, oh no. I can't believe it. I thought the eggs were tea, because up North we call tea, dinner, so I thought breakfast might be tea, like bathroom's toilet. Oh no, Mr Davis.'

I was talking gibberish, making no sense at all.

'I've eaten Mr Davis. No, I mean I've eaten your scrambled eggs, Mr Davis.'

The expression on his face contained no hint of comprehension as he tried to reconcile what I was saying with what he was seeing. As I stood back up Clive said,

'OK, Gary, no problem, I've got a bagel over here.'

'Ohh,' I practically wailed and again threw myself to my knees. 'Mr Davis. Oh Mr Davis, I can't believe it, I've eaten your bagel, too.'

As I knelt there like I was on stage singing 'Pray', he walked over to the telephone.

'Ah yeah, I know I've ordered scrambled eggs, and they've been delivered, but I need one more egg and a bagel. Yeah, I know.'

He never bothered to ask me if I wanted any more which is a shame because I really fancied another bagel.

I slowly regained my composure as we began discussing the album.

'Mr Davis, I have this tape of songs here,' I said, reaching into my pocket.

'Yes, fine Gary, but I've got two songs I want *you* to listen to.'

He then played me a song called 'So Help Me Girl' and another called 'Fall So Deep'. Both were country songs. 'I think you should record these songs,' said Clive.

'Well, Mr Davis, I'm a songwriter and—'

'I know you are, Gary,' said Clive, interrupting me. 'But sometimes songwriters need to broaden their horizons and take on other people's work.'

'Well, yes,' I stammered, 'but in England I'm a really respected songwriter.'

This continued back and forth for a few more minutes, but I knew that he knew that I knew the game was up. Clive spoke and I listened. I was to record some cover versions to make my album more marketable across a broader demographic, or whatever bullshit marketing terms he trotted out. His parting question to me was, 'Is there anyone in America you'd like to work with?'

'Well yes, there's Diane Warren.'

'My next meeting's with Diane, I'm sure we can fix something up.'

I never did play him my songs.

I had flown to Los Angeles hoping to impress him. Stupid me. There I was thinking I was the star when all along it was Clive. I was distraught, and when I got home I told Nigel what had happened.

'Well, you know what I think. I would prefer to have two songs written by someone else on my album and have everyone in the world believing in me and have a chance of breaking America.'

'That's fine, Nige, but it's not your album, it's mine.'

'Suit yourself, Gary. It's either that or an album written by you that no one is motivated about.'

I was defeated. 'OK, Nige, I know. If that's what we need to do then let's put it into action.'

But I was determined to exact a price. If Mr Big Shot wanted me to do his bidding he could pay for it. I called Clive, 'There are two more people I'd like to work with on this project.' I said, putting him to the test. 'One is David Foster and the other is Walter Afanasieff.'

'No problem, Gary, I think we can make that happen.'

It's hard to say now whether it was the insecurity of going solo, without the lads to back me up and offer support, but I was beginning to feel as though Nigel wasn't behind me in the way he should have been. Perhaps it was just that the management tactics that he used to pull off such brilliant coups for the band felt embarrassing for a solo act. At the end of May I flew to California for an international A&R conference, where I was going to showcase some of my new album – the few bits Clive did like. Nigel, Dawn and I flew on Virgin to Los Angeles but we had to make an emergency landing on Baffin Island because of a technical problem. All my BMG supporters were on the plane, including Hugh Goldsmith and Simon Cowell. After a long delay we were re-routed and finally arrived at Laguna Beach where the conference was to be held. It had been a long journey and the hotel was fine for everyone – except Nigel. He decided he didn't like it and had everybody running around trying to put us in another hotel. I felt Nigel was showing me up; he was behaving as though we were still in the Salford Van Hire Transit.

After the show Clive came to see me. 'So, Gary, I've got you some dates with David Foster next week and before that Diane Warren wants to work with you.'

'Well, I'm also here to shoot the video for "Forever Love" with Sophie Muller.'

'No problem, Gary, do that, and then go to Diane and after that go to David's house.'

So I shot the video at the Chateau Marmont on Sunset Boulevard, with Gwyneth Paltrow and Keanu Reeves, who was nursing a broken leg and looked enormous, watching. The next day I went to work with Diane Warren, a songwriting legend. She's probably written more hits over the last twenty years than any other writer and for that reason alone I was desperate to meet her. Elton, Tina Turner, Barbra Streisand, Britney Spears, Chicago, Whitney Houston, Céline Dion, and LeAnn Rimes are just a few of the big names who have sung her songs.

Diane and I agreed to meet for dinner at a Thai restaurant on Sunset; she was about fifteen minutes late and the waiter came over almost as soon as she sat down.

'Are you ready to order, sir?'

'I'll have the Pad Thai.'

'Miss Warren?' asked the waiter

'I'll have the noodles, hold the oil, hold the sunflower . . .'

It was hold this, hold that. There was going to be an empty bowl by the time the food appeared. But that was nothing compared to what happened next. She reached into her pocket and pulled out a live parrot, which she popped on to her shoulder.

As we talked I have to admit I was a little preoccupied, but not nearly as distracted as some of the other diners, who stared at Diane open-mouthed. She had by this time taken the parrot off her shoulder and was rolling it around in her hand, talking to it while trying to maintain a sensible conversation with me. Then the parrot started hopping around the table, perching on the pepper pot and sitting on the soy sauce.

'Excuse me, Diane, but there are people looking at us.'

'Really? There are people looking?' said Diane as if amazed. 'Excuse me, waiter, can I have two pieces of bread?'

The bread appeared and Diane picked up the parrot and popped it between the two slices. She then held it up and said in a loud voice to everyone in the trendy Hollywood eatery, 'Parrot sandwich, anyone?'

After that the meal continued fairly normally by LA standards.

Diane said she would pick me up the following morning at my hotel and then we could do some writing together. Next day, when her Range Rover drew up, I opened the passenger door to be confronted by a seat literally overflowing with cassettes. There were dozens of them.

'Diane, shall I move them?'

'No, no, don't move any of them because you're going to mess with my head. Just sit on them.'

As I climbed in and sat down I could feel tapes cracking and breaking as I tried to perch on the seat without putting my entire weight on it. One tape was sticking in my arse so I pulled it out. Written on the cassette was 'Unbreak My Heart'.

'That's one I've just done with Toni Braxton, wanna hear it?' Diane said.

So there we were listening to this terrific song as we drove north from Sunset up into the Hollywood Hills. Diane lives in a beautiful house, just by the Hollywood sign, but the first thing that struck me as I walked in was that it was a loner's house. Given that Diane normally only writes by herself I was flattered that she had agreed to write *with* me, even though I knew it was only because of Clive. She told me that every song she wrote was about her father – she was devastated by his death and had never got over it. Listen to 'Because You Loved Me' knowing that, Céline Dion singing, and you'll hear it in a whole new light.

Diane is consumed by songwriting like no one else I have ever met. I love it, but I'm not consumed by it. I love the whole thing, and not just the writing. I love being on stage and in the studio, in fact, I adore every aspect of making music. It's why being given a second chance is so important to me – this time around I'll appreciate it even more than I did the first time. Of course there's pressure, but it's a very positive pressure, unlike the anxiety that was growing inside me during that summer of 1996.

Diane and I wrote a song called 'My Commitment' and after we finished it I took the short trip up to the Malibu Beach Hotel, where Dawn and I were to stay while I worked at David Foster's house. Despite my worries I was getting into the romance of it all. After all, these were the people I had always wanted to work with, the biggest names in American songwriting. I might have eaten his breakfast, but Clive had delivered.

For me as a songwriter and aspiring producer, working with David was a brilliant opportunity. He had recently made 'I Will Always Love You' with Whitney Houston. When I got to David's studio I was expecting to do one of the songs Clive had given me and one of my own. As we were about to start on my song, David said, 'Clive sent me this great song and suggested we do this one, too.'

It was the country and western song Clive had played me in the bungalow. They're playing a fucking game with me here, I thought. They think I'm stupid.

'This is the one, man, just listen to that, it's great. Let's do it,' said David.

'What about my song?' I whined.

'You know what? Let's just do this one,' said David.

Of course, by the time we had finished there was no time to record my song. I was so pissed off. At the end of the week we flew home and I sat on the plane deciding that perhaps I could take or leave America. It had been great working with David and Diane, but I was ready to go home.

In the build-up to 'Forever Love' coming out I was everywhere: French TV, the Lottery show and then two days after that I was in Rome playing a great gig on the Spanish Steps. I pulled out all the stops to promote it and it was huge. The week 'Forever Love' went in at No. 1, the Spice Girls went in at No. 3. A week later they knocked me off the top and I went down to No. 2, but the track stayed in the charts for three months and sold something like two million copies. On its third week Robbie's 'Freedom' went into the charts at No. 2 and stayed in the charts for ten weeks. We were neck and neck, yet the press had already started to write him off.

In early July, shortly before the release of 'Forever Love', I was at the Conrad Hotel doing interviews. In the middle of one with the *Sun*, Chris Healey interrupted to say I had a phone call. I knew it must be important because Chris never interrupted me like that. As I came out, Chris closed the door in such a way as to make me understand it was very serious.

I picked the phone up.

'Mr Barlow?'

'Yes.'

'This is the Fraud Squad.'

The policeman asked me whether I was the owner of a building in Manchester. I was; I had bought it from Simon Orange. It was for investment purposes and the building was leased to a government organisation. The lease was for twenty years and with the rent I'd get the building would pay for itself three times over and I'd also be able to sell it at the end of the lease. I'd bought the building from the company Simon worked for and they had bought it from someone who needed to sell it quickly. The building was then valued at £550,000, Simon's company had bought it for £300,000 and sold it to me for £400,000. It turned out that a person they had bought the building from was suspected of defrauding the Health Authority and that the Fraud Squad were investigating him. They thought this guy had sold the building too cheaply and assumed he had received some undeclared cash as part of the deal.

At the time I didn't hear any of this: my head was too full of the whispers I'd been hearing against Simon. After all, for the previous three years Simon had had power of attorney and full control of my money and everything I owned: he even signed my cheques. I thought all my money was gone.

As soon as the interview ended I cancelled everything I had planned for rest of the day and went to see my lawyers. They told me that we needed to arrange a squad of lawyers and accountants to go to the offices of Simon's company in Manchester immediately and freeze all my financial dealings with them, and that's exactly what happened. Life was so busy and stressful – I was leaving on a trip the next day – that I gave them the go-ahead and didn't deal with the fallout.

Simon and I had been really friendly – he used to come round to my house for dinner parties all the time – and he was Jason's brother, so I had every reason to trust him. But my career at that time was like spinning plates, and every plate was a country I was trying to sell records in. I regret now that I didn't take the time to make a second phone call to Simon – today I would drop everything and go to see him myself. I'd insist on us sitting round a table and talking it through. It would have saved us all a lot of strife if I'd done just that. As it was, I simply said to the lawyers, 'Get every penny of my money out of there as fast as you can,' and I didn't return Jason's calls, which still makes me feel guilty even now.

My lawyers ended up suing Simon's company to get back the £100,000 profit they had made on the building. The company gave in because even if they had gone to court and won, Simon would have lost his licence to operate, as I had persuaded him to take my power of attorney, which is against the rules of the Financial Services Authority. It forced his company into a situation that eventually led to their decline.

Sometime later I found out that they had done nothing wrong, both in respect of the sale of the building and the Fraud Squad investigations or in any of the other investments Simon had arranged on my behalf. Simon had in fact looked after my finances very well, and the only thing that my accountants could find amiss was the fact that I had given Simon so much control – control I insisted he should have. The accountants said I was lucky that nothing was missing given the scope Simon had had. In addition, the building in question turned out to be one of the best investments I ever made.

Simon's business recovered – he's still a successful businessman – but I very much regret how I handled things. I thought I was the one giving Simon all the trust, but he had also expected my trust in return.

At the end of July, two days after 'Forever Love' came out, Dawn and I went to Venice to celebrate her birthday and stayed at the Hotel Cipriani. We had a wonderful time; despite the problems, life was looking good from where we sat overlooking the bay in Venice. When we arrived home we found our whole trip had been documented by the paparazzi. While it didn't ruin it for us, you can't help but wonder where they were hiding and what else they saw.

A month later we moved into Delamere Manor. Our Ian and the builders had worked on it for about twelve months, getting it just the way I wanted and it was lovely to move in finally. Because Dawn was busy with work, we had been living at my flat close to Battersea Bridge in London most of the time.

A little while later, on the day I was due for a sitting at Madame Tussauds I got a call from the therapist Beechy Colclough. He was ringing to tell me that Rob was at Elton's in a hell of a mess.

'We're getting a doctor,' he said, 'but Robbie wants you to know that when he's better he wants to talk to you.'

'OK,' I said. 'Well, he's got my number and I'll be here.' I asked Chris Healey to buy a *huge* bunch of flowers and take them down to Woodside for Rob. Chris came back and confirmed that Rob was in a bad way, and later that evening I got another call from Beechy.

'Gary, hello. I've got Robbie here. He wants to talk to you.'

Rob came on. It was a similar conversation to the one we'd had a couple of months earlier – I'm sorry for all the things I've said. I want to see you when this is all over.

I said, 'No problem, mate, no problem. I haven't got a problem with any of that. Good luck, I hope it works out.'

I have to hand it to Clive, he didn't give up easily. I had more sessions lined up with Trevor Horn at SARM West Studios for another of Clive's covers, Johnny Bristol's 'Hang On In There Baby'. I then went to San Francisco to work with Walter Afanasieff, the second half of my dream-team request, on 'Never Knew', which at least was one of my songs.

In early October I got a call saying, 'Gary, I'm really excited. I've found you another song.'

'Hi, Clive, that's great,' I said while thinking, I don't want a fucking song. I don't want any of your songs.

'This track's fantastic, it's written by Madonna.' This time at least I was eager to hear the demo.

I was worried. My publishing agreement was based on the fact that I would write 75 per cent or more of my album. If any other people's songs got on to the album I wouldn't get an advance as it wouldn't qualify as my album. And yet, while all this was going on, Nigel didn't seem to care. Perhaps he didn't have a vision for my solo career in the way he had done for Take That, or perhaps he was out of his depth with the American style of doing things. Either way, he seemed to have lost his bite and I decided we needed to have it out.

'Hi Soozi, I need to have a meeting with Nigel this evening.' Soozi was his PA and pet dragon; at least that's what he called her.

'Nigel can't see you tonight, he's going out with a casting director.' And with that she put the phone down.

I thought, that's it, and the next morning I called my lawyer. 'Get me out. That's it, I'm finished with Nigel. I'm fed up with this. It's a joke.'

It didn't even feel like a big decision. The result was a fax from my lawyers to Nigel saying I was terminating my agreement with him. Of course it was no way to deal with the situation, or with someone who had done so much for me, but all I can say by way of explanation is that I was desperate. Nigel and I had reached the point where we were never going to see eye to eye. It was such a frantic time for me, it was a case of act now, think later – and later I came to see that I'd behaved badly.

I called BMG later that morning and spoke to Hugh Goldsmith and Jeremy Marsh. 'I'm leaving Nigel, how do you feel about that?' I asked

'Well, I'm sure our feelings are clear on Nigel. We've enjoyed our relationship with him, but it's been rocky.'

'I've heard that Simon Fuller is pretty good, but I don't know him well and I wonder if you could help me there?' Simon had recently taken on the Spice Girls and was making a real name for himself.

Hugh said, 'Listen, I've got a meeting with him this afternoon. I'll talk to him and let you know what he says. Just so you know, we have Annie Lennox on BMG and he looks after her, we think he's amazing. As your label, we will make this happen for you.'

Perfect. That would mean that Simon would be able to deal with Clive Davis because Annie was signed to Arista as well. A week later I met with Simon and he was mad for it. At the same time, though, he wasn't what I'd expected. Striking looking but softly spoken, he didn't initially seem as powerful as he turned out to be.

I played Simon what I had recorded and he gave me an A&R perspective on it – he thought there were some mixes he could hear working better on it than others – and of course he loved 'Love Won't Wait', the Madonna track. Over the next week or so Simon got into conversation with Clive and they decided they wanted Stephen Lipson to make the record. OK, I thought, I give in, and we set about recording it. Simon was very much part of making that record and was delighted with it when it was finished in January. Clive and everyone else decided that 'Love Won't Wait' would be the second single. I, on the other hand, didn't like it – I don't like the way my voice sounds on it. For the first time I wasn't speaking up, which is very unlike me. Everyone seemed to have something to say about which direction my career should be heading and I was having to let go of things and trust other people's opinion. It felt like I could no longer trust my own.

By now six months had gone by since 'Forever Love' had been released, and that's a long time in pop. Added to which, things with Nigel had developed into a legal brawl since sending the fax. The same thing had happened between Rob and Nigel, so I knew that Nigel wouldn't, for understandable reasons, let things drop, but I still didn't cope well with it at the time. I wanted and needed to focus on being creative, but I was being sidetracked by business. Simon said all the right things, but there was a fundamental difference between his approach and Nigel's: he wanted me to do *everything*. It seemed like I was at the opening of every envelope.

Because my relationship with Dawn was still in the early stages I was too proud to talk to her about what was going wrong. I wanted to shelter her from the harm of it. I was used to gritting my teeth and getting on with things, but I was also used to things going well. This was like a football team that always won the treble losing four league games on the trot – to me it was inexplicable.

When we had finished the single, Simon announced, 'I want you to be on the BRITs.'

'I fucking hate the BRITs,' I said.

Sure they'd been good for Take That, but it's the music industry's night of rampant self-obsession, which was the last thing I needed just then. Nevertheless I agreed to present an award with Louise Nurding from Eternal. Meeting everyone and getting good reactions from people made me feel better. Here comes the second wave, I can feel it, is what I told myself.

That night at the BRITs, after I presented the award, Simon found me backstage. He came towards me waving his mobile in the air and mouthing, 'It's for you, Gary,' across the crowded room. He handed me his phone.

'Hi Gary, Clive here.'

'Er, hello Clive.' Why's he ringing me now?

'I'd like you to perform at my pre-Grammy party.'

'That's great, when is it?'

'It's tomorrow night.'

Which is how I found myself on Concorde the next morning.

When we arrived at JFK a car took Ian Pirrie, the guy Simon Fuller had sent in his place, and I straight to Manhattan and Arista's offices on Seventh Avenue. I was whisked upstairs to Clive's office, where eight people were waiting to greet me.

'Gary, welcome,' said Clive. 'Hey, this is a big night for Arista and a big night for you!' Simon had told me all about it, so I was really up for it – at least America would be mine, or something like that.

'We need to get over there to rehearse, but before we go I'd like to play you something.'

As the chief upper turner downer leapt into action I thought, oh no, not another cover. A heavy dance track started and all the guys in Clive's office started moving and dancing around. I was too embarrassed to look at them. As I was listening to the track all I could think was, this is fucking awful. Then I heard my voice. Clive and his crew had remixed 'Love Won't Wait' into something barely recognisable, and it seemed to go on for ever and ever. When it finally finished, the plant pots stopped jiggling around and Clive fixed his eyes on me through his shades.

'Well, Gary, what do you think?'

'Yes, Mr Davis, Yeah . . . it's . . . it's OK.'

'That, Gary, is what you are going to perform for us tonight.'

He made it sound like I was on *Stars in Their Eyes*!

My mind was racing. I'd spent an afternoon recording it weeks ago and had done not a thing with it since – no TV performances, nothing. I hadn't even listened to it after I'd recorded the vocals. Now Mr America expected me to perform it on the biggest night of my solo career. There were about thirty-eight bars before my voice came in. What was I supposed to do on stage while all that was going on?

'Oh no, oh no, I don't like it at all.'

'No problem, Gary, let's hear it again' said Clive, demonstrating his selective deafness, a skill he expertly coupled with America's favourite management technique of never saying no. On it went again and the plant pots were up dancing. The second time it sounded even worse.

'Mr Davis, you know what?'

'Come on everybody, we're going to rehearse,' rallied Clive, at which point he got up and led us out of his office, down in the elevator and out the building. We were all following him up Madison Avenue heading for the Ritz. Clive was out front, the plant pots and the chief upper turner downer behind him, with Gary from Frodsham trailing in their wake.

'I just don't like this record,' was all I could say to Roy Lott as I caught up with him.

'We'll speak to Clive. Don't worry, Gary, we'll just get there and get organised, there'll be no problem.'

At the Ritz there was a group on stage, but Clive cleared them off. I was given a radio mic and took centre stage. As I looked out I could see Clive standing in the middle of the room and he'd got a radio mic as well. Maybe it was going to be a duet!

'Gary', said Clive, 'why don't you sing "Back For Good"?'

I heard them getting the sound right just as I got to the end of the song.

'That's good, yeah, that's very good. OK, here we go.'

All of a sudden the dance track started.

'Mr Davis, Mr Davis, can I just have a word?'

I could see Clive turning to Roy Lott, who incidentally would later spend millions trying to break Robbie in America, as if to say, 'What's he going on about?' Clive indicated to cut the music and walked up on to the stage. He came and stood very close to me.

'Gary, when this song starts you've got to move. You've gotta move, you've gotta dance and you've gotta sell this record. You've gotta be one side of the stage to entertain them and then the other.'

Instead of objecting I just said, 'Right.'

The track started up again, and like an idiot I began moving around, all the while trying to work out where I was supposed to come in. Halfway through the verse I joined in – better late than never, but it was excruciating. I looked out and saw Clive pointing for me to move towards one side of the stage. I'd go where he told me to go, then he'd point to the other side of the stage; I was so busy darting from side to side I missed all my vocal cues – not that I had any idea where they were. As I finished I turned to have one more go at Clive, but he was nowhere to be seen. It seemed he had left the building.

'Where's Clive?' I asked.

'Oh, he's gone for an interview with CNN and then he's got ABC. It's a big night for Clive,' said Roy Lott. 'In fact, I need you, follow me.' He led me through some doors.

'But Roy, I need some time to learn the lyrics to the song, I don't have any idea what I'm singing up there.'

'Don't you worry about that, Gary.'

From the empty performance room I was taken into another room which was heaving with people.

'Gary, this is MTV.' A girl immediately started to interview me. As I tried to answer her questions my thoughts were running on a reel: This is a disaster. I need a tape of that song so I can at least learn it. Get me out of here.

After about an hour of non-stop interviews and schmoozing I was panicking. Another hour went by and I heard an announcement, 'Ladies and Gentleman, in fifteen minutes please take your seats.'

Shit! I turned to one of the Arista plant pots.

'How long before I'm on?'

'You've got about twenty-five minutes.'

'I need a fucking tape of that song quickly, I need to get my gear ironed. Get me out of this room and into mine now.'

No tape could be found, but I did at least manage to change into my stage gear. At that moment who should arrive but Ian Pirrie, Simon Fuller's man on the spot. He strolled into the room looking all washed and brushed-up and wearing a fucking kilt. I've nothing against kilts, but this event was supposed to be rock and pop, and how come he had had time to get ready?

'Gary, that's the three-minute warning,' said a plant pot.

I seriously considered doing a runner. Just as the sweat started to pour off me I heard, 'There's a young guy from the UK who's come over here having already had a huge hit with "Back for Good". Please welcome . . . Gary Barlow.'

As I started there was a little applause and I thought, OK, this is good. As I looked down I could see Bobby Brown, Babyface, Whitney Houston and Aretha Franklin in the front row, then I noticed George Michael and Chaka Khan. It was like a musical *Who's Who* but they seemed to love 'Back for Good'. As I finished there was some applause, and even a few woo woos from the front third of the audience.

Pesh, pesh, boom, pesh, pesh – I was frozen. I didn't know what to do as I desperately tried to work out where to come in. It was, of course, the wrong place – it wasn't the verse at all but the bridge. Not knowing the song meant I couldn't fast forward and work out how to redeem the situation. I was lost. I went from one side of the stage to the other, feeling and looking like a total prat. Nine minutes is a slow death on stage and as it neared the end it went into a fade. The audience offered nothing, not a sound. I walked off the stage to the sound of my own footsteps.

Somewhere in my head I could hear Clive introducing the next artist. Simultaneously I was aware that for the first time that day I was completely alone – not a flunky or plant pot to be seen. My suitbag and holdall were there and I picked them up and walked out of the Ritz. I had been given a ticket for my car and driver which I handed to the doorman.

'Your car will be about ten minutes.'

'You know what, mate, I can't be bothered to wait.'

Despite the fact that it was pouring with rain I walked back to my hotel. I got soaked – to say I hardly noticed would be a bit dramatic, but I sure as shit didn't care. As I walked I knew it was all over. Back in my room I just sat there – I've never heard so much silence in New York.

12

I'm Not Invincible

14 April 1998

I'm flying back to the UK after spending months doing radio breakfast shows, drive-time shows, mid-morning shows, weekend shows – just about every radio show in every state in America. What's made it worse is that my PA and mate Chris Healey has not been with me. The label thought it would be too expensive to take him, and instead agreed to fly me First Class. But I reckon this could be the last time – we didn't get a record higher than 42 in the Hot 100 all the time I was there. My contact in the UK tells me that it's going be a rough ride from this point on as Robbie is being loved by all and playing the press game very well. 'Let Me Entertain You' has been in the charts for weeks. They tell me not to think about him, but I need to; I need to think how I'm going to get my audience back.

I'm leaving America early. I should have been there for another two months. Two days ago I was in a radio station in Spokane – like where the fuck is that? – when I lost it. 'Who else is doing this crap?' I complained, 'We're up at 5 a.m. every morning doing these shitty shows that no one listens to.'

My promo guy Ken pointed to a board on the wall that detailed who else was due at the station to do the breakfast show for the rest of that week. Tuesday: Jewel. Wednesday: Sarah McLachlan. Thursday: Faith Hill. Friday: Puff Daddy. Shit, shit and shit again. This is how you sell records in America. I was actually lucky *to be on this show. To bring it home to me I got a call when I was on air from a British woman.*

'Oh my God, what the hell are you doing in Spokane? People here have no idea how big you are in Britain.'

That's when I knew I can't do this. I miss Dawn and home too much. I want to be in my beautiful house which I haven't seen for months. I need to go and get my career at home back on track. I need to make a new record and put Robbie back in his place. He's been having a free ride all this time.

Finally in June 1997, eleven months after 'Forever Love' had topped the charts, my album, *Open Road*, came out. With Clive's help I had made an album for the American market with barely a thought for the UK. The hiatus had taken all the steam out of my career, not to mention knocking my confidence. I absolutely believe in the power that confidence gives: it aids creativity, allows you to overcome almost any obstacle and is an essential ingredient in the alchemy of pop.

I know now, and I knew then, that the album wasn't my best work; people bought into the record because they were still interested in me. The album did pretty well – it sold over two million copies around the world – but it was a long way from where I needed or wanted to be. In a sense the reviews of the album proved that my instincts had been right. One British paper described it as an album of 'thuddingly dull ballads and lacklustre cover versions aimed at the US market'; it sounded, they said, like 'the feeble ramblings of a washed-up old crooner in a cardigan'. Ouch!

Right after the album, 'So Help Me Girl' was released and made No. 11 on the singles chart. Robbie's third single, which came out the same week as mine, got a few places higher. But

Rob's single was not the third single from an already released album and he was busy working his career and profile in Britain. I was in a corporate holding pattern and close to slipping off the radar.

Despite the Grammys, despite everything, Clive was not yet finished with me. Whatever I thought about his ideas for me, I have to say that he cared. There's no question in my mind that he believed I was worth it. When I signed to his label he gave me his direct line and I could call up day or night to speak to him. He'd always take my call, listen and try to deal with things. Having put me to work writing with some of the best in the business, he remained focused on me being big in the USA. When 'So Help Me Girl' came out in the USA I went back to New York and then on to California. This was the start of weeks and weeks in America, some spent working with other writing partners and producers that Clive had lined up, including Montell Jordan, Jermaine Dupree and Babyface, but the majority spent working America. I learned so much while I was there: how the charts work, how you get airplay and how you break records in the US, which basically involves packing your bag, getting on a plane and going to every city in every state.

On one of these promo trips, having refused to let me take my old pal Chris Healey to the US, Arista assigned me a minder called Ken Laine. He was a real promo guy: loud and proud, untroubled by either boundaries or intuition. Because Ken Laine sounded like John Wayne I used to call him John. It was the kind of thing that would have become a running gag in Take That, and Chris would have found it hilarious, but every time I said, 'Hey, John' he'd say, 'It's Ken.'

This went on for months, day in day out.

Ken, or John, was some travelling companion. He had a remarkable ability to embarrass me on a daily and sometimes even hourly basis. We were in Seattle with an hour to spare, so we decided to visit a record shop. In the singles department I saw a guy picking my single off the rack. I slowly backed away so as not to disturb him and I was half an aisle away when I heard John Wayne say, 'Hey, man, are you buying that? Wait one minute, my friend, the artist's here. Hey, Gary, GARY, get over here! This dude is buying your single!'

I couldn't get to the exit. He'd got me. He dragged me back to introduce me to the by now red-faced guy. Then to top it all, out came John Wayne's camera. 'Wait till they see these in the office!'

To be fair, John had a shit job. He was doomed to spend months with a miserable British bastard who moaned constantly and didn't want to do anything, least of all what he needed me to do. He was miles away from his family, getting grief from his boss because the single wasn't being played on all stations, or as it turned out any, and yet, despite everything, he seemed happy.

He came to see me off at the airport and say goodbye, and probably good riddance.

'Well, thank you for being part of the end of my career. See you, John' were my parting words.

'It's Ken!'

Furious at having had to travel every inch of America when I could have been at home promoting my single, I parted ways with Simon Fuller. I was used to Nigel's 100 per cent support, while Simon was hardly ever around. Perhaps I hadn't appreciated the value of Nigel's exclusive focus on us. Once the Spice Girls took off and I began reading about Simon brokering five-million-dollar deals with Pepsi-Cola, I realised what I was missing. It was a curious time, summed up for me when the Spice Girls movie came out at the end of 1997 – with a scene where they take a pop at me. Simon couldn't even protect me from his other acts. He was very fair, however, and only charged me for expenses.

I needed a new manager who was used to working with me and who understood what I was trying to do. I persuaded Kristina Kyriacou, then head of marketing at BMG, to come and work with me as *Open Road* was released. We set up GloBe Artist Management to handle my affairs both professional and personal, as I needed someone to take over where Simon Orange had left off. All too soon I realised my mistake: by taking Kristina out of BMG I had lost one of the few people at senior level in the UK who was a real champion of mine. However, even if I had had the best manager alive I was still doomed because by now Rob was really getting going.

To begin with, when all that bollocks started appearing in the press about Rob and me, how he hated me and how I'd ruined his life, the media hoopla didn't matter much. None of the press helped Rob's career until 'Angels' came along and through most of 1996 and 1997 Rob's career was, like mine, stalling; neither of us had hit the premier league.

The first time I heard 'Angels' was at the end of November 1997. I was in Frankfurt with Chris Healey for a TV show and we were backstage when Rob's video came on. For the next four minutes or so I stood and stared at the screen, watching his beautiful video. When it finished Chris said, 'That's pretty good, isn't it?'

'Chris, it's very, very good and that's what's worrying me.'

At that moment I was both happy and sad. Sad because I didn't have anything like 'Angels' in the bag and happy because I thought that maybe now Rob had a smash hit on the way, he would leave me alone.

I couldn't have been more wrong. What would I have done if I had been in Rob's shoes? I hope that either I would never have mentioned his name again, or that I'd have thrown him a lifeline every so often; but Rob used me in the worst kind of way. It seemed like whenever he had nothing else to say in an interview, he would toss out a Gary Barlow put-down. Even during 2005 he was still pulling them out of the hat. I'll never forget watching the BRITs and seeing David Walliams and Matt Lucas dressed up as Howard and I to present an award to Robbie. Quick as a flash

Robbie said, 'But I was the talented one.' Every time Rob had another hit I thought, perhaps it will end now, but it never did. Don't get me wrong, I had, and have, the competitive instinct, too. When I released my first two singles and they went in at No. 1 – Rob's first two went in at No. 2 – I was out there celebrating. But I like to think I'd have known when to stop.

Because the whole thing was conducted in the papers rather than face to face, there was no escaping it. I'd walk down a street and someone would say, 'How's Robbie then?' Or go into a shop and the assistant would put on one of Robbie's tracks. I knew I was the butt of Rob's jokes, but soon it felt like I became the butt of everyone else's too. It would almost have been better if we'd had a proper stand-up fight: I'd rather have had it out face to face and given him a bloody nose – I could have taken it on the chin much better. Instead I felt as if I'd been stitched up, though it was hard to know whether by the press or by Rob.

In December 1997 I played the Concert of Hope and Rob was there. The press claimed we had made up, in fact we hardly had a chance to talk to each other, and in any event there was a camera crew following me around. It was the last time we spoke until we were staying in the Conrad Hotel in May 2006.

While 'Angels' remained in the singles charts for most of the winter of 1998, I slogged around the world promoting *Open Road* anywhere and everywhere. I went to the Far East for several weeks of promotion. Besides Tokyo and Kuala Lumpur I went to Korea. I was at Seoul airport waiting to board a flight to Singapore and was talking to several young girl fans when I noticed one of those electric cars coming towards us; we were in its path so I said to the girls, 'Watch your back.'

They all replied, singing in unison, 'Watch your back for good!' It was a truly funny moment during a period where most things only seem funny in retrospect.

Clive continued to suggest people I could work with to come

up with that elusive magic record. Every time I tried writing with someone and it didn't work out as well as we'd hoped, it would chip away at my confidence. They didn't just drain my self-belief where songwriting was concerned, it was more personal than that. I would arrive in New York for a photo shoot and be met by someone from Arista's promo department. We would get in the car, and on the way into the city promo-man would get on his mobile and I'd hear him say. 'Yes, Sean, he's heavy again.'

Believe me, they'd seen nothing yet.

Quite early on I could feel that my second album was never going to work. I was being pushed and pulled in every direction, and told, 'You should be this . . . you should be that . . .' I got to the point where I just thought, who am I? What is this music I'm making? And yet I had to see it through, for myself as well as contractually. If I had backed away from it I would always have wondered what might have been. But it was without doubt the most stressful time of my life – I'd lie awake at night, imagining the crash down the road, anticipating the pile-up and knowing I was heading towards it.

In March 1998 I embarked on my first UK tour since leaving Take That. Danny Betesh had booked a dozen dates, including the Royal Albert Hall and London's Hammersmith Apollo. When they went on sale in the late summer of the previous year they had sold out almost immediately, so I was really looking forward to them. Before the UK dates I also played throughout Europe, and being back on stage, doing what I had spent the majority of my adult life doing, helped lift my spirits.

With a successful tour behind me, and in anticipation of my new album, we scheduled more dates for later in the year. But with the subsequent hold-ups with the second album, the gigs were rescheduled for April 1999 and then postponed a second time. They finally took place in December 1999, and with all the delays they sold poorly.

Shortly before starting the tour I did an interview with the *Sun*. I told them the private jets and limos were gone; I was just going to be a road rat with the rest of the band and travel on the tour bus. I joked and said, 'It isn't all hardship because I've bought myself a £1,700 Versace duvet for my bunk.' The *Sun* loved the story and were going to run it as part of a double-page feature the following Monday. In between I did another interview with the *News of the World* and mentioned the duvet again. They then got a picture of a Versace duvet and ran the story the day before the *Sun*, upstaging them. The *Sun* were furious and I knew straight away I had made a big mistake. I worked hard to make it up to them by giving them exclusives and competition giveaways but afterwards I wondered if I had contributed to my own bad press.

Having been so well supported by them throughout the Take That years and the early part of my solo career, it came as a shock as well as a disappointment when the papers turned from friend to foe. Nigel had often told us in the early days, 'If you've only shaken their hands once, go back and do it again; make sure the press knows who you are and like you.' But I had yet to learn how to manipulate the press nineties-style. Now it seemed like all the press wanted was flaws and redemption, which Robbie offered in spades.

I did an interview with the new showbiz editor of the *Sun*, Dominic Mohan, and it was a disaster. I answered a question in the middle of the interview about drugs, and instead of it featuring as a small part of the bigger interview, they made it a front-page story, twisting the whole thing around: TAKE THAT GARY'S DRUGS SHAME. I BINGED ON COKE AND ECSTASY ran the headline, alongside an ancient picture of me looking fresh-faced and about sixteen. It made me sound like I was trying to shake off my clean-cut image. From then on it felt like open season. Each time my name was mentioned it would be coupled with 'pop flop' or 'has been'. The bile and vitriol worried me, and I wondered what I'd done to deserve it, but I didn't comment. I kept my mouth closed, soldiered on and in doing so lost the public's sympathy.

The press loved Robbie for his frailties. In September 1998 'Let Me Entertain You' entered the charts at No. 3, while *Life Thru A Lens* stayed in the charts for the whole of 1998, and yet despite this success Robbie continued to be seen as the troubled artist. People love that, especially here in the UK and his greatest weakness became the most attractive thing about him and a big strength. It was hard at that point not to wonder if Robbie was hyping up his drugs problem because I had seen so little evidence of it when we were in the band. If that makes Rob sound manipulative, well he is.

The difficulty for me was that by virtue of his downs Robbie was on the up. He was always a lot more modern than me, a lot cooler, and maybe I was jealous because I wanted to be cool – I don't mind admitting it but I didn't want to pay the price Robbie seemed to be paying. If that meant I had to be the boring one, then so be it. I had things in my life that I wanted to protect, above all else my relationship with Dawn.

I had all these plans for how I would ask Dawn to marry me. I was going to propose in New York, but in the end I couldn't wait. I popped the question – no ring, no getting down on one knee – as we were waiting for a Chinese takeaway to arrive at our flat in London. How crap is that? It was more of an agreement than a question. I want to do it again – I want to take her to Vegas and renew our vows, maybe for our tenth anniversary, and get it right this time.

Robbie or no Robbie, the stories continued to run unprompted. In the autumn of 1998 I went to a lunch party at the Ivy organised by Elton for David Furnish's birthday. I was seated at the opposite end of a table from George Michael. George sat there with a cap pulled down low over his face the whole way through lunch. I said hello and he blanked me, but I didn't make much of it. I had to leave early to rehearse at the Albert Hall because that evening it was Elton's Aids gala and I was doing a duet with Ronan Keating.

The following morning there was something in the papers about a feud between George and me. What feud? I didn't get it until I found out about an interview he'd done with Q magazine in which he'd said, 'Gary Barlow doesn't have any talent.' What did I ever do to him other than admire *his* talent? Apparently a few weeks later George went on London's Capital Radio to apologise.

Elton knew none of this until after the lunch, and when the article appeared he called me and said he was playing a show in Manchester and would I like to go on stage to sing with him? My mum and dad were going to the show, but they didn't know I was appearing until Elton said, 'Ladies and gentlemen, I want to bring on stage now a great friend of mine, Mr Gary Barlow.' And I went on and sang 'Sacrifice' with him.

At the start of 1999 I was still hoping that my career would magically be reinvigorated. I appeared on Michael Parkinson's TV show at the end of January performing 'Stronger', a song I'd written with Graham Gouldman from 10CC. The only problem with that was it would be six months before it was released in the UK, and in the meantime Robbie's 'Strong' was released. You can imagine what the papers made of those titles.

My second solo album was a long way from finished so I returned to America a couple more times. There was one advantage to Clive's relentless plans for coast-to-coast coverage. A statement came through one day about air miles. I phoned up and asked, 'What are these air miles on my card?'

'Let me just have a look at your account, Mr Barlow. Oh, you have 78,000 air miles.'

'What does that mean? I'm going to New York in a couple of weeks, can you get me there?'

'How many passengers will there be?'

'Four.' Dawn, myself, my mum and dad.

'We can fly you there First Class return and you'll still have 48,000 air miles left over.'

That's me all over – plenty of money in the bank but I still love a freebie. Thank you, Clive!

We had a brilliant few days eating our way round the city, and when it was time for my mum and dad to fly home, Dawn and I waved them off in a cab and ran straight round to Tiffany's to buy a ring.

When 'Stronger' finally came out it redefined disappointment. Where I had been used to doing national TV, the Radio One *Breakfast Show* and top level stuff, I was reduced to Cardiff's Red Dragon road show and other similar gigs throughout the summer season – the kind of gigs Take That were doing in 1991 before we had a record deal. I didn't say much, but I took it very hard and retreated into myself. I stopped taking Chris Healey places with me because I was too embarrassed to have anyone there watching. And I noticed that it worked both ways: people had stopped talking to me about how my career was going. No one needed to.

By the Autumn BMG had lined up 'For All That You Want' as my second single from the album. It didn't even make the Top Twenty, despite me doing the National Lottery TV show and a live gig with Radio Two in Sheffield.

But it wasn't all bad. I managed to achieve one of my lifelong ambitions, one of the few left in my Filofax: on 5 September 1999 I turned on Blackpool's lights. Being a northern lad, Blackpool matters to me; it's one of my favourite places, probably because I used to go there so much as a kid. Maybe it reminds me of the beginnings of my success as a solo artist, but whatever it is I LOVE it.

When you arrive in Blackpool and pull up at the first set of traffic lights the first thing you're likely to see is a woman with tattoos all over her. If you see a woman over thirty pushing a pram she's probably the grandma, that's the kind of place it is. Radio

Two had phoned and asked if I would like to do the honours and I was met outside Blackpool and given a police escort all the way up the prom. When I was introduced to the people organising the event they told me that there were a couple of other artists, including Martine McCutcheon, who were going to turn the lights on with me.

'I'm sorry, that's not the deal,' I said, suddenly climbing on my high horse. 'I don't care if I'm first on the bill or don't sing at all, but I want to pull that lever all by myself. In fact, if I don't I'm going home.' How mature.

I think they may have had to telephone Terry Wogan to ask his permission, but whatever they did to make it happen, I had my moment.

As I was driving back out of Blackpool accompanied by my police escort – all seven of them – I suddenly realised that I was missing something. I couldn't leave Blackpool without having fish and chips.

'Hey up, I haven't had my fish and chips,' I said to the driver.

We pulled over and the police motorcyclist drew alongside. ' 'Scuse me, mate,' says the driver, 'he wants fish and chips,'

'What?'

'He wants fish and chips.'

'He wants fish and chips,' said the policeman into his microphone.

'OK,' I heard him say. 'OK, follow me.'

We swung around and soon pulled up outside a fish and chip shop – oddly enough it was the one I usually go to. The limo and seven police bikes with flashing lights were all parked outside while the driver went in to get my fish and chips. And yes, they were delicious.

The press's final nail in my career coffin was a piece in *Private Eye* that I never even saw. It was a memo circulated around BMG, suggesting that it was time they 'rebranded the product' – the product being me. They wanted to give me a more laddish image and talked about my love of Grand Prix racing and other things that were designed to give me street cred and cool. Instead it made me look like a puppet and the label look controlling. While I don't think all my fans were *Private Eye* readers, it contributed to my sense that people in the industry were starting to write me off. Kristina, my manager, was struggling to change minds already closed by the media backlash against me. Years later she wrote to me in an email: 'Was there anything either of us could have done? On reflection I think we both know that that no matter what you recorded and wrote, and no matter what "spin" I put on it, the situation was completely out of our control . . . The pressure on you was enormous! So much of what happened was completely unnecessary, grossly unfair and completely impossible to respond to.'

Later that year, before the release of my second album in October 1999, BMG were forced to issue a statement about my future.

> We are currently preparing the next single release, 'Lie To Me', which will follow his new album *Twelve Months, Eleven Days* . . . Gary is a very important artist on the BMG roster and we look forward to a long and fruitful relationship with him.

It felt like a massive, very public put-down. Having meant so much to that label in the past they now had to defend my reputation. While the cycle of pop means there is always a younger, faster, better model coming up, it still hurts like hell. It makes you realise what an amazing job Elton and a handful of others have done in maintaining their careers at the top.

At BMG it seemed that anyone who had any history with me was either working on other projects or had been fired. Nick

Going solo: 'Open Road', 1996

Above: Delamere Manor

Right: 12 January 2000. Dawn and I snuck off and got married in Nevis in the Carribean

Above: Little and large: Dan and me in Hawaii

Right: Dawn and the little rascals

We're back, 2006

KEY103
KEY103
Beer Tent
Beer Tent

Raymonde had elected to work with Mark on his solo career, so my A&R man was Simon Cowell. Having always got on with Simon, I was happy to work with him, but Simon's view was that I should have made another 'Forever Love', while I wanted to move on. To be honest, though, anyone would have failed me on *Twelve Months*; I failed myself. As you can tell from the title, it took an age to make and it cost me a small fortune – and I'd be the first to say that it doesn't sound like £800,000 well spent. I had gone from being someone who worked quickly to someone who seemed incapable of finishing anything. There is a relationship between speed and creativity, there's no question about it. If pop music takes that long to make, it's no longer pop. The whole point of pop is that it's in the here and now, it captures the moment. It's not just about fashion and being on the cutting edge, it's more about immediacy and capturing the essence of what you do.

When the album was finished Simon called Nicki C. and asked her to come to his office to listen to it. Nicki was left there alone for an hour listening to the album and when it was over she was called into a meeting and told that if she didn't have any ideas on how to promote it they would get someone else to work on it. Nicki was furious, being one of the few people left at the label who had worked with me from the outset. She had endured girls spitting at her in the early days of the band, been called vile names when we were huge – and been pivotal to our success. She said that unless she was working on my album she would quit – she resigned later that day.

Even before *Twelve Months, Eleven Days* came out and spent a mere seven days in the charts, I knew it was going to bomb. It was nothing to do with it being good or bad, although I know it's far from my best work. But even if I had had ten 'Angels' on that album it still would have sunk without trace. My visibility was so low I'd lost touch with my audience and they'd lost touch with me.

There's something awful about waiting for the inevitable. I felt alone, with no champion at the label, no friends in the media and no effective management – even Chris Healey had moved on. The power of hindsight allows me to rationalise all of this, and now it doesn't matter, but back then it was devastating.

Of course Rob kicked me while I was down. In an interview he said that he had bought my record but took it back because it was crap. Why would anyone as successful as Rob was then bother saying that? Why did he so want to make me unhappy? I know the insecurities fame brings, and I suppose that explains, in part at least, why he did it, but he was a shit nonetheless.

To escape the media flak I went with Howard to Dubai to take part in a go-cart race – anything to avoid reading or hearing the slights in the press. I got back to hear that 'Lie To Me', my next single, had been pulled from release. With that I embarked on my final solo tour in the run-up to Christmas. It wasn't looking good.

On 12 January 2000 Dawn and I got married in Nevis in the Caribbean. It was no big bash, in fact, I think Dawn and I spent all of half an hour planning it.

We'd sat down to discuss the wedding, and had started talking about marquees on the lawn when we worked out that with the size of Delamere we'd need 150 security men.

'Forget it,' said Dawn. 'Gary, I want to enjoy the day, for it to be our day and not everyone else's.' As usual she was right.

'Why don't we do what my brother did when he got married?'

Ian and Lisa had gone to the Caribbean to tie the knot, so that's what we did too. It was just our mums, dads and brothers. We talked about who should be my best man.

'You know, Dawn, I want my dad to do it,' I said.

The wedding was very low key in a small resort where Dawn and I spent a week before everyone else arrived. Dawn's brother designed her dress and I had suits made for my dad and me on

Savile Row. On the morning of the wedding we received a lot of press calls, so we ended up bunging our clothes into a bag and sneaking into the clubhouse, which was where we eventually got married. We changed in the toilets, got married, changed back and then went out for dinner. That's why, when you see pictures of me on my wedding day, I'm carrying a suitbag! Afterwards Dawn and I flew to the K Club on Barbuda for our honeymoon. It was paradise, but all week long Dawn kept saying, 'It was beautiful, but I wish we'd had a party.'

I had been arranging it since November. While we were on honeymoon the mums did the family guest lists and a friend of mine and a friend of Dawn's organised the rest. When we touched down in London we were knackered and went straight to our flat in London, then later we took the train to Manchester.

Dawn's friend's words were ringing in my ears: 'Make sure Dawn has some kind of warning so she looks the part.' But all Dawn wanted to do was sleep. I was down in the smoking carriage phoning to check the security guards had arrived, the marquee was up, the drink had arrived . . . Between napping in London and dozing on the train, Dawn must have slept on and off for twelve hours. She had a nice sleep crease down one cheek, and looked kind of groggy.

'Babe, could you go and sort your make-up out? You look a bit of a wreck,' I said.

'I just want to go home to my bed,' said Dawn, putting her head back down.

'I'm your bloody husband, please, just do it.'

She did and of course she looked gorgeous. When we arrived at the station a car picked us up, and as we drove through the gates at Delamere I kissed her so she wouldn't see we were going in the wrong direction. Instead of going to the house the car drew up outside a marquee in the grounds where 200 guests were waiting.

It was really relaxed, with everyone in jeans, and all the band were there, except for Rob and Nigel – no celebrities. Frodsham's finest caterers served meat and potato pie followed by apple crumble and Howard as the DJ spun dance records all night. It couldn't have been more perfect.

It wasn't long before reality knocked at my door. Granada Television called to ask me to dinner; they had something big for me to consider. I thought it was to talk about a music series, but instead they offered me a part in *Heartbeat*. It could at least have been *Corrie*! I thought it might help me recapture middle England, but it was a disaster. I played the part of a soldier, my hair styled into a duck's arse quiff, who is picked up by Bill Maynard's character, and as we're driving in his car I tell him stories about my army life. The programme ended with me getting arrested, which proved to be just the opening the reviewers needed. Almost every newspaper carried a review on the Monday, and everyone had a different way of saying I was crap – and you won't find me arguing with them.

It was the day after the episode went out that I got the call telling me I'd been dropped.

13

Writing It Out

April 2000

This is it. I've reached it, the place that people talk about. The trouble is that people talk about it after they've been here – after they've got over it, survived and returned to tell the tale. It doesn't seem half as bad with hindsight. But when you're in the middle of it – right here, right now – it's shit.

I'm slobbing about, unshaven, in the same bloody tracksuit every day. No one calls or stops by, and I wouldn't want to see them if they did. I'm smoking a pack of Marlborough Lights, a packet of Silk Cut Ultra and probably fifteen spliffs most days – but who's counting? At the end of the night I only smoke half my last joint so that when I wake up I can have the other half before reality sets in. One half of my brain really likes this existence and the other half is really disgusted and disappointed with myself. Who ever said grass made you creative was talking bollocks.

The only time I half straighten up is when Dawn comes home from work. As soon as she leaves I fall back into this never-ending cycle. I want to work, I just can't get anything together. I'm spending my days going nowhere. What used to take about ten minutes now takes me all day, and most of the night. I'm going to bed, or falling asleep in the studio, at about 4.30 a.m. By the time I wake up it's usually midday. I find myself studying my old songs, their structure, and their lyrics, just to try and find the art I've so completely lost.

I can't stop crying. Just when I think I've finished, I start again. I'm only pulling myself together for Dawn's phone calls. I wish I could write something – but I don't want to sit at the piano in case it's the same as last time. Instead I'm watching its silence. How can something go from being so easy to virtually fucking impossible?

Five months after I was dropped by BMG, on 16 August 2000, our son Daniel was born. Talk about putting a new perspective on things. Dan was, after Dawn, the best thing that ever happened to me. It was the strangest time – to have something totally fantastic and life-changing happening just as another part of your life is going in a direction you really don't want it to. If I hadn't been dropped I would have still been recording and performing, it's what I love and live for, but Dan's arrival took my mind off the fact that all that was gone. My career had vanished almost overnight, but everything in my home life was wonderful.

I remember getting home from the hospital at 2 a.m. and how quiet and dark it seemed driving through the gates of Delamere after the drama and excitement, worry and joy of the hospital. I think it would be fair to say Dan's birth wasn't a bed of roses – especially not for Dawn. It was a bit of a horror show, a lot of waiting and a lot of blood. Poor Dawn spent twenty-four hours in labour and Dan was a big 'un at 9lbs 1½ oz. Up until the last hour or so Dawn was so calm and loving to me, then all of a sudden cavewoman took over – us men were out of the picture and it was face to face with Mother Nature! But by the time I left the hospital, she was beaming, with Dan red and wrinkly and swaddled up in the plastic cot beside her bed. I knew she'd be a great mum. Two weeks after Dawn and I got together I told her that one day we'd have a boy called Daniel. Now here he was. I wanted to call the world and announce it, even though the world was sleeping. It was the first time in months I had some good news to tell.

That day I was dropped from the label I had to face up to what I had known was coming for the previous eighteen months. After my humiliation at Clive's pre-Grammy party, everything had changed. When I got back there had been no calls, nothing from anyone in Arista. Neither Clive nor Simon Fuller ever mentioned that night. The reports must have been so bad that no one dared bring it up. From the outside the music business looks so together, so professional, but that night it was chaotic; I've told people that story since and found myself nearly in tears. It was failure on an enormous level from which I didn't recover until November 2005. It felt then like the end of everything, as if the dream was over. I continued working on my two solo albums, I kept up the show, but my approach after that day was very different. Everything became tentative. I'd go on TV shows – shows that I would have dominated in the past – and be petrified before I walked on. I took on board everything that anyone said about my albums even if it went against my instincts. It was like somebody had reached in and pulled out a whole load of machinery that was vital to who I am.

When BMG finally pulled the plug, I went home to Delamere, drew up the bridge on my fortress, and tried to work out what to do with my life. The first thing I did was nothing. There are people who have fallen into deeper depressions but for me to come to a full stop was a big thing.

Most people, when things are going badly, need their friends around them. Not me. I wanted to close the door and be left alone. There was a four-month patch where I didn't leave the house once. Nobody came by and I didn't want them to either.

When I'd bought Delamere it was as if I became head of the family – and I'm the youngest. I'd taken care of everything – a house for mum and dad, a house for Ian and Lisa – and had only let them see the good bits; now there was no hiding the fact that things weren't going well. My family rallied round. Dawn could see I was finding things difficult but she said nothing, confident that I would find my own way out of this. My mum, though, took my negative press very badly and found it hard to see me vulnerable. According to her I deserved everything good that happened. I'd worked so hard for it, how come things had gone wrong?

During this period I occasionally had conversations with people about a new record deal, but it was clear that neither they nor I had our hearts in it. There was one practical issue that needed addressing, however – my deal with Virgin Publishing. EMI Publishing had bought them out, and while there were still people there who tried hard for me, I felt I needed a change. It made sense to look for a new deal, but would anyone want me? I talked with Celia McCamley at Sony Publishing and liked her approach.

'Gary, you're at a crossroads,' she said, 'and you need to work with someone who's dedicated to making it happen. I'm going to work my arse off for you.'

Her first move was to get me writing *with* people and *for* people, doing what any good publisher should do, and I even began having some positive thoughts about a career as a writer.

With my state-of-the-art studio, track record for hit singles and years spent working with what seemed like every producer and songwriter in the business, I was all set up to write for other people. I worked with both Steps and Victoria Beckham at this point, and though it may not have been my best work because my confidence was at such a low ebb, at least things were starting to happen.

Then I got a call from the manager of Steps: 'I've had one of the papers on the phone, Gary, and they've told me that if we use any of your songs on the new album they'll refuse to put the band in the paper. I'm afraid we'll have to stop working together, Gary. I need the press on my side.'

Another paper had asked Victoria Beckham if she was working with me and reported that she had denied it. If that's the case then quite what she was doing at my house, in my studio, I'm not sure. David used to come and pick her up after we'd finished! All of this made me feel like a leper. People were obviously embarrassed even to be associated with me. And then there was the most devastating blow of all. Madame Tussauds announced that they were melting down my waxwork dummy: they needed the wax to make Britney Spears. Why only Britney? They could have made the whole of Destiny's Child.

With all the zeal in the world, Celia was struggling to find me work. One day we met up and she said, 'Gary, we have a problem. I've been sending your songs to labels and they've been bouncing them back to me. They won't even listen to them – it's got to the point where I don't put your name on the tapes.'

You can imagine how that made me feel. If my career going into meltdown felt bad, this was even worse. People were saying I had no future, no chance of earning a living, but most of all they were saying I was a rubbish songwriter. Celia was still talking, but I was oblivious and only caught the end of her sentence.

'. . . Gary, the only thing you can do is leave the country.'

'What? Leave the country? Why? Dan's only a baby. What do you mean?'

'I think it would make sense for you to get away and work somewhere else for a bit. Britain needs to forget about you.'

'But I don't want to be forgotten!'

'Gary, you have no choice. As a songwriter here in Britain you're dead. I have three places you can go: Nashville, New York or Los Angeles.'

I went home to talk to Dawn.

'Let's go to LA,' she said quickly. 'Dan's no problem, he's a baby, so there's no schooling to worry about.'

When I called Celia back she immediately said, 'Just get yourself there and call our office. I'll have everything set up for you. I've already mentioned that you might be coming and the LA office is excited about having you around.'

Sony helped me find an apartment and within six weeks we were off – it felt like a new start after all the bad vibes at home. To celebrate, I gave up smoking on the flight, going from forty a day to nothing – although I kept a pack in my pocket, untouched, as my talisman. I felt proud of that move.

It turned out to be a trip full of challenges and surprises. When we arrived we found that Sony had arranged a beautiful apartment, Sea Colony II on Neilson Way, with a living room that looked out on to the ocean. We'd brought two suitcases and nothing else, but we loved the fact that we weren't rattling around that huge house in Cheshire.

'Gary, I'm off to the supermarket.'

'Do you know what? I'll come with you.'

We even held hands as we walked around: we were free to do as we liked for the first time in years. When Dawn was at the checkout I was still going up and down the aisles, looking at what you could buy. I remember being fascinated by the choice of toothpaste – a lot changes in ten years. About the only place I was recognised was on Sunset Boulevard, where there were Brits wandering around. The relief of living in Santa Monica, where Dawn and I didn't have to check round every corner to see if there was a cameraman waiting, was just brilliant and it helped rebuild my confidence. After a few weeks I thought I should get down to work and went into Sony's office on Colorado Avenue. The first people I met were Jim Vellutato and a lady named Katherine Carey, who both gave me a lovely welcome. It was just what I needed.

'We've set up meetings for you with some of our writers who are fans of yours and who would be interested in working with you.'

Fans? 'I didn't know that was going to happen.'

'That's not all, Gary. There are people at Warner Publishing who want to work with you, too.'

Within a week I had a diary full of dates with songwriters, and our six-week trip to California was soon extended to twelve weeks. Best of all, I discovered writing again. And the people I was working with weren't writing for Steps, they were aiming a lot higher in the musical stakes.

This time I could appreciate American songwriting from the

other side. In Britain it's a background role, but over there songwriting is a serious profession, something with real value. In LA people don't laugh at you when you say you're a songwriter or a film producer or whatever, it's a city with a real creative vibe.

My mum and dad came to visit and we began to make friends with people locally. Almost without trying we started carving out a new life for ourselves. Most of all it was enjoyable. Before we left England, going to a restaurant had become a huge logistical nightmare; now we ate our way round Los Angeles. I think that's when I really became a foodie. I don't think we used the kitchen in the apartment for anything more than the odd breakfast – the labels were still on the pans. It wasn't us being lazy, it was just that we could go out and not be hassled.

One day I got a call from Eliot Kennedy from Five Boys Productions in Sheffield, who I'd worked with on the second Take That album. He was in town to see some other songwriters and suggested we meet up. Eliot had been one of the few people who got in touch with me during the dark times – just to say hello and how are you – and he had also given me an opportunity when no one else had. Just before I left for Los Angeles he had asked me to work with a new band called Blue. Eliot arrived at my home studio at Delamere with a young songwriter named Tim Woodcock, and he and I worked on a track together. While we were in Los Angeles, Blue's album came out with my track, 'Girl I'll Never Understand' on it and went triple platinum.

Eliot and I went for dinner and almost immediately it reminded me of what I was missing from back home: a really good laugh. We started writing together while he was in Los Angeles. It was so easy – three songs in an afternoon, no big deal. Eliot is like me in that he writes melody and lyrics; he's a real bread-and-butter songwriter – and I mean that as a total compliment. Many of the writers I'd met in LA wrote either lyrics *or* melody, top line or track. I hadn't yet met any all-round songwriters.

Eliot went home and we kept in touch by phone and email while I continued working with various people in LA. One day in July I got a call from David Massey, a senior vice president at Sony Records. He was the son of Lulu's manager and he had tried to sign Take That in the USA but was pipped to the post by Clive Davis.

'Gary, I'm organising a writers' camp at Bearsville near Woodstock to which I'm inviting fifteen of the best songwriters from around the world and I'd like you to come. I want to get you all writing for our acts. Will you come?'

'Of course.'

That night I was chatting with Eliot online when he told me he'd been invited, too. The next morning I called David Massey's office to ask if we could work together.

'No problem, we'll put you together in the same writing group.'

Dawn and I had been making arrangements to fly home as our visas were about to expire, but instead I put Dawn and Dan on the flight to London and flew to New York and then on to Bearsville – I was due to fly home after I finished.

Bearsville turned out to be everything I hoped it would be – a really buzzy place to exchange ideas with writers and performers who were enthused by what they did. It gave me renewed impetus and at last I felt like I was getting back in touch with what I was good at. As the week was coming to an end David Massey pulled Eliot and me to one side and said, 'I've had a word with Tommy Mottola and Sony want to offer you two a production deal as writer/producers.'

Eliot and I hadn't even discussed working together. He was already a successful writer/producer with his own set-up back home. Maybe he wouldn't be up for it.

'Are you joking, Gary? Of course I want to work with you.'

I didn't have to be a solo act, I would have a partner – someone who made me laugh, whose talent I respected and who thought I could actually bring something to the party. My backstage phase was about to begin.

14

Backstage for Good?

When we were living in Los Angeles I made a list of people who, for different reasons, I wanted to contact when I got home. There were some I needed to apologise to for being a right pain when we'd worked together and others I just wanted to catch up with. At the top of the list were Nigel and the boys.

As soon as I got home in August 2001 I began working my way through my list. I had nothing specific to talk about, I'd just missed everyone. Even before we went to LA, the pressures of my doomed solo career had meant there hadn't been time to hang out with the boys. We all decided to meet up, and with some persuasion from Nigel we arranged to do it at his place. I think Jay even contacted Rob's agent to try to get him to come. I pulled up in the drive and there was NMS 1, Nigel's Porsche, alongside Jay's nice old Mercedes.

It should have felt weird – it had been more than five years since the band had split – but strangely it all felt quite normal. The four of us have the kind of relationship that springs back to the way it was whenever we see one another – we just start laughing and don't really know why. It's probably because we shared so much for so many years. Yet while everyone was joking about, I could see in their eyes that they were shocked at how much I'd changed. Living the good life in Los Angeles had piled the weight on. And, for some reason which must have seemed genius at the time, I had shaved my head. I thought it would make me look thinner, but in fact I looked like a big red tomato. Normally Jay would have been the one to say something; if I'd been slightly overweight he would have said, 'Look at you, you fat bastard!' The fact he said nothing was what really brought home to me how large I'd got. The only person who mentioned it was Chris Healey when I saw him a week or so later. 'You've chubbed up a bit' was his take on my fuller figure.

We sat around bantering and, once everyone finished staring at me, it became obvious that Nigel had something to say. He'd been hovering on the edge of his seat ever since we sat down. He had prepared a speech.

'Listen, lads, it's great to see you all. You know that documentary that was on Channel 4 last year?'

Of course we all knew about it, Nigel and Howard had both been in it and it painted a far from complimentary picture of us all. Nigel obviously felt like they'd done him down, which they had, and he wanted a chance to put the record straight.

'I think the time is right for us to make a documentary, don't you, lads?'

Immediately I stood up. I think I wanted to make my point as forcibly as I could.

'No. Listen, I've got to tell you all right now, I don't want to do a documentary. In fact, I don't ever want to be on the TV. Not now, not ever again.'

Nigel looked puzzled. It was as if he was thinking, why wouldn't you want to be on the TV again? surely it's something you were born to do? as if I had no choice. None of us had ever said, 'I'm not doing that' to him before, and I didn't leave it at that, either, I was very definite about it – it was quite an outburst.

'I'm telling you now, I don't want to do it. I'm never going to be in the public eye ever again.'

Needless to say it put something of a dampener on the

conversation. We had another cup of tea and then we all dispersed – Nigel couldn't wait to get rid of us. Having had his idea scotched he had no reason to have us hanging around. The whole meeting was typical Nigel: he can never do anything without an agenda. If he goes out for dinner, it's to do a deal; he never just meets someone to have a good time. And he certainly isn't big on small talk, in fact, when he hasn't got anything specific to tackle, conversation with Nigel is hard work. I left feeling a bit empty-handed, without quite knowing why.

Driving home, and for quite a while afterwards, I was perplexed, because my memory of the band and how we got on was very different from what had happened that day. I'd always thought it was unbelievable that five people who didn't know each other before they were thrown together managed to get on so well. For the six years we were together we had looked after and loved each other. I enjoyed their company, their warmth and their humour, I loved everything about being in that band. When we were on the road, if Jay was busy I'd go to Mark's room, and if he was busy I'd go to Howard's or Rob's room; once we had been inseparable. It was just like living on the estate when I was a kid. All the lads are nice people who are good to be around and all of them have infectious characters. Since leaving the band, the way things had panned out with Rob had made me question everything I'd believed in: our friendship, my talent, the way things had been. I used to think, what the fuck did I ever do to him? but I had always thought my friendship with the other lads was still intact.

It wasn't on the drive home, but a few days later that it dawned on me. There was something both Jay and Mark hadn't said: they'd been thinking something but they hadn't said it. I'm usually good at picking up vibes and something definitely hadn't felt right. But as I didn't see the lads again for a while I didn't dwell on it.

Eliot and I had established True North Productions, based at Delamere. He lived in Sheffield, so he drove over every day to work in the studio. We both got a huge kick out of the whole thing. Eliot, having started out writing songs in his bedroom like me, had ended up running a business, and had to some extent lost sight of being a songwriter. Coming to LA and working with me had reignited that flame. For me, working with Eliot gave me some much-needed credibility; because of him people were prepared to work with me. I felt like I had been offered a new direction and a new identity. Now I was Gary Barlow, songwriter, producer, husband and father. It was great to be over the apathy and hopelessness of the last few years.

But working with Eliot had its side effects, too. He's a big lad, six foot six, and he loves his food as much as I do. I'm five foot eight and only have to brush past a bag of chips to pile on the pounds. We'd have huge breakfasts and lunches, with loads of pastries, and I matched him butty for butty – an evil shared is a beautiful thing! Our weakness was sweets, but also portions. We'd eat the most enormous helpings. It felt great, after all those years of having to watch my weight in order to look good on stage, not to have to worry about being in front of a camera or in the public eye. Anyway being slim wouldn't make me a better songwriter. It was all about being relaxed and being myself – at least that's what I told myself.

The fat was a protective coating. As I got bigger I found I didn't need a hat or sunglasses, I had my disguise wrapped around me. If I was ordering something I would never give my name, I'd just say I'd pick it up and pay with cash. I didn't want them to recognise my name, see me and make the connection.

One day just before Christmas 2001, I was walking around the bed when Dawn said, 'Babe, I think you should go and see the doctor.'

I knew what she meant immediately. I was wheezy and out of breath with even the slightest exertion. It would take me three rolls to get off the bed and I was reduced to wearing XXXL tracksuits. But it was the first time Dawn had said anything. I looked down and all I could see was stomach. I hadn't dared stand on the scales, but I forced myself to do it. Sixteen stone eight. I booked an appointment.

The doctor put me on his scales, and according to them I was even heavier. 'Gary, I know you're aware that you need to lose a bit of weight,' he said 'but I have to inform you that you're clinically obese. Do you think that somewhere inside of you there could be some depression driving all this eating?'

He offered me help, but I was determined to do something about it on my own. He asked to see me again in three months' time. Having taken that all-important first step I was then 'papped' by the *Daily Mirror*'s photographers coming out of our local pub. The article included gems like 'Back for Pud' and 'Relight My Fryer'. Of course it hurt, but their writers are clever.

I faced the truth: the bigger I got, the smaller I felt inside. Hiding away for so long had changed me: I was fragile, vulnerable and unable to cope. My family background also trapped me; my parents are very proud of me, but I only know that because they tell other people – we're not a family that communicates much. When things got hard it would have been completely alien to me to go and see a therapist. I didn't like admitting weakness, or despair – I always wanted to be strong for everyone else.

I had found a way of coping with it all. I had kept myself together somehow and managed to get back on track, but I had paid a price. I didn't break down, become an alcoholic or an addict, but I suffered and I made others suffer with me, no one more than Dawn. I was painfully aware, looking at Dawn who is so beautiful, of what she had had to put up with living with me. It's only with Dawn's help that I have managed to become more open. I was angry with myself and determined to change.

So much about my life was fabulous. I had Dawn and Dan, and then in May 2002 Emily came along. With Dan's birth the labour was so traumatic that I can't remember what emotions I felt – mostly relief that he'd arrived and they were both OK, I think – but with Emily it was completely different. My family is full of boys in twos – Ian and I, Ian's Liam and Lewis, so we just presumed we'd have another boy. Emily was born in two hours – I was there doing the whole husband bit when out she popped. As she came out, the midwife practically threw her to me. I had her in my arms and was looking down at her as the midwife said, 'Oh, and by the way, it's a girl.'

'What?' I just lost it and started to cry. Dawn kept saying, 'What are you crying for? Look at the pain I'm in! Stop it, man! Pull yourself together!' But I just blubbed away.

'I've got a daughter! Brilliant!'

One of the great things about having the studio at home is that I get to savour every minute of the kids growing up. Their first steps, their first smiles, first words, first haircuts, I've been there for it all and I feel very, very privileged. I love being a parent and I never stop messing around and playing with them. I've got friends who are dads who, when we sit down for dinner are the furthest away from the kids, but I love being right next to them – I'll join in the colouring, I'll be daft with them. I'm very tactile with my kids and I'm always kissing them. I never had that at home, but I'll still be kissing them when they're fifty, I love it so much.

Professionally things were going much better by now. After the success of working with Blue before I went to LA, we got another crack with them on their third album, which is how 'Guilty', which became a big hit, came about. We also had a big slice of luck when David Massey called me about working with Lara Fabian, a Belgian-born multi-lingual singer signed to Sony. Our next call was to work with a sixteen-year-old Australian called Delta Goodrem and then after that Charlotte Church. Eliot also wanted to work with Donny Osmond, and we gave him his biggest hit in thirty years.

One of the best things that happened to me during this period was just after Mark won *Big Brother* in November 2002. I got a call from Island Records to say that Mark wanted to come and work with us. I've never asked Mark whether it was his idea, but it was a beautiful thing that he did and I was flattered beyond belief. 'Four

Minute Warning' came out of that and made No. 4 in the charts – it was Mark's first hit in six years. It's amazing to think that he joined Take That without much singing experience, never having written a song or played an instrument. Since leaving the band he's really worked on all of that and developed his voice and his career. Mark stayed with us at the house for a week while we made the record and we had a great time. Mark's always himself, he has time for everyone and is totally charming. It's easy to see why he was the most loved guy both in the band and on *Big Brother.*

Working with Eliot moved me up the production ladder, and one thing I learned from him was how to take bits and pieces of songs and work them into something better. However, I had to come to terms with an inevitable consequence of professional songwriting: once you start turning songwriting into a business you begin to lose something. I was in danger of becoming like some of those American writers Clive had sent me to work with; I found myself turning out formulaic songs in a bid to please the A&R man – but does he really know better than I do?

Of course I wanted to write hit records, and not just for the money – the excitement is just brilliant – but the sad thing for me as a songwriter is now that songs are products that have to hit sales targets, there are too many fingers in the songwriting pie. It used to be that one or two people wrote a song, but now there are often four, five or six names credited. Diane Warren's passionate, individualistic approach way is the best, writing by committee just drains the creativity out of the whole thing. The music business is constantly asking itself why the excitement has gone out of music, why kids aren't turned on by it like they used to be. It's the process. Records take for ever to make these days, and by the time the record eventually comes out everyone has forgotten why they made it in the first place. The music business has become more about business than show business. For Take That keeping the showbiz element has always been uppermost in the mix.

Despite this, if you'd ask me whether I missed performing then I would have told you, as I told Nigel and the boys, no, not at all, never again. But my real feelings about it were brought home not long after Emily was born. We'd been working with Donny Osmond in Salt Lake City, and things had gone so well that we'd finished early.

'I've got an idea,' I said to Eliot. 'Let's go to Vegas.'

Within an hour we had our flights booked. Donny said, 'Guys, if you're going to Vegas you have to see a Cirque du Soleil show called *O*.' He was so insistent he even booked us the tickets.

The show was incredible, a bizarre but wonderful mixture of sychronised swimming and acrobatics. It was full of humour and excitement, the staging was unbelievably technical and the music was amazing. Once it started I don't think I moved or breathed for twenty-five minutes. I could only gasp, and by the end, when all the cast walk forward and sink into the water, I leapt to my feet, applauding and crying. I must have seen the show seven times since then, and it gets me every time.

But that first time, as I left the theatre, I felt very churned up. It brought back to me the sheer joy of performing, the magic that happens when you really connect with your audience. On one level it took me back to how it had felt to be on stage with Take That. What it felt like to take an audience on a journey and have their emotions in your hand, to be able to make them laugh or cry. We'd had that in Take That. I'd had that in Take That, no matter how deeply I had buried it.

My confidence had taken too many knocks and to perform I need to feel wanted. When the label dropped me, I'd been offered pantos, West End shows and celebrity appearances but I turned them all down. I'm not thick-skinned enough to accept any old offer and go through the motions. When I said I never wanted to perform again, I believed it – I thought the desire would pass and I could be happy behind the scenes for ever. And yet the more I said it, the more aggressive I became. You don't have to be a shrink to see that I was in denial.

With Dawn's support and example I began to tackle my weight. I wish I could tell you I lost it in a week through some miracle diet, but sadly I lost it in the usual way: I ate less and exercised more. I took up running, hired a nutritionist and educated myself. I even tried the Atkins diet. You'd have thought that hanging out with someone as health-conscious as Jason all those years I'd have picked up something, but no. It took turning into a sixteen-stone jelly man to teach me what I should be eating. It was hard and bloody boring! My only problem was I plateaued – my goal was thirteen stone, but I got stuck at fourteen.

Being busy and occupied with home life meant I hadn't seen anything of the other lads in ages. One day in early 2004, I was in the middle of moving into our new flat in London when my mobile rang. It was Jay.

'Hello, mate,' I said. 'I'm sat here in my new flat in London.'

'I'm in London, too. Where have you moved to?'

He was just around the corner.

'Shall we get some lunch?' he said.

'Yes, definitely.'

As I was walking to the restaurant I was excited: I'd really missed Jay. Jay's so different from me – he'll think and think and think about things until they can't be thought about any more, but it means he always has an interesting perspective. After catching up, Jay asked me a very leading question. 'What do you think of the old days? Do you think about them much?'

'Not really, Jay, but I miss them a bit.'

Jay seemed to turn grey at this.

'What's up, Jay, are you OK? You're worrying me.'

'It was bloody difficult working for you and Nigel. You were a nightmare.'

I was so shocked. I just didn't expect it.

It was no secret that I was the leader in Take That. I'm squirming as I write this because I hate the thought. Gary, the sensible one, the worrier. I have been described as all of those things, and at times I was all of them. The truth is I didn't earn the role, but it was like that from the start. Nigel held me higher than everyone else and he didn't hide it. It even felt like the other boys didn't mind, although in retrospect how could they not? I think it was harder for Jay and Rob than it was for Howard and Mark, but I think they all resented feeling their contribution was less valued and valid. While I thought, as usual, that it was up to me to look after everything, to them it felt like I was taking charge. Throughout our life as a band I was driven, pig-headed, single-minded, selfish, domineering, devious and extremely ambitious. I can see all of those things now; I couldn't then. The other four lived, worked and travelled with me, they experienced and shared things with me and were on the receiving end of me. Back then, although I was a friend to everyone in the band, for me it was all about *my* career and *my* experience.

It wasn't just Nigel that made me separate from the rest of the band, my financial position also created a divide. Thanks to my publishing deal, by the time Take That came to an end I was seven times wealthier than the others. All the Take That songwriting credits for the songs I'd written came to me. Now I regret my unwillingness to share; it wouldn't have hurt to have given everyone a piece of the action. Even one song!

I guarded my songs too jealously. I'd worked so hard to learn my craft that I wasn't about to hand them out willy-nilly. Not for one second did I even consider that it could have been fun for us all to get involved. Today things are different. I'm writing this after we have spent a day working together. Somewhere between Mark and Howard a melody gets written, then Jason starts pecking away at the laptop, off-loading lines of lyrics. Nowadays I can sit and enjoy the process unfolding in front of me, happy to contribute every now and then. Martin Barta, the manager I took on for my songwriting and producing work after I was dropped by BMG, also helped me to see that things can be straightforward if you set out to make them that way. Martin's one of the real old-time gentlemen of the business and doesn't go in for gossip or scheming – it makes life a lot less complicated.

After getting back from LA I'd seen and apologised to many people for my behaviour when I was in the band – Mark Cook our make-up artist, who I always dismissed, and the Take That photographer, whose life I made hard work when I was in the band, were a couple of them, The four people I hadn't talked that time through with were the boys. As Jay and I sat there discussing things, much of what I have just said was going around in my head. Jay and I touched on many of those issues and with Jay there's no hiding place when it comes to things that need to be said. With all my self-obsession I'd failed to see how different my experience of Take That was to his and the others'. I felt mortified and couldn't wait to get the bill.

Out of the blue I received a call from Nigel. After a few brief pleasantries, he got down to business.

'Gary, BMG want to do a greatest hits CD. They reckon they can shift 60,000 copies at mid-price through the supermarkets and they want to know what we'll do for it?'

'What do you mean, what'll we'll do? Nothing, I guess.'

The upshot of this conversation was that Nigel insisted we have a band meeting. It was eighteen months since we'd all last met and this time we assembled at Nigel's sister's house. No sooner had we all sat down than Nigel pulled out some papers and passed them around. There were ten or twelve sheets with NMS MANAGEMENT right across the front one. I caught sight of Mark's face as he flinched. Mark, like me, had his own manager, but Nigel had just waltzed in and taken charge again. While Mark stared at the sheaf of paper, Jason looked horrified.

I looked around the table and picked up on everyone's body language. It was as though I'd never seen it before, but instinctively I knew it had always been that way. I suddenly realised that Mark was intimidated by Nigel – every time he talked Nigel would interrupt him and Mark just let him talk right over him – while Jay looked like he was sitting next to the big bad wolf. He looked physically ill, and I could see that simply being in Nigel's company had that effect on him.

Nigel, of course, was oblivious to this. He was just engrossed in being back with his boys.

'I'm going to get us the best deal ever and make us all a lot of money. They will do as they're told.'

His delivery was going at a hundred miles an hour and he was saying all the wrong things. Everyone round the table was asking questions, and we were saying, 'No. No, we're not doing that.' Or 'No, we won't do this,' but nothing made any impact. It was as if the clock had been turned back. When we finished talking, without resolving anything, Nigel produced another piece of paper and handed it round.

'I've got a questionnaire for you all to fill out.'

'Questionnaire? What's this?'

'It's from my lawyer. I'm suing a newspaper and you've all got to testify for me.' There were some very unpleasant questions on it, and as we sat there filling it out a nasty pall settled over the meeting; it was almost as though our reputation was being soiled, not Nigel's.

As I drove away from the meeting I couldn't help thinking, same ol' Nigel. He thinks if he speeds things up enough he'll get what he wants. I thought back to my conversation with Jay. I'd been trying to face up to the reality of how it was for the others in the band and had gone to the meeting thinking they must all hate me. Consequently, on the way to Nigel's house I'd decided to tone down my act and not say much. Suddenly I was very conscious of how I behaved.

My phone rang.

'Who does that Jason think he is? Did you hear what he asked me in the middle of that meeting? He asked me how much promotion will we get? Can you believe it? He's just a painter and decorator.'

'Nigel, I can't talk right now, I'm driving.'

How could we work together on a greatest hits package when there was so much past between us? Did we even want to work together again? From a business point of view I wanted the CD to come out: it would be great to sell a few records. I thought it would benefit us all, but first and foremost I was probably thinking of myself. It would be good for the catalogue, great for some publishing royalties and we'd all earn a few quid, which would be cool. Then I began to think back to what people had actually said at the meeting. Mark had been the most reluctant. He'd said, 'I can't give you an answer today.' He had his own career now and it was going in a very different direction to Take That. Perhaps because I hadn't said much or given any indication of what I wanted, it made everyone else unsure.

One of the nicest things to come out of our success – and having the time to enjoy family life – was our place in France. In February 2003 we bought a house in Nice. It started off as a whim. I'd always thought that you bought a house, lived in it and that's that, but one day Dawn and I were playing about on the internet and started looking at where we could fly to cheaply from near us. We were just having a bit of fun, dreaming of a place in the sun, but once we found flights going from Liverpool to Nice we began to think we might look for an apartment there. So we made a trip, started seeing a few places and fell in love with the third place we saw. It was bigger than we intended, a house with three bedrooms and a swimming pool, but it was on the top of a hill, with views across the ocean to Cap Ferrat, and even had a studio for me to work in. We wanted somewhere we could escape to for the whole summer and this was it.

Apart from our little London flat, it was the first place Dawn and I had owned together – Delamere was very much mine – it became our first family house. Whereas Delamere was all heavy antiques and quite grand, this house was decorated with blond wood and modern classic furniture made by David Linley, and very bright and airy. The first summer we had a wonderful time just keeping to ourselves and enjoying the place. I also found I loved going there on my own in February, for four or five days, when it's a bit rainy and cold. I'll head down to a restaurant with a book, and although it's out of season, Nice still feels vibrant and alive because it's a city. As time went on we started to meet people in the area and we've now got a great social life there – a lot of our friends have boats so there always seems to be trips to St Tropez and down to Cannes and Monaco, and it's always a great gaggle of adults and kids.

We were staying in Nice in the summer of 2004 with my mum and dad. I had sent them off with my mobile phone because they didn't have one, and told them to answer it if it rang. As they were wandering round they were bemused by the number of wind chimes they heard – of course it was my mobile. Mum answered it.

'Hello? Oh. Right. OK, love, OK, Elton, I'll tell him.'

Elton was at his house in the south of France and wanted Dawn and I to come for dinner. Elton had met Dawn just once, at his White Tie and Tiara Ball a month or so earlier, and although we'd had the house a while I'd only recently mentioned that we'd bought a house down the way from him. Dawn was shy of coming for dinner or lunch at Elton's house - I usually went on my own - and it took a lot of persuading to get her to go.

'There'll be fifty people there, babe, he won't even notice us,' I told her.

'Promise me I won't have to sit next to Elton.'

'Don't worry, we won't – we're not interesting enough. We'll be on a table down the other end of the room.'

We pulled up at Elton's in our Hertz hire car and walked into find one table set for four. Dawn came out in blotches almost immediately. She needn't have worried, though. It was Elton and his old friend Bob Halley and together they're a real double act. We spent the whole night in stitches

15

Take That Back

Also on Nigel's agenda at that last meeting was another proposal to do a documentary, but this time I hadn't shot him down like I had the first time. The others too seemed more enthusiastic – in some ways they seemed more positive about that than they were about the greatest hits album. With some clear blue water between where we were in 2004 and where we'd been when we split up, and a good many phone calls between us all, we came to the conclusion that the time was right for a retrospective.

In June 2004 Nigel phoned me and said, 'Listen, it's getting late for that documentary if we're going to get it out for Christmas with the CD. What about releasing the greatest hits at Christmas and the documentary at Easter?'

'Nige, I think the two go hand in hand. We should only do them together.'

I rang round and we were all agreed. I could tell Nigel was a bit disappointed, but I knew it was the right decision. Ten minutes later he was back on the phone.

'The label aren't happy. The guy that is steering this project doesn't even know if he'll have a job next year because they're merging with Sony.'

'Well, Nige, I guess it's just not going to happen, then. I don't think any of the boys are that bothered either way.'

And that's how we left it. I came off the phone thinking, I wonder if he's rung the other lads? Probably not.

Close to Christmas I got another call from Nigel.

'Sony/BMG want a meeting in the new year to discuss the greatest hits and the documentary, are you up for it?'

We met with the label on 14 January 2005. This time there was a definite air of anticipation as Nigel and the four of us walked into the room. We sat down and BMG went straight into their presentation. They had produced a mock-up sleeve, a little video piece and made up an advert – it all looked beautiful. There were a couple of fit birds from the marketing department at the end of the table, and everyone was talking the talk.

'If we get things right from a marketing point of view and select the TV shows and radio carefully, we think we could shift 100,000 albums and maybe 20,000 DVDs,' said one of their marketing people. We thought that sounded pretty good, especially as the CD was essentially the same as the one we released when we split up.

There was one small problem to overcome. Nigel had been developing the documentary idea with Fremantle TV, but BMG wanted Simon Cowell's company Psycho to do it. Nigel was quick to point out that they had never made a documentary, though he agreed to meet them. But – and with Nigel there's always a but – he showed us up by saying things like, 'What this means for the boys is just making piles of money. That's what it's about.'

No it's not, I thought as I sat there, that's not what it's about at all. I'm thirty-four in a few days' time, not nineteen. This is something I'm looking forward to doing. I was back to feeling good about myself, my weight was down and I could even see myself back on TV.

The four of us decided to meet up at my house and discuss how we wanted the documentary to be. It was a completely different experience to working on Take That the first time around. We were all adults now, with views, opinions and ideas, and it made the process much more dynamic than I remember things being during our first incarnation. Mark contacted Rob, and to our amazement he agreed to appear in the documentary – not with us though; in the end he did his piece first. We also made a pact and agreed that because the four of us were putting ourselves out there, we would stick together. If any of us was unhappy with something in the documentary, we would all stand together.

20 January 2005; Dawn took me out to dinner for my birthday. We went to the best, most popular restaurant in Cheshire. It was a Thursday night and we were sat there, on our own, with thirty empty tables around us. There was one other couple down the other end, and all we could hear was our voices and the sound of the cutlery scraping against the plates.

When we got to the end of the meal I said to Dawn, 'Babe, I've got to be honest, I don't think I can live up here any more. I feel like we're dying.'

We were living in his vast house in the middle of nowhere and our nearest neighbour was a road away. Maybe it was being with the band again and enjoying the feeling of things happening around me, maybe it was the boost that going to LA had given me, but I didn't want to barricade myself away any more.

I thought Dawn was going to go mad. She burst into tears.

'Gary,' she said, 'I've been desperate to do this for three years.'

I remember getting home from that dinner and walking round the house in silence, just looking at the rooms and all the mounds of stuff I'd accumulated. There were CDs from floor to ceiling – there must have been 15,000 of them – and so much furniture, not to mention paintings and ornaments. If there had been an empty corner I'd filled it. The whole house was stuffed. It's going to be impossible to move from here, I thought, but in a way that spurred me on even more. I just decided, there's no way I'm going to be held prisoner by all this stuff. It has to go.

The idea of selling Delamere was enormous. Delamere had saved me when times had got bad, living so close to my family then had meant they were there to support me and look after me, and I loved being near them. They, along with Delamere, had helped me pull myself together again. It wasn't just Dawn, Emily, Dan and me I was uprooting, we would be dislodging my parents and Ian and Lisa. It was a tricky topic to bring up and has been hard to see through. My mum still can't talk to me about it. She wanted to live there for ever. Even though they are now all settled in fabulous houses not far away, it will take time for them to adjust.

For years I had been thinking how come I can't remember things? I would get up from a chair, walk across a room, and by the time I'd got to the other side I would have forgotten why I had gone there. The fact was my mind was so clogged with stuff that I couldn't think straight. I wanted life to be simpler. The antiques and paintings went to Sotheby's to be auctioned and we only kept what we loved. It was life laundry and hugely cleansing. Goodbye mini Elton, hello Gary B.

We spent that summer in France, and by the end of August I was aware that we needed to start filming the documentary, but we hadn't yet finalised which production company to use. Nigel called and said, 'We've got a slot on ITV in November and we've got the production company. It's Simon Cowell's company. An old friend of mine, Nigel Hall, runs it and he wants to meet with us.' We arranged to get together at the Hilton near Manchester Airport in early September.

Before Nigel Hall arrived, we sat and discussed the latest news on the greatest hits package. Nigel said that there was a remix of 'Relight' and the rest of the album was the same.

'What? A remix? Is that the only new thing?'

'Lads, that'll be enough. Most people will have lost their old copy by now.'

'Nige,' I said. 'That's not true. We've gotta give them something new.'

'What about that song we all loved, "Today I've Lost You"?' suggested Mark. He was right, we did love it, especially Jay.

'I'll dig it out, but it has to be ready in a fortnight so we're going to have to motor. We'll need someone to produce it,' I said.

'Who was it that produced "Back For Good"? Was it Chris Porter?' asked Jay.

'It was.'

'Then that's who we should get to do it.'

Nigel immediately got on the phone to tell the label the good news, and to ask for a £20,000 budget to get it recorded.

'We'll need to hear an MP3 of this song first,' said the man at Sony/BMG.

'I don't think you understand what I'm saying, we've got the song, we all love it and we want to make the record next week. The boys are ready. It's a new Take That song on their greatest hits.'

'I hear you,' said the guy at the other end, 'but we need to hear an MP3.'

'Here's what I'm going to do,' said Nigel. 'I'm going to pay for it and you're going to have to license it from me, otherwise I'm going to give it to EMI. How embarrassing will it be for you when Take That release a single at Christmas and it's not on your greatest hits CD? Goodbye.' And with that he put the phone down. 'Listen, boys, I'm telling you now, I'm transferring the money to pay Chris Porter. Get the band in, we're going to record it.' That was Nigel at his brilliant best.

A fortnight later I recorded my vocal for 'Today I've Lost You' in my studio with Chris Porter producing. The following Monday I went down to London to watch the strings being recorded at Abbey Road, and later that week the lads did the rest of the vocals at Metropolis Studios.

Almost from the minute Nigel Hall arrived with his producer and the director of the documentary, David Notman-Watt, they started grilling us. This was clearly not going to be a BBC2 at 11 p.m. on a Sunday night style documentary, they were very tabloid.

'Lads, don't worry.' Nigel reassured us. 'I've worked it into the contract that I'm the executive producer. By law, you four can't have approval over it, otherwise it wouldn't be a constructive documentary, but as executive producer I can take out any bits I don't like, and I'm going to do a sub-agreement with you guys that says if you tell me to take something out I will.'

But their Nigel outsmarted our Nigel. It turned out that Nigel Hall was an executive producer too.

We shot my bit of the documentary at Delamere on 22 September 2005. I had worked out very clearly what I wanted to say. I wanted people to like me this time. Fresh in my mind was the thought that last time around people didn't feel good about me, and I wanted to be different. When it came to it I couldn't do it, I just reverted to being Gary from Frodsham. There was only one thing that changed: whereas before I'd always been guarded when I spoke, this time I was more honest.

It was around this time that I took a good long look at Nigel. Something was different. 'Nige, what have you done to yourself?'

He'd had another facelift to go with the two he'd already had.

'What did you do that for?'

'I don't want the camera to go from one of you lot to me and for me to look old,' he said.

On 2 November, Howard, Mark and I were in a bar in Kensington, not far from my flat, when Mark brought up the idea of touring. His manager Jonathan Wild had had a call from a promoter named Simon Moran, and they were interested in doing a Take That tour. Mark was quite excited by the idea. He had hundreds of ideas and got us all really enthused. The more we talked about it, the more carried away we got until, at about 1 a.m., Mark called Jay. 'You've got to get here as soon as you can, mate, we have a plan.' When Jay arrived the chat continued. Like the rest of us, he was interested and excited, but with a few reservations.

Nigel's take on us getting back together was, 'Never re-form, Abba never re-formed.' That thought haunted me, but we went ahead and met Simon Moran anyway. I represented the boys, and before we knew what we'd done, we'd agreed to a tour. Having been out of the touring game for a while, Nigel contacted Clear Channel about promoting the tour to give us something to compare to Simon Moran's offer. Their expert told him that 'public opinion' felt that Take That as a four-piece, without Robbie, had no chance of selling tickets. How could Simon Moran be so sure we could sell so many shows? Maybe Nigel was right.

We finished filming the TV show on 13 October at Cliveden. The hardest bit for me – and for all of us – was when they sat us down on the sofa and filmed our reaction to Rob's contribution. It was one of the most horrible positions I'd ever been placed in. There we were, receiving this personal message from someone who'd spent an important chunk of his life with us, and there were TV cameras on us. I felt very exposed and couldn't really take in what Rob said. But three weeks later, when we went to Manchester to view the finished programme, we were pretty happy with the way things had turned out. There were only a few minor changes to made before it was aired on Wednesday 16 November.

On Monday 14 November the production company arranged

a mini-premiere for the TV documentary at the Coronet in Notting Hill Gate. We were, of course, invited along with wives, girlfriends, friends and journalists. It was the first time we had appeared in public as a band since our press conference on 13 February 1996.

It took me right back to our first gig – Mark, always the Take That stylist, had done his research, bought a copy of *Vogue* and told us what to wear: 'I want you all in white shirts, black suits, no ties; very brat pack.' The four of us were asked to arrive at the cinema in a limo, and as we approached Notting Hill there was complete silence. Suddenly Mark said, 'Shall we just go to the pub and give it a miss?'

We were inches away from bailing out when ahead of us we saw light beams illuminating the sky. There were police in the middle of the road, and as we drew up we heard the unmistakable sound of excited girls – about 200 of them. I could have kissed them one by one. Beyond the girls was a pack of photographers jostling for prime position. God my heart was beating fast! I looked around at the boys and saw them take on that confidence we have when we're out as a group. We were strutting our stuff, waving and signing and kissing the fans. Yes, the boys were looking great. Click, click, snap, snap. News cameras, *London Tonight*, MTV, VH1 and *GMTV* were all there supporting us. What a feeling. We had been convinced no one would turn up – how wrong we were.

Inside the Coronet, the press loved the film and were oohing and aahing and even singing along. It captured the euphoria, hysteria and madness of those years. Nigel, on the other hand, hated it. At many points during the documentary there were jokes and comments made at his expense, and a couple of times, as the audienced laughed at them, I caught his eye. It looked like someone was driving a stake through his heart. Sadly, after the screening finished he disappeared and wasn't seen again all evening.

We, however, like old pros, attended the after-screening party. It was at this that I got a real flavour and insight into 'public opinion'. We were surrounded by high-powered editors and radio producers. They had been our fans in the old days and now they were grown women, with responsible jobs and wedding rings – and they were popping their cards in our back pockets! The question on everyone's lips was, 'When are you going to tour again?'

Two nights later, when it aired on TV, I sat watching it at Delamere, eating a bowl of porridge. I went to bed as normal and the next morning caught a train to London. Before leaving home for the station I turned on my phone to find thirty-five text messages and seventeen voicemails. For the next thirty minutes I read and listened to a phone full of compliments, and a message telling me that the documentary had the evening's highest viewing figures – 7 million.

Suddenly I sat tall in my seat on the train, I was proud to be me. One by one people came over and said how much they'd enjoyed the documentary. Good luck, they said. I hope you go back on tour. You should make a new record.

I'd waited a long time for this.

Everyone seemed to like it except my mum.

'It's not for me, Gary. No thank you, not for me at all. If your nan was here I can't imagine what she would have to say. No thank you, not for me.'

I think the honesty was too much for her and probably reminded her, as it did me, of some difficult times.

A week after the screening I was at JFK, coming back from a couple of days writing in New York, when my phone rang. It was Jay.

'Gaz, something's happened.'

'What is it, what's up?'

As we were talking I heard the call-waiting alert – it was Nigel.

'Go on, Jay.'

'I had a meeting with Nigel and I've asked him to resign. Then

Nigel said to me, don't you think that's a band decision? So I said, you might be right. It might be a band decision, but if the band decides they want you, I'm out.'

No wonder Nigel was trying to get through to me.

'I can't do this tour if he's looking after us, Gaz. I *won't* do this tour if he's looking after us. From this moment on I don't want any business dealings with Nigel Martin-Smith.'

'OK, OK, I'll be home tomorrow. Let's talk about it then.'

We had all said we couldn't imagine being backstage without Nigel, but maybe that was unrealistic. We had all grown up too much. Now I realise that there was a big part of me that felt relieved that Nigel wasn't going to be involved. I knew it would be a different tour without him, but it might be a more enjoyable one.

We were due to announce the tour dates at a press conference in less than two days' time. The night before the conference we stayed at the Berkeley Hotel in London. Given what was going down with Nigel, we arranged to talk it out that night. It wasn't as simple as deciding whether or not we wanted to tour with Nigel, it was more a question of were we going to do the tour we were about to announce the next morning at all.

Around about 7 p.m., I was pacing in my room, wondering whether this was just night-before nerves. We'd been given a long, impressive list of who was coming to the press conference, and it was to be broadcast on Radio One. When we'd all gathered, I looked at Howard, Jay and Mark and thought, we could get slaughtered here. Maybe I was getting cold feet.

Having avoided Nigel's calls in New York, I'd been avoiding them ever since. I wanted to hear what the others thought before I spoke to him. Sitting there talking, I understood very quickly that there was no bringing Nigel back. This was it. I'd parted company with Nigel once before and knew how nasty it could get. This time we had no legal obligation to tour with Nigel, the contract was all emotional – he had been such a huge part of the band's past. It only made it harder. And yet it soon became clear that everyone was up for the tour; the only necessity was agreeing we could do it without Nigel.

'We've got to think about how we're going to handle this,' said Jason. 'We're going to announce this to the world tomorrow and we can't go back on our word. Once we've announced we're going to tour, we've got to go through with it.'

We all agreed and understood what the consequences were.

The next morning everyone was on edge. Jay, who had spent the most time out of the limelight, was quiet and nervous. We all knew it was time to get out there. The press was waiting.

The press conference felt ropey and unconvincing. It was like we were all solo artists. Up until that point we had felt so good I'd just assumed we'd click right back into our old roles. We'd done the documentary, we'd done *GMTV* and Radio One and now, within twenty-four hours of us pulling it off, it felt like we were falling apart. We came off stage, did a few one-to-one interviews and then went backstage into our room. Suddenly the security guys began clearing everyone out of our room – Howard was on his knees, crying, he was overwhelmed by it all. Jay sat hugging him, looking as white as a ghost, and Mark, who had seemed the least fazed by the press, looked as worried as I felt. I sat there with my head in my hands thinking, I've been out of the limelight too long. I can't handle it. This tour's never going to happen, we can't deal with it. This is big shit happening here. And we hadn't finished; there were more interviews to do. It was one of those situations where you want someone to carry you a million miles away.

When it was all over we said our farewells and I got the train home. I didn't see or talk to anyone else from the band for a week. I did talk to Nigel, however. He was in tears, his world had been taken away. Nigel had loved us boys. He'd gone further for us as a manager than anyone else would have done. He didn't only give us his undying attention and love, we'd been the sole focus of his career. He'd fought so hard for us, and pissed off so many people in the process, that when it was over no one wanted to work with him again. With Nigel you're either for him or against him. For Nigel as a manager, it wasn't a case of moving on to the next young talent. We were his moment, his career, and now he wasn't going to be part of our future. It wasn't a decision any of us found easy or pleasant to make, but it's been part of us growing up. There was too much water under the bridge for us all to fall back in line and be dictated to.

We were managerless with a tour to plan. Simon Moran, the promoter, had to talk to someone about rolling out the dates for the tour, and the others elected me to deal with it. We had agreed to put some tickets on sale and hold back some of the dates in case we sold out. I had been getting dozens of texts from people after tickets. A guy I bought a car from eight years earlier even sent me his Mastercard details, expiry date, everything. The others were getting a similar reaction, and yet we couldn't acurately gauge how well the tickets would sell. Simon had absolutely no doubt we would sell out, it was the four of us who were sceptical.

Simon called me the day before the tickets went on sale on Friday 2 December and said, 'Tomorrow morning the tickets go on sale at nine o'clock and I need you to have your phone on. By quarter past nine the first nine dates are going to have sold out and I'm going to need to call you to say can we put the next nine on sale. Then by half past, when they've sold out, I'll need to call you to say can we put the rest on sale.'

'Yeah, right, Simon,' I said, laughing. 'Promise me you won't put any more dates on sale until I've talked to you.'

'Gary, I definitely won't, I swear.'

On the Thursday I had a meeting in London and afterwards I

went out with some friends for dinner at a nice restaurant in St James's. It was probably the tension, but one drink led to two and it was quite late when I got in. In fact, I wasn't in the best shape, I even slept in my clothes. I know when I've had a heavy night because I sleep on my back and when I wake up it feels like someone has poured sand into my mouth. I looked at the clock. It said nine twenty-five.

Bugger! Simon! I'd turned my phone off. As I switched it back on, in my hungover state I initially thought there were no messages, but when the network logo disappeared the screen started flashing like a strobe. You have one voicemail, you have three voicemails, four voicemails, you have twenty-eight voicemails and sixteen missed calls from Simon Moran.

'Simon, it's Gary.' I sounded like Jack Duckworth.

'Fucking hell, I told you . . .' he began to shout.

Easy now.

'We hung on trying to get you but we had to let them go.'

'How many have you sold?'

'We've sold out nineteen dates. I'm sorry, I just had to roll the dice because by quarter past nine six nights at the NEC had gone. I need to know, can we roll out the full twenty-six?'

I replied, 'Go for it.'

The BT computers went down in Manchester and the network crashed in the north west because of people phoning the MEN Arena. We were really in it now. I immediately got on the phone to the others. Jason said, 'Man, it's all over the radio. Big queues at the MEN.'

Radio One carried the story about sales for Take That shows going faster than any other ever. By ten past ten Simon called me back and said, 'That's it, we're clean. All the tickets have gone everywhere. There isn't a single ticket left.'

'Fuck, that's unbelievable,' was all I could say.

'What shall we do? Put another thirty dates on sale?' said Simon.

'No, let's not do anything.'

'I'm going to have a think over the weekend, but there's more tickets to be sold.' And with that Simon rang off. The following week he came back and suggested we do five stadium dates.

Once the tickets sold there was a big change in all of us. It was as though we had accepted the responsibility. On the day of the press conference I'd very nearly run down to the bookies to put seven grand on us not touring. I'd thought the Take That magic had gone. Just before Christmas we did Jonathan Ross's TV show, and for the first time we actually got the interview right, at least by our standards. We were on our way back to becoming Take That.

Dawn and I finished the year by going on a Disney cruise from Miami with the kids. The night before we left we went to Elton John's hen party at Soho's Too2Much Club. Bryan Adams sang 'Big Spender', Bill Clinton pre-recorded a speech, the Pet Shop Boys and Scissor Sisters front man Jake Shears performed and Lulu and I did 'Relight My Fire' together. It was quite a do.

It was also quite a contrast to the new me. Delamere was on the market and I'd bought a semi-detached house in London – a very nice three-bedroom semi, but no pop star's mansion. I'd also sold my Mercedes – now I have to rely on the wife for a lift. I don't even have a little red Ford Orion any more. When I was working in London, staying at our flat, which I'd done a lot lately, I'd begun taking the bus. I'd even got myself an Oyster card. I went about my business in London, walking, riding the bus or taking the tube, just like everyone else and I loved it. It was all part of getting a grip at last.

16

Take That Take Two

Sunday, 9 April 2006

Two weeks to go and I'm amazed. Driving by myself gives me time to think. I'm on my way home from the dentist. All kinds of things are running around my head, but the dominant thought is just how bloody exciting my life is at the moment. It's not just because the tour starts two weeks today, but also the fact that once we finish the tour I'm going to be leaving home for the first time. I've always lived within a few miles of the street where I was born. My parents, my brother and his family live in houses in the grounds of Delamere Manor. It's not that I have a burning desire to get away from them – far from it – but it will be brilliant for us to embark on a whole new life.

After all the lows I had in the period after BMG dropped me, things have completely turned around. Less than a year ago Howard, Jay, Mark and I were looking at a situation where we were going to get £70,000 each for doing the documentary – that was pocket money back in the old days – and BMG were looking at a mid-price re-release of our greatest hits. They thought we'd sell 100,000 copies and then quietly slip back into obscurity. Now, with the tour and the chance to make a new album, it really is a case of everything changes.

My Take

I'm thirty-five years old and I've never felt more professionally in demand than I do now. Both Universal and BMG have been vying for our attention and we feel like we can achieve anything. I thought my recording career was over – it's amazing to be valued again.

And the touring! At one stage I thought it was just me and Mark who wanted to tour, but Jay, having been the least excited about it, is now totally involved with everything. Throughout rehearsals he's been pushing us to be the best we can be, and he's pushed himself harder still.

I know we're going to love being back on stage. I think we'll enjoy it far more than last time around. While we all suffered some kind of post-Take That stress syndrome, it was really only Jay that didn't seek out the rush you get from performing – Mark and myself pursued it through our music and Howard through being a DJ.

8.30 p.m., 23 April, Newcastle Metro Radio Arena. I can't wait. To think that's the city where we did our first big gig, and now we're back. It's going to be fantastic.

The four of us flew to Vegas on 8 January to spend five days together. With all that had happened in the run-up to the tickets going on sale, it turned out to be a great idea. Not only did we get some inspiration from seeing some of the shows, it was also a chance to have fun together. We'd go out to dinner and sit around our rooms conjuring up ideas for the show. In fact, in true Take That fashion, most of the ideas came from us, which takes nothing away from Kim Gavin – who else would we have chosen to put them into practice?

When we came back from Vegas, we didn't see each other for the rest of that month. It was like a little test to gauge how things were going to be. At the end of the month we got together to work on our dance routines. The first day we walked into rehearsals and Howard did a spin on his head – not bad for thirty-seven!

While we were in London we auditioned for dancers. Dawn,

having a bit of an inside track, was going to be one of them. That's not favouritism, she'd been training for weeks. Getting into shape like that requires real dedication; she was an inspiration and I felt so proud of her.

Although the tickets had sold beyond our wildest expectations, we still had worries. We constantly asked ourselves and each other whether we were doing the right thing. How was it going to turn out? Would people laugh at us? Not that we had any option but to continue. Jay questioned whether or not we could even do it as a four-piece, but of course we'd already done our biggest ever tour with just the four of us after Rob left. I guess all of our thoughts were clouded to some extent by how successful Rob had become in the meantime. I wasn't the only one who felt I was living in his shadow.

The tour inevitably led us to discuss whether we should get back into the studio to make a new album. BMG, which by this time had fully merged with Sony, had been our label for fifteen years, and as soon as they got wind of what was happening they began courting us. We weren't under contract to them, but Sony/BMG own our entire back catalogue, which put a certain pressure on us to sign with them. But the vibe we were getting from them wasn't as positive as we felt it should be. We had more confidence now. The *Greatest Hits* re-release had sold over a million copies and we'd earned far more than their modest advance, but it wasn't about the money. It was as though they saw a new Take That album as just a continuation of the *Greatest Hits*, whereas we saw it as the start of something new and exciting.

I decided to go and see David Joseph, who is the managing director of Polydor, which is part of Universal. He had started out as a PR Manager at BMG, and was one of those guys who would always take the time to say 'Hi' and 'How's it going?' He'd also kept in touch with our careers over the years. I recently saw the video of our break-up press conference in Manchester, and as the camera panned along the line of the four of us, there's David in the last shot – it must have been an omen.

I sat in his office and said, 'We're thinking of recording again, what d'you reckon?'

I expected him to talk around the subject for a while, but instead he was very direct.

'Gary, we would love to do this. We would really love to do this. I'm saying this without checking with my chairman, but I'm sure we want this.'

Forty-eight hours later we had an offer, and it was an offer we couldn't refuse. Rob Stringer, the head guy at Sony/BMG, realised they had fallen behind in the race and pulled out all the stops, but Polydor were too far ahead. Besides, it felt like the right thing to do to draw a line in the sand with BMG. A new label meant a fresh start. We had dealt with some fabulous people at BMG over the years, but by 2006 none of them were left at the company, and it's the people you deal with that make a label what it is. Added to which, I still had a bad taste in my mouth after the way I was treated by BMG when my solo career came to an end. When it came down to it, though, it wasn't me who made the decision, it was Jay who sealed it.

'The guys from Polydor are cool. They're not desperate and they're just the sort of people we like doing business with. They're decent.' They had a vision for our future whereas Sony/BMG were reacting to our past.

So as well as planning for the tour we had to start writing songs, not that I'd ever stopped. However, this was a different kind of pressure. I didn't want to go back to working the way we'd done before. Mark had developed his songwriting, Howard had some great ideas and Jay as always offered some quiet insights and ideas for songs. We decided that if we were to do an album all of us would contribute to the writing, performing and production; it would be the first real Take That group effort. I say 'if' because for a long time during the late winter and early spring we harboured doubts. In our negotiations with the labels we said that if we weren't happy with what we had produced we would hand them back their advance and just not bother. Maybe it was nerves, maybe it was not wanting to let anyone down and maybe it was a way of not raising the stakes, and the label's expectations, too high.

When the question of who should produce the album came up in band discussion, I was the first to say 'not me'. I wanted to enjoy making this record. It's hard work producing – proper work, the kind my mum and dad would be proud of – but it's a lot of responsibility. I didn't want to be the one left in the studio long after everyone else had sloped off home.

We've got an amazing guy called John Shanks and I'm loving it. I really trust him to get it right and it feels like the album I've always wanted to make. Nobody's telling us how to sound, we're just doing our own thing.

When we first talked about the tour and what it was going to be, it seemed so far off, like a speck on a distant hillside. But the closer we got, the more detail we could see and the more real it became. I no longer had the kind of over-inflated ego that looked on centre stage as my natural place, so I had to think myself back into that frame of mind and work out how I was going to deal with performing again. If I was having trouble with the concept, Jay was really struggling. He had utterly convinced himself he would never appear live again.

At rehearsals we had endless conversations about how embarrassing it was going to be dancing on stage again, and when you break it down to basics, it is faintly ridiculous. When we got near the end of the tour, though, we all agreed we were sad that it was nearly over – Jay was showing off as much as ever, my arms were spread wider than I thought possible and Mark and Howard were back to how they used to be, only much, much better.

Another thing that gave me a real buzz was how hard everyone worked on their vocals. There was no way that we could have sung 'How Deep Is Your Love' live in the old days. Beverley Knight stood in for Lulu on 'Relight My Fire' and did a brilliant job – she was a great sport, agreeing to do everything we suggested, and even my mum thought she was the right choice for the song.

One of our goals from the tour was to get amazing reviews. We needed all the press behind us if we were to be a success. I had the feeling that there was a lot of goodwill for us from most sections of the media, but bitter experience had taught me how things can change in an instant. A change of heart can occur at the editorial level for the strangest of reasons, and the jokes would have been all too easy if we'd failed to live up to people's memories of Take That. As a result, we spent the extra money we made from the ticket sales on producing a better show. The average pop tour costs around £8 million and we wanted to go well beyond that – stools, after all, are fairly cheap. What we wanted was not to clean up personally, but to reinvest in our futures.

The stage was set, the rigging, trussing and lights tested, the sound checked. I looked out at Metro Radio Arena and thought, the next time I'm on this stage it's for real. On the morning of the day before the first show I got on my scales and I was thirteen stone exactly. I hadn't weighed myself in ages, I'd been so busy it had just dropped off my radar. Bloody hell, I thought, after all this time everything is coming together for the first gig.

When I went into the canteen at around 6.30 p.m. I said to myself, I'm going to have rhubarb crumble *and* a jug of custard on the side. Then it hit me: I couldn't eat it. One minute I was sitting at the table chatting and the next I had to get up and go and be by myself. I sat in my dressing room alone just thinking. It wasn't that I wasn't together, I was totally in control. But . . .

When the others arrived in the dressing room I could sense that they felt the same way. I'm usually the one who rallies everyone, but that night I thought, fuck this, I'm not going to take responsibility, and everyone else took on that role.

'Come on, Gaz, let's get this going. Come on, you'll be good.'

As soon as they started I thought, it's going to be OK. It's the same in every band: there's always one person who's the worrier, and in Take That it's usually me. If it can go wrong it probably will, is my view. I'm the one fiddling with the amps, looking around, double- and triple-checking that everything's all right. I can't help it, I'm like that with everything in my life, I just want things to go well. I'm like that with my family, too, and Take That are my extended family.

The opening, of course, was planned for maximum impact. When we were revealed at the rear and walked on to the elevated platform that lowered us on to the stage, it was an incredible feeling. It felt like our last gig had been weeks ago, not eleven years. When 'Once You've Tasted Love' started, my feelings almost overwhelmed me, but as soon as I sang one line all the nerves disappeared and I started to enjoy it. I looked into the other lads' eyes and I was twenty-four again.

Together with Kim Gavin we'd worked on a production that was a cross between theatre and rock and roll, but not so theatrical so that it looked cheesy – well, that was the aim. The idea for the boy band sequence was Jason's. We wanted to take the mickey out of being a manufactured band and out of managers who have a list of rules – it even makes fun of my dancing! People have said that it's better these days, but that's because I'm not doing as much and it's so well choreographed that I'm hidden away. We wanted to acknowledge where we had come from, to accept that we had been a boy band, but at the same time to move on. As I said in an interview before our first gig, when we were asked about being a boy band, 'We're not, we're a man band now . . . wanna see my belly?'

Mark went to see Robbie and he agreed to do the hologram we used in the opening of 'Could It Be Magic'. Using the hologram of Rob was very important to all of us, and it was great that he agreed to do it. It certainly worked brilliantly in the context of the show. It had a lot of impact because none of us, and by that I mean Rob and Take That, spoke about it publicly beforehand. We wanted it to be a surprise for the fans on the first night.

Howard's idea was the tango – he got us all to watch the movie *Moulin Rouge* – and it was the sequence we were most worried about. None of us are trained dancers and it was bloody hard to do. All through rehearsals we would say, 'Ladies and gentlemen, the tango tits.' Lifting someone is hard and dancing with someone is a real challenge for me. I just kept thinking, get this over with and you can get on with the rest of the show. It was a brilliant way of making 'It Only Takes A Minute Girl' work thirteen years down the road.

We used the Christians' 'Harvest For The World' as our inspiration for giving 'Everything Changes' a makeover. It was important to have it in the set and it was also a great way to get Jay playing his guitar. All our personalities were there in different parts of the show, and we deliberately chose to perform the songs together on stage, so that no one person took the limelight.

We had the idea to walk back from the B stage to the main stage after the 'Beatles Medley', 'How Deep Is Your Love' and 'Love Ain't Here Anymore' because we wanted to get closer to the fans. It was a challenge to get Newcastle Metro Radio Arena to agree to it, but we were so glad they did as the reception was just unbelievable. Of course, ten years on our audience has grown up a bit: they're throwing G-strings now, not Toblerones and teddy bears.

We've always scripted our shows like pantos – 'Hey up, everyone, look over there.'

'Where?'

'Over there.' But this time we each had a slot to ad-lib, saying whatever came into our heads, except for Howard. When we came up with the idea I could see it was worrying him. When he worries he really frowns – he looks like he's in agony – so I said, 'How, just plan what you're going to say, then. There's no point in letting it ruin the show for you.'

So he goes on and lays bare his soul. He'd thought about it really deeply: 'Ten years ago I said we'd be here for ever, then six months later we split up. But in the meantime I've had my two daughters, and you've got to respect that . . .' It was really heartfelt and moving, and it kind of summed it up for me. Howard was always the quiet one – you'd do an hour's interview and he wouldn't say a word – so for him to say so much, and so well, made me feel like the band now had room for all of us to be ourselves.

When we got to London for the Wembley gigs on 8 May there was an enormous bunch of flowers from Rob waiting at the Conrad Hotel. Jay and Mark had been getting text messages from him for a couple of days. We were standing in the hotel and Mark's manager Jonathan Wild, who was now our manager, said to me, 'Robbie lives up there,' pointing to the Belvedere at Chelsea Harbour. My room faced straight on to it. I stood on my balcony looking up at it for about fifteen minutes, trying to see which one Rob lived in. Daft as it sounds, I was trying to imagine what he was doing and what he might be thinking.

On the night of our first Wembley gig Jason received a text saying, 'I was going to come over but I'm a bit tired.'

The next day Jay told us, 'I've had a text from Rob, he's coming tonight.'

Having not seen him in so long I'm not sure what I felt. That night after the show we had decided to stay at Wembley for a bit of an after-show party with our guests, rather than rushing back to where we were staying as we normally did. We ended up staying a lot longer than we'd planned, but when we got back to the hotel Rob was waiting in the bar.

He had been sat there for an hour, having got a table where he could watch the entrance. As we walked in, he stood up – I'd forgotten how tall Rob is – and we all hugged. Everyone's eyes were on us, so Jay said, 'Let's go upstairs to a room.'

We went up to Jonathan's room and sat up talking until well after three. Our cases had to be packed that night because they were going on the coach to Dublin the following day, so the other lads and I took it in turns to go off and pack our bags. At one point it was just Rob and me in the room. Everyone has always said how they felt sorry for Rob, but to be honest while I can see some of his issues and problems, I've never actually felt sorry for him – until that night, that is. He was so nervous he was twitching, eating and drinking non-stop. He couldn't stop asking questions and wanted to know everything about the show – how it started, what we did, every imaginable bit of detail. Most of all, though, Rob was intrigued by the crack the lads and I were having together.

As I'd walked into the hotel I hadn't had time to think about how I was going to react to Rob. Time may be a great healer, but still, whenever I thought of him I thought, you absolute fucking cunt. I've never had anyone do so much damage as you've done. No one has said or done such awful things as you have said and done to me. No one has even come close. Yet as I sat there I felt nothing. I looked at him and thought, you're just a bloke like the rest of us. That person I'd seen on TV and detested for so long was just ordinary and no different from the lad I met all those years ago. There was still tomato sauce all down his top from dinner.

Rob asked about our new album and even wanted to hear some of it, which made me feel a little uncomfortable. It brought back all those feelings from the head-to-head we'd had when we'd gone solo. I immediately went quiet, and I think Rob sensed it and quickly moved on. Most of all it felt bizarre. It could have been me sitting where he was, but it wasn't, and I was glad. With everything that Rob has – all the money, all the fame, all the trappings of success – he's not a very positive person. I'm certainly much more upbeat, and I like to think that my competitiveness is with myself. It's why I like running rather than tennis, because it's not about beating an opponent. That's healthy, at least I think it is.

We talked about how much we were enjoying touring, and Rob said how much he loathed it and hated performing, but then when Jay suggested he come and see the show, 'There's no need to be on stage, just come and watch,' Rob replied, 'I couldn't come and see the show because I'd be itching to be up there. In fact, I'd have to come on stage.'

I mentioned how careful I was while touring, careful to get enough sleep so I could sing and didn't let the others down and careful to avoid getting a cold, and Rob said, 'That's why I hate touring 'cos it's all down to me. I can't afford to get ill or anything.' Typical Rob: he's a mess of contradictions.

Howard talked about how down he'd felt at one point and I could see Rob was itching for him to finish so he could ask me if I'd ever felt like that. I told him about being dropped from the label – I'm not sure whether he enjoyed hearing about it or not, but he did say that his period of feeling absolutely awful was right after leaving the band.

To lighten the mood someone suddenly said, 'Have you got taller, Rob?'

We all got up and stood next to each other.

'Look, it's Take That,' said Rob.

No one contradicted him.

Given Rob's feelings about Take That, his obvious dislike of all that we stood for, I guess he saw me as the embodiment of the band. I'm also aware that I was often the one with the vision for the band. I set the path I wanted us to follow. Not to take anything away from Mark, Howard and Jason, but Rob was the only other person in the band who was like me. Maybe we're the Cain and Abel of Take That.

Being with Rob again reminded me of how I used to be: completely self-obsessed, working, working, working just to stay where you are, blind to the world. Whatever way you look at it, being in Take That the first time round had absolutely nothing to do with what passes for real life. It came to me earlier this year as I was out running in Hyde Park. A girl came towards me sobbing into her mobile and as I wondered who or what was making her feel that way I realised I'd never know because I'd never see her again. A few minutes later a couple came towards me hand in hand and clearly newly in love. Life was going on all around me. Later that day I went into the studio with Howard, Jay and Mark and we talked about what I'd seen, the result was a song called 'It's All Life'.

We were all, to some extent, required to disconnect from life during Take That take one. Real life became invisible somehow, particularly for me, and now I saw that same disconnection in Rob.

At three I went off to bed, but of course I couldn't sleep. One thought kept going round and round in my head. Rob had said, 'Yesterday I had my binoculars out and I spent two hours trying to spot you in the Conrad.'

I guess he must have missed my fifteen minutes on the balcony.

On the last night of the first group of three Wembley shows Rob was sitting in the same seat waiting for us when we got back. He came upstairs again, but pretty soon we all ended up down in the bar. We had some great conversations and compared notes about our lives. Rob, like me, doesn't like cars that much, and we laughed about what we'd spent our money on. Once you get past the point when you can pay all your bills the whole thing becomes daft. Rob said he had spent two weeks in his flat without going out once because everywhere he went people gawped at him. Maybe he'd won in the career stakes, but I was the one with the Oyster card.

Although Rob had met Dawn before, it was so long ago that neither of them remembered it. The next day I got a text from him saying, 'I'll have to get me one of those wives, they look good.' I reminded myself yet again, as if I need reminding, how much I love Dawn and how much I value everything about our relationship. No matter how many friends you have, how great they are or how much you trust them, there is nothing so wonderful as a loving partner. Dawn being back in our show has been a terrific experience for both of us and it's something I have yet again to thank my mum and dad for. They have been amazing about looking after the kids while we've been away on the road. While we went home at every opportunity, and stayed there whenever we were within easy driving distance, we couldn't have done it without their support. My life and career have come full circle – Mum and Dad always were, and always have been, there when I needed them.

We've done it. I'm not backstage for good, we're back for good. Having been a solo act, I can tell you it's very difficult and that's one reason why being together in Take That is so fantastic. We support each other. While I'm capable of being on stage by myself, it's so much better being part of a band. As Take That we mean so much more. We are more than the sum of our parts. Take any one of us away and it wouldn't work. At one point Nigel wanted to replace Jason with Shayne Ward. It's bad enough that Rob's not there, but without him we are still Take That; if anyone else went missing we definitely wouldn't be. From five to four still worked – maybe that was part of Nigel's masterplan all along; it wouldn't surprise me. He was right about so much.

I love the camaraderie of being on the road – being with musicians, the crew and everyone else that makes a Take That show an event. We used to think we lived in a bubble during the

Take That years, this time around I feel we've enveloped the audience in our bubble. There's humour, we don't take ourselves too seriously and there's a lot of positivity, fun and friendship. I think we've even surprised the cynics.

I'm really looking forward to what happens next . . .

Full Circle

7 July 2005

I woke up with a start – I'd overslept slightly. The clock said 8.17 and my train from Euston was at 9.18 – I always allow at least an hour to get there to be on the safe side. I sprang out of bed, showered quickly and dressed. I stared at the clock and wondered if I should even bother trying to catch the train; it was 8.28. I stuffed my computer and other gadgets into my bag and five minutes later I was standing on the platform at Kensington High Street tube station. It seemed unusually busy.

The train pulled in and it was so packed that I headed up towards the front, hoping to find a carriage with fewer people in it. No luck, it was going to be a squeeze no matter which carriage I got in. Being one of the last to board, I stood in the doorway. It was nose to nose, and as we pulled away everyone leaned on one another for stability. We bumped through Notting Hill Gate and Bayswater, and as we arrived at Edgware Road Station the train braked heavily.

As we slowed there was a deafening, deep bang. It was so loud I felt it in my jaw. Instantly I was afraid. I was jolted to the floor of the train, along with almost everyone else who had been standing. Some people had bitten their tongues and there was blood around their mouths. The carriage began to fill with smoke, plumes and plumes of it. I was terrified. People were screaming and crying – the sound of panic – and as I stood up my legs turned to jelly. It was hard to see as there was only emergency lighting. I helped the guy next to me to his feet.

Still the smoke kept coming and I too started to panic. I thought, we must be on fire and there's no way off the train. We were all going to burn alive. I looked through the window of the train door and all I could see beyond the smoke was a brick wall. Some other guys and myself were trying to prise open the doors, and despite using all our strength, and fear, we could only move them about four inches. We pushed our faces into the gap, trying to get some air. People were shouting now, and a couple of guys on the opposite side of the carriage had found the emergency hammer and were trying to break a window. The problem was the train was so full of people they couldn't get a big enough swing to smash it. Eventually, after four or five attempts, it broke, filling the carriage with air.

After about five minutes the smoke began to clear. What had happened? Had we hit a train? Maybe it wasn't a fire, maybe it was just dust and crap that had been lifted up by that enormous bang? Just then there was a cry from a woman sat by the window. I looked around and what I saw will stay with me for ever. Next to us was what looked like another train, but it had no roof or side. The seats were exposed, and although it was dark I could see bodies lying across them. There was an old black guy sat in one of the chairs just gazing around. He didn't appear to be hurt, but he was in shock. There was a woman lying on the floor of what had been the carriage. She was slipping in and out of consciousness. Several people, including myself, threw bottles of water across, and we talked to them through the broken windows. A lot of people couldn't look and sat with their faces in their hands. Others sat quietly, some saying prayers.

The smell was terrible: smoke and what I assume was burning flesh. Fifteen minutes after the explosion one or two emergency service people appeared. Horrified by what they found, they headed back for more help. In our carriage things were quiet and I noticed for the first time that everyone around me had a black face. Although I desperately wanted to get away from the scene I knew those poor people on the train opposite had to be treated first. What had happened?

'It must have been a bomb,' someone said.

Somebody else said, 'It's Al-Qaeda.'

I looked again at the woman who was lying on the floor. Someone's daughter? Someone's mother on her way to work on a day like any other? I began to understand how lucky I'd been. I get that train; I travel anti-clockwise on the Circle Line all the time. That could easily have been me. But here I was, looking at someone else's tragedy. I counted seven bodies, and as the woman was carried out on a stretcher, I prayed that she'd be all right.

Half an hour later the interlocking doors on our train were opened. Slowly we filed through the carriages and off down a little set of stairs at the front of the train and on to the track. I could see we were about a hundred yards from Edgware Road Station. On the track was wreckage from the other train, a couple of doors all crumpled and black. It looked like they'd been blown off and our train had run over them. On the station platform we walked past a number of bodies covered in white blankets. There were people sat on the floor, covered in blood and dazed.

I climbed the stairs along with everyone else and the last few steps up to ground level were beautiful. I felt relief as daylight hit my eyes. Almost automatically I checked to see if there was a bus to take me to Euston so I could catch my train. As I was standing there I thought, I could have had Dan or Emily with me on that train, but at the same time I didn't remember seeing any children on board. While I was waiting to leave the train, one of the things that had flashed through my mind was that there was no one there to look after us. I wanted to be held and taken care of. I always tell my children, 'Don't worry, the big daddy will make sure nothing happens to you.' Well, today we all needed someone. What about those poor people I'd left down there? Their families would be frantic, wondering where they were.

Every bus was overloaded with people. I tried calling Dawn on my mobile phone but the network was obviously jammed. Everyone was talking about bombs all over London, and I'd been just feet away from one of them. I suddenly realised that there probably wouldn't be any trains leaving Euston that day. I also noticed people looking at me strangely. It wasn't a look of recognition, it was because my face was black, too.

Almost without noticing, I began walking through Hyde Park back to my flat. It seemed like hours since I'd been on the tube, but I could still smell the fire and burning flesh, it wouldn't leave me. Bizarrely, I desperately wanted a cigarette – the first time I'd even thought about smoking in five years. In my head I could hear the sounds of pain and agony on that train. I thought, I've got to get out of London and back home to Dawn and the kids, to things that are familiar and safe. What kind of a world is it where people on their way to work step on a train and get blown to pieces? They timed it right, just at the height of rush hour, and now London seemed to be at a standstill.

Eliot had stayed at the flat and luckily he was still there.

'Can I borrow your car to get home?'

'Yes,' he said without hesitation.

Within minutes I was heading out of London on the A40. For the next three hours I was glued to the radio news. I wanted to hear that the lady on the floor of the train had lived. For some reason they kept reporting that the bomb on the train had gone off at 9.20 but it was actually 8.45. I made it home on adrenalin, I guess.

Although I'm fine, my mind keeps flashing back to what I saw. I've managed to sleep but woke two or three times with a jolt, an echo of the jaw-wrenching jolt of the bomb. I've been part of something that will be in my head my whole life. I don't know how to process it, what to make of death and horror close up. I've become a news junkie, and, whenever anything to do with 7/7 comes on, I'm hooked.

I don't know why there or why then, but I started to cry in the shower. I stood there for about thirty minutes and cried and cried. My mind kept returning to that lady lying on the floor. Who had she left behind? I could have been in her place. Thank God I wasn't. I'm here. I can't stop kissing my children. I've never been so happy to be alive.

ACKNOWLEDGEMENTS

Having never written a book before I had no idea what it was going to be like. Believe me it's a lot harder than writing a song! A few years ago when I first started writing things down I had no idea whether I would actually finish it, let alone see it published.

I had no plan as to how I was going to research my book, but there were things that I needed to know that only other people could help me with. I got in touch with lots of old friends and I would like to thank them for being honest with me, and sharing their memories – both good and bad. Chris Healey, James Gentles, Paul Medley and Kim Gavin have been with me for much of my life on the road and, apart from what they have added to this book they have been great guys to be around. Others who have given me their insights, as well as information, have included, Nick Raymonde, Kristina Kyriacou, Simon Orange, Richard Bray, Danny Betash, Jon Kutner, Chai Ying Yau, Nicki Chapman and Simon Moran (thanks too for having the vision!).

I firstly want to thank my ghostwriter and mate, Richard Havers, for being one amazing human being. His enthusiasm and commitment have been continuous from the day we met. I couldn't have done the book without him. A special thanks to Simon Kenton at Idols for all his help with the photographs in this book. There's no one who knows more about Take That pictures than Simon. A big thank you to Philip Ollerenshaw who not only took the very first pictures of Take That, sometime during the last century, but also took the cover shot of my book.

In the 'without whom' category there's Wayne Critchley, my accountant, who has done his usual efficient job in keeping on top of things and Richard Bray, who besides helping with the story, is also my lawyer. Christine Havers had to listen to hours and hours of tapes of Richard and I in conversation and then try to make sense of what we were talking about – thank you. Jonathan Wild was at the Take That gig at Flicks and is now our manager – somewhere in between he even found time to become a lawyer. Jonathan has helped me at every stage with the book and is also doing a fabulous job with the band.

Eddie Bell, Pat Lomax, and Paul Moreton at my literary agency, Bell Lomax, have been fantastic in being with me every step of the way – if anyone needs a good agent give them a call; they're in the phone book. At Bloomsbury there is a whole host of people who have contributed to making this book happen; most of these people I have not met and might not know what they have done but thank you for everything. I would like to single out a few by name, Alexandra Pringle, Minna Fry, Katie Bond, Sarah Morris, Jessica Yarrow and Penny Edwards. Victoria Millar, who edited the book, deserves an extra special thank you.

Mum and Dad, Ian and Lisa were all with me in 'Ramsay Street' and have been through so much with me. In our family we don't talk about things very much, but this is my chance to publicly say how much you all mean to me, how much you've helped me and how much I love you. Of course that goes for Dawn too. She is the best wife any man could ever dream of having and I owe her more than words can say. I hope Dan and Emily will read this book in years to come and understand a little more about their dad than they might have done without me having written it.

Not last, and certainly not least, there's Nigel. If you've read the book before reading this you'll know that I say things about him that are not always complimentary, but who would feel any different, given what I went through? Was he a good manager? Yes. Was he sometimes wrong? Yes. But he was our manager and Take That would have been nothing without him. Above all else, I've tried to be absolutely fair and honest, but I'm sure Nigel will read some things about himself that he will not recognise, but they are my take. I owe Nigel a huge debt of gratitude, one that he might not feel I've repaid but one of which I'm constantly aware. Without Nigel this book would not have happened, because Gary Barlow would still be in Frodsham.

Music, Take That and what we do is not real life. It's magical. As soon as you begin to believe it the magic will disappear. I have to thank the boys for bringing a very special magic back into my life. Howard, Jay and Mark, you are great, the best.

I never believed I would ever stand on stage again, with my arms spread wide. So I have finally to thank everyone, especially the fans who never thought it would happen, who welcomed us back – with open arms.

PICTURE CREDITS

Plate section one

All images courtesy of the private collection of Gary Barlow

Plate section two

Unless otherwise stated, all images © 2006 Philip Ollerenshaw/Idols

Pages 2 (far left), 6 (third from top) and 7 (first row, left and sixth row, right): © 2006 Tom Howard/Idols

Page 5, top: © 2006 Moy Williams/Idols

Plate section three

All images © 2006 Philip Ollerenshaw/Idols

Plate section four

Page 1: © 2006 Philip Ollerenshaw/Idols

Pages 2, 3, 4 and 5: courtesy of the private collection of Gary Barlow

Page 6: © Getty Images

Pages 7 and 8: © Guido Karp-FansUNITED.com

A NOTE ON THE AUTHORS

Gary Barlow was born in 1971. He was the lead singer and songwriter for Take That, the most successful British band since the Beatles. The band broke up in 1996 and since then Barlow has garnered further acclaim as a songwriter for artists such as Charlotte Church and Blue. Take That reunited in 2006 for a massive UK tour and to record a new album. Gary Barlow lives in London with his family.

Richard Havers has written regularly for radio and TV and launched Turkey's first commercial radio station. His books include the acclaimed *Sinatra* (2004) and, with Bill Wyman, *Bill Wyman's Blues Odyssey* (2001), which won the 'Handy Award for Literature', and *Rolling with the Stones* (2002).

A NOTE ON THE TYPE

The text of this book is set in Bembo. This type was first used in 1495 by the Venetian printer Aldus Manutius for Cardinal Bembo's *De Aetna*, and was cut for Manutius by Francesco Griffo. It was one of the types used by Claude Garamond (1480–1561) as a model for his Romain de L'Université, and so it was the forerunner of what became standard European type for the following two centuries. Its modern form follows the original types and was designed for Monotype in 1929.

UNITED SERVICES CLUB
Prescot Road
Members Notice

Thursday, October 12
SINGALONG with Bill & John
Saturday, October 14
PANIC STATION
First class cabaret band
Sunday, October 15
★ STAR NIGHT ★
GARY BARLOW
Brilliant all round entertainer
Star of the future
PLUS
JIMMY CARROL
very funny comedian
both artists not to be missed
Monday, October 16
Star Country and Western Night
KENNY JOHNSON & NORTH WIND
Please be early on all nights
SHOW STARTS AT 8PM
Tote No's 4 & 36 x28

ST. LAURENCE CHURCH
HARVEST SUPPER
at the Church Hall
on Friday, 5th October 1984
7.30 - 12 Midnight
Music by GARY BARLOW on the Organ
Ticket £2.50

THE WEEKLY NEWS
SCHOOLBOY STAR AIMS FOR E.M.I CONTRACT
Runcorn WEEKLY NEWS

Tel:- Frodsham
Karisma
KEYBOARDS and V

Halton Royal British Legion
Main Street
Runcorn
☎ **Runcorn 64860**
Members Notice
Friday, June 23
AVALON
Fabulous duo
Saturday, June 24
SUNSET SOUND
Group
Sunday, June 25
Lunchtime:
HAL NOLAN
Top TV comic
Evening:
GARYS FAREWELL
Tote Nos 10 + 34
x12

TAKE THAT

THE BRAND NEW SINGLE
"DO WHAT U LIKE"
RELEASE DATE: 22 JULY, 1991
ON DANCE U.K. RECORDS
VIA TOTAL / BMG CAT NO. DUK 02

ELECTRONIC ORGANIST
Gary BARLOW
Tel:- Frodsham 33657
"Ravenscroft"
London Road,
Frodsham.